A JOURNAL OF
Trans AND
Queer Studies
IN **Religion**

VOLUME 1 • NUMBER 1 • MAY 2024

Queering and Transing Origins
Context, Compass, Access

JOSEPH A. MARCHAL and MELISSA M. WILCOX

Welcome to *QTR: A Journal of Trans and Queer Studies in Religion*, a project intended to increase and transform both the production of and access to knowledge about the full range of rich and complex connections between religion, gender, and sexuality. This transformational access and its accessible transformations are a long time coming and could not have come at a better and more urgent time.

All too often, accounts of our increasingly polarized political and cultural landscapes take for granted that to be religious is to be intolerant, and that to be progressive—an umbrella label under which LGBTIQ people are assumed to sit—is to be against religion. Yet evidence of interest in the intersection of religion, spirituality, gender, and sexuality is all around us, in a rapid proliferation of academic work as well as in the voices of many LGBTIQ cultural leaders, who experience religion or spirituality as an essential aspect of their lives and find their most important activist work to be that which is religiously rooted. The assumption of antipathy between camps is furthered by a lack of platform, a lack of resources, anti-LGBTIQ biases, and unimaginative perspectives on religion that have for too long plagued many institutions of knowledge. The history of trans and queer studies in religion demonstrates that these popular and persistent narratives, or at least the ones that are most loudly espoused and amplified, are woefully incomplete and thus inaccurate.

Scholars whose research challenges such limited perspectives have worked for decades in relative isolation from one another, gathering together at times during meetings focused on broader shared interests but rarely having their own dedicated spaces in which to develop, share, or publish their work. This lack of space has also prevented robust and collaborative connections between scholars, activists, artists, and those who wear more than one of these hats; yet we know—and can see all too clearly in the devastating speed with which core protections have been dismantled in recent years—that such collaborations, such networked spaces, are critical for social change. This journal, we hope, will provide one such space: a crucial hub for connecting academic and other public infrastructures for a more sustainable shared future. *QTR* and its

QTR • A Journal of Trans and Queer Studies in Religion • 1:1 • May 2024
DOI: 10.1215/29944724-11208893 © 2024 Joseph A. Marchal and Melissa M. Wilcox

developing companion website at queertransreligion.org will not only expand access to these conversations, but also widen the conversations themselves to enfold a broader range of participants and interlocutors yearning to seek knowledge and build community. In this introduction, we provide a very brief overview of trans and queer studies in religion, recount the collaborative histories that led to the journal's development, introduce the journal itself, and orient readers to this inaugural two-issue volume. We are thrilled and honored to have the opportunity to bring this important new work to the world, and we look forward to all of the ways in which *QTR* will foster expanded conversations and much-needed transformations in the world.

Queer and trans studies in religion is a diverse field—or a twinned set of closely (inter)related fields—that has formed at the intersection of queer studies, trans studies, and religious studies. This suggests, queerly, transitively, even loopily, that *QTR* requires more than one narrative of origins—particularly as its roots stretch back much farther than most people suspect. These fields began developing in their current form just as queer theory and transgender studies were both taking shape, beginning in the early 1990s. By the mid-1990s, books were reaching publication that made use of emerging queer theoretical paradigms to think about religion, and transgender theological writings were beginning to appear as well.[1] Conference space for such work was often limited to occasional, specialized conferences or to specialized units within larger conferences, such as the Gay Men's Issues in Religion (now Gay Men and Religion) program unit within the American Academy of Religion, and venues for publishing articles were almost entirely limited to special journal issues and edited volumes. Since that time, the field has grown from one whose proponents held their reception in an unmarked basement hotel room, a field graduate students were dourly warned away from by their advisors, and one that saw the regular denial of tenure to scholars who refused to heed those warnings, to a field in which there is a sustained pattern of growth and interest, a field that is increasingly featuring in doctoral exams and job descriptions, and a field that sees numerous, cutting-edge monographs and engaging classroom resources published year after year.[2]

Despite a century-old pattern in European and European-derived cultures of understanding (and thereby mandating) queer and trans lives to be at odds with religion, these three fields of queer studies, trans studies, and religious studies have much in common. Moreover, particularly within religious studies, scholars beyond queer and trans studies in religion have begun to realize the importance of these connections. At the 2019 American Academy of Religion/Society of Biblical Literature Annual Meeting, for example, there were more than twenty separate paper sessions or plenaries focused specifically on queer and/or trans studies in religion—a total of roughly eighty papers. An additional twenty-one papers appeared in panels that had a different focus, indicating that over a hundred scholars and several artists showcased work on queer and/or trans studies in religion at this one conference.

Both the panels and the individual papers ranged widely in terms of the specific religious tradition or traditions they engaged, their methods, and even the rank and location of their authors. This diversity and breadth of coverage is indicative of a subfield that has come into its own, influential not only within its own ranks but in its wider cognate fields as well. At the turn of the new decade (in the Gregorian calendar), one could observe both a wealth of supply of and a steadily growing—and even broader—demand for publications on trans and queer studies in religion.

Queer and trans studies in religion is a transdisciplinary field, meaning that it does not only combine disciplinary approaches across boundaries; it explodes those very boundaries. Indeed, it is well positioned to do so, having developed from three fields that are themselves transdisciplinary. Put simply and perhaps self-evidently, religious studies is the study of religions and related phenomena. Though some scholars recognize a sharp divide between the study of a religion by its own practitioners for the purpose of improving its practice (sometimes termed "confessional") and the study of religion by outsiders or by insiders taking the stance of outsiders for the purpose of improving general knowledge about religious phenomena (sometimes termed "non-confessional" or "descriptive-analytical"), from a queer theoretical perspective this divide smacks too much of positivist obsessions with an unreachable objectivity that in reality serve to obscure entrenched power dynamics. The field initially took form at the intersection of what we know today as sociology, anthropology, phenomenology, history, linguistics, and philosophy, hailing as forebears figures as diverse as Friedrich Schleiermacher, Émile Durkheim, Max Weber, W. E. B. Du Bois, and Arnold van Gennep; from this lineage alone it is possible to see in what methodological breadth the study of religion is rooted. Still today, religionists both hail from and contribute to all of the above-listed fields, as well as art history, literature, area studies, gender and sexuality studies, and ethnic studies, to name a few.

Queer studies grew out of the narrower field of queer theory, a term that was coined by literary critic Teresa de Lauretis in 1990 to mark a new approach to gay and lesbian studies that would be more inclusive of critical approaches to race, class, and gender.[3] This new approach has rightly been credited to the work of a number of women-of-color feminists and womanists writing in the 1970s and 1980s[4]—the key ancestors of the field—and although what developed from de Lauretis's conference failed initially to live up to her aspirations (she disowned queer theory in 1994 as "a vacuous creature of the publishing industry"[5]), at its best queer studies has become exactly what she envisioned and more. A broad field today that ranges from history to media studies and even—like religious studies—dips delicate toes into the natural sciences, queer studies continues to refuse definition and delimitation but can generally be understood as the study of nondominant (especially but not solely non-heteronormative) desires, bodies, and sexualities.

Similar to the early roots of queer studies in the writings of activist women of color, trans studies grew directly out of trans activism.[6] Unlike queer theory, trans studies has been grounded from the start in a wide range of academic disciplines, from history and anthropology through literature, arts, and—again—the natural sciences. It focuses in particular on the ways in which bodies and selves both encounter and resist a variety of cultural strictures around the sexed forms they are expected to take and the social roles that are expected to accompany those sexed forms.

At the convergence of all three of these fields are scholars from a range of the traditionally recognized twentieth-century disciplines who bring the perspectives of religious studies, queer studies, and trans studies to bear on each other. Some have trained in one or more of these fields; increasingly since the late 1990s it has also been possible to train specifically in queer and trans studies in religion as part of a degree in religious studies. Many scholars in this subfield have backgrounds in cognate fields, and have come to trans and queer studies in religion as an area of specialization within their own field. This convergence, therefore, like a convergence of rivers, produces rich soil in which to germinate a wealth of insightful scholarship.

The project that became *QTR*, then, can be traced to many points of origin. One might be when Danielle Dempsey, Kathryn Phillips, and Melissa Wilcox sent out the call for papers in the summer of 2018 for what would be the first annual UCR Conference on Queer and Trans Studies in Religion at the University of California, Riverside. Among the responses to that call was a query from Joseph Marchal asking how they could support the conference and wondering whether the growing prominence of queer and trans studies in religion meant it was time for a journal dedicated to these fields of inquiry. Since questions like these had been intermittently posed for years, informal conversations about a journal began in earnest that fall. These conversations, and the enthusiastic participation of so many colleagues at that first QTSR conference, were clear and strong barometers of the potential audiences, contributors, and overall value for increased academic organizing in this area of study. A second town hall at the 2019 annual meeting of the American Academy of Religion and the Society of Biblical Literature brought another startlingly large and enthusiastic audience, along with early interest from Duke University Press. Collectively and collaboratively, into and through a global pandemic that exposed so many of the reasons why our work in these fields matters so very much, we began to envision a journal that would serve scholars, artists, and activists working at these intersections.

QTR is the fruit of collaborative planning and attempts to respond to the needs of an international and transdisciplinary community of scholars, as well as to offer public-facing scholarship to support and educate the many and varied communities in which we all live and work. It follows other new and newly redesigned journals in featuring formal academic articles, but presenting them in an accessible format, most especially as a fee-free and open-access source of the latest knowledge about trans and queer peoples and practices within religions. It honors a long-standing tradition of activist and inclusive scholarship by embracing not only a wide range of methods but also a wide range of modes for communicating ideas and a capacious understanding of what constitutes knowledge. In addition to offering research articles of the highest quality and reviews of the leading-edge scholarship that is coming out of these fields, *QTR* includes original creative works such as poetry, fiction, and visual art. The companion website will feature shorter, more bite-sized writings as well as audiovisual materials, including but not limited to field recordings that might illustrate a published article, original musical compositions, audio files and transcripts of interviews with authors, and occasional podcasts related to featured articles. We are excited to put queer and trans methods into play not only in the research we publish, but in the very design of the venues in which we make it public.

Trans and queer bodies and forms of knowing have repeatedly been marginalized, silenced, and made into the objects rather than the subjects of knowledge. These forms of physical and intellectual violence are rapidly rising again, even as the forces of white supremacy and religious nationalism seek at times to recruit a narrow population of white, cisgender gay men to their cause. To us, and to all of those with whom we collaborated in creating this journal, these newly rising tides of violence and repression make it critical that the work featured here be broadly accessible to audiences around the globe, and that our work be informed by an ethic in intersectional justice. Thus, producing an open-access journal was key to our vision from the start, as is our dreamed future of a multilingual intellectual and activist space. What many readers may not know, however, is that open-access publishing does not remove the paywall but simply relocates it to the author's side. Given the precarity of the majority of trans and queer scholars and artists, producing an open-access journal by charging contributors thousands of US dollars for the right to publish was no solution at all. We dreamed, instead, of a journal with no paywalls for either contributors or audiences, a truly free press; Duke University Press found excitement in that vision and put together a budget that, if met, would allow them to produce the journal with no fees charged to contributors or audiences. Once the Henry Luce Foundation stepped in to cover the majority of these costs for the first five years, this growing collective of scholars was able to launch *QTR* as we had envisioned it.

This inaugural volume took form out of a workshop held at UC Riverside with the generous support of UCR and the Holstein Family and Community Chair in Religious Studies, the UC Humanities Research Institute, and the Henry Luce Foundation. The theme was *Queer and Trans Studies in Religion in the 2020s: The State of the Field*, and participants were invited to contribute either a selection from their own current work as an example of the state of the field or a broader commentary on the state of the field as a whole or of their specific subfield within it. It was May 2022; for many of us, this was our first travel in more than two years. We were relieved, uneasy, exhausted, and inspired to be gathering again and discussing our work in person with like-minded scholars at all levels, from senior faculty members to precarious contingent faculty to brand-new graduate students. Our conversations were thoughtful, engaged, and broad ranging; nearly everyone who brought a paper to the workshop went home to revise and rethink, producing the papers that comprise much of the inaugural two issues of *QTR*. Participation in the workshop, of course, depended on a scholar's availability, both to travel and to write; some of those we invited were able to accomplish one of these but not the other in the first part of 2022, and in some cases they later wrote papers for this volume. Others opted to serve as inaugural editorial board members rather than inaugural authors. Our book reviews and creative contributions were invited and hand selected to contribute to our theme. Thus, the volume that launches the journal offers a series of snapshots of the state of trans and queer studies in religion as seen from certain angles in a particular place and time. There are inevitably lacunae. There is limited engagement with premodern sources here, for instance (as even our colleague working in Rabbinics focused his article on how Jews figure in prominent modern approaches to the history of sexuality), or with Native studies, and there is a lean toward the Global West despite our attempts at breadth. Some of this reflects the longer engagement of queer and trans approaches in areas like the history of sexuality, religions of North America, theology, and biblical studies (reflecting some concentration within the study of Christianity and Judaism). We are actively working on the development of special issues for volumes 2 and 3 that will correct these and other imbalances. We warmly welcome and enthusiastically encourage submissions from scholars working in any and every time period, regional or globalized position, or religious tradition.

Nonetheless, the conversations taking place in this first volume offer an extraordinarily rich and complex picture of the burgeoning fields of queer and trans studies in religion. Our inaugural issue leads with Orit Avishai's consideration of the ways in which some queer activists—in this case, Orthodox Jews—are defining themselves *into* existence, while Ahmad Greene-Hayes turns his attention to two famous trans activists whose religious lives have often been soft-pedaled or defined *out of* existence. Janet R. Jakobsen then offers characteristically thoughtful methodological reflections on how and why we should be engaging trans and queer studies in religion in the midst of what she terms a "legislative hurricane" of antitrans and antiqueer bills, both in the United States and worldwide. Şahin Açıkgöz's consideration of the exclusions enacted by transnational framings of trans activism offers one example of the types of analysis Jakobsen is encouraging, pointing as it does to the erasure of "the pious trans subject" which is all too often defined out of existence. Finally, Max Strassfeld's article reaches into the history of queer studies in religion to offer a Jewish trans studies assessment of the ongoing usefulness of John Boswell's work in an intensifying antitrans and anti-Jewish environment. A reproduction of Joy Ladin's powerful poem "Shame," from *Shekhinah Speaks*, and the always thought-provoking work of SA Smythe round out the contributions in this inaugural issue, followed by insightful reviews of two important new works in the field: Carlos Ulises Decena's *Circuits of the Sacred* and Omar Kasmani's *Queer Companions*. In volume 1, issue 2, along with more provocative creative contributions and book reviews, you can look forward to a capacious overview of queer and trans Jewish studies (and a provocation regarding the colonialist and Christian imperialist foundations of religious studies), engagement with a Black trans archive, a consideration of indigenous African gender epistemologies, musings from Black queer ethics to reframe freedom through fugitivity, and a reconsideration of the role of churches in radical gay activism in the United States.

Queer and trans studies in religion is a labor of love and a labor of life for many of us in the field. No matter how arcane or abstract the details of our work may be, we are all keenly aware of its real-life impacts. Most of us know that the work we do can be, and is, a matter of life and death. This awareness, these commitments to the urgency of our work, have led to the creation of this journal as a communal, collective effort. We stand on the shoulders of our forebears, our mentors, those who believed in us, those who believed in the work but were forced to stop doing it or never lived to see it through to completion. We move forward with the support and enthusiasm of our editorial board members; of the six-member editorial team; of the graduate students and emerging scholars who were at the workshop and who were not, whose work is included in this volume and whose work will be included soon; of the staff members at UCR who have supported this project in ways ranging from development assistance to travel planning. Alongside each person whose name appears on the masthead is a community. We do this collectively; we do this for those who came before, for each other, for those who will come after us. We do this with and for you. We hope you are as delighted as we are with *QTR*, and we hope you'll contribute to making it an ever-stronger resource. Welcome!

Joseph A. Marchal (any pronouns with respect) is professor of religious studies and affiliated faculty in women's and gender studies at Ball State University. Most recently, they are the author of *Appalling Bodies: Queer Figures before and after Paul's Letters* (2020) and serve as chair of the Society of Biblical Literature's first-ever Committee for LGBTIQ+ Scholars and Scholarship.

Melissa M. Wilcox (any pronouns) is professor and Holstein Family and Community Chair of Religious Studies at the University of California, Riverside, and author most recently of *Queer Religiosities: An Introduction to Queer and Transgender Studies in Religion* (2020) and *Queer Nuns: Religion, Activism, and Serious Parody* (2018).

Notes

1. Key examples of this work include: Goss, *Jesus Acted Up*; Eilberg-Schwartz, *God's Phallus*; Alpert, *Like Bread on the Seder Plate*; Jordan, *Invention of Sodomy*; and Mollenkott, *Omnigender*.

2. For further context on these developments, see introductory works like Marchal, "Queer Approaches"; Marchal, "LGBTIQ Strategies of Interpretation"; and, esp., Wilcox, *Queer Religiosities*.

3. De Lauretis, "Queer Theory."

4. See, for example, Combahee River Collective, "Black Feminist Statement."

5. De Lauretis, "Response," 297.

6. For further introduction, see Stryker, "(De)Subjugated Knowledges."

References

Alpert, Rebecca. *Like Bread on the Seder Plate: Jewish Lesbians and the Transformation of Tradition*. New York: Columbia University Press, 1997.

Combahee River Collective. "A Black Feminist Statement." In *This Bridge Called My Back: Writings by Radical Women of Color*, edited by Cherrie L. Moraga and Gloria E. Anzaldua, 210–18. New York: Kitchen Table, 1983.

De Lauretis, Teresa. "Queer Theory: Lesbian and Gay Sexualities, an Introduction." *differences* 3, no. 2 (1991): iii–xviii.

De Lauretis, Teresa. "Response: Habit Changes." *differences* 6, nos. 2–3 (1994): 296–313.

Eilberg-Schwartz, Howard. *God's Phallus and Other Problems for Men and Monotheism*. Boston: Beacon, 1994.

Goss, Robert. *Jesus Acted Up: A Gay and Lesbian Manifesto*. San Francisco: Harper San Francisco, 1993.

Jordan, Mark D. *The Invention of Sodomy in Christian Theology*. Chicago: University of Chicago Press, 1997.

Marchal, Joseph A. "LGBTIQ Strategies of Interpretation." In *The Oxford Handbook of New Testament, Gender, and Sexuality*, edited by Benjamin H. Dunning, 177–96. New York: Oxford University Press, 2019.

Marchal, Joseph A. "Queer Approaches: Improper Relations with Paul's Letters." In *Studying Paul's Letters: Contemporary Perspectives and Methods*, edited by Joseph A. Marchal, 209–27. Minneapolis: Fortress, 2012.

Mollenkott, Virginia Ramey. *Omnigender: A Trans-Religious Approach*. Cleveland: Pilgrim, 2001.

Stryker, Susan. "(De)Subjugated Knowledges: An Introduction to Transgender Studies." In *The Transgender Studies Reader*, edited by Susan Stryker and Stephen Whittle, 1–17. New York: Routledge, 2006.

Wilcox, Melissa M. *Queer Religiosities: An Introduction to Queer and Transgender Studies in Religion*. Lanham, MD: Rowman and Littlefield, 2021.

Making Unlikely Queer Worlds
Gay and Lesbian Orthodox Jews in Israel

ORIT AVISHAI

Religion and queer lives are often thought about as antithetical, but for some LGBTQ+ persons disaffiliation is not an option. Instead, religious LGBTQ+ people seek to carve out livable spaces within their faith traditions: they make what queer theorists call "queer worlds." This article describes the making of one such queer/religious world and considers the plausibility of applying the lens of queer worldmaking in conservative religious and political contexts that do not seem to conform to queer visions of counterculture and counter-publics. The article draws from a larger project on the activism, identities, communities, and lived experiences of Orthodox LGBT Jews in Israel, with a specific focus on Orthodox gays and lesbians. The article considers how respondents negotiate with and transform religious (and religious adjacent) everyday spaces, practices, and discourses as examples of religious queer worldmaking, with the implication that religious acts are among the range of creative acts that are part of queer worldmaking. The article makes an empirically informed case for a queer worldmaking project that is grounded in everyday religious practice, ritual, and scriptural interpretations.

KEYWORDS conservative religious traditions, Orthodox Judaism, queer religiosities, worldmaking

> Queer worldmaking is . . . a mode of being in the world that is also inventing the world.
> —José Esteban Muñoz, *Cruising Utopia*

> My dream is still to have a Jewish home. It won't be the same home that I imagined. But it will be a Jewish home and God will be a part of it. You see, I had to change the story.
> —Efrat, a twenty-six-year-old lesbian woman

In 2004, Rabbi Shlomo Aviner, a stalwart of conservative Orthodox Judaism in Israel,[1] declared that "there is no such thing as a religious homosexual." The rabbi was nominally right. Lacking visible religious LGBT[2] role models, and in the context of almost universally unquestioned assumptions that Orthodox and queer lives were incompatible, many LGBT Jews left the Orthodox fold—thereby confirming the rabbi's stance. But under the surface, changes were brewing, and by the end of that decade Orthodox LGBT persons had launched

QTR • A Journal of Trans and Queer Studies in Religion • 1:1 • May 2024
DOI: 10.1215/29944724-11208902 © 2024 Orit Avishai
This is an open access article distributed under the terms of a Creative Commons license (CC BY-NC-ND 4.0).

9

advocacy organizations, formed networks and social groups, and began to innovate Jewish ritual spaces, learning, scriptural interpretations, and theology. Fast-forward another decade and Orthodox LGBT persons are visible (if not fully accepted) in (some) Orthodox communities, challenging with their very (queer) presence previously undisputed definitions of the family and what it means to be "Orthodox." In queer theory parlance, they made religious queer lives, formerly socially invisible and culturally paradoxical, plausible and livable.

Each of these developments can be analyzed vis-à-vis different bodies of literature: social movements and activism, identity development, theological innovation, the social construction of reality.[3] This article argues that they can also be understood as a process of queer worldmaking: a productive, creative, and ongoing process of rejecting cisheteronormativity by enlisting a range of social practices, cultural productions, and political activities to create new social contexts, scripts, and rituals. Queer worldmaking typically references rhetorical and performative strategies. This article argues that religious (and religious-adjacent) acts, including everyday ritual practices and scriptural interpretation, are among the creative acts that are part of queer cultural worldmaking.

The article builds on queer worldmaking scholarship to document how Orthodox LGBT persons "change the story" daily through improvisations associated with their marginalized status.[4] Like other LGBTQ+ persons, they create a local counterculture, but the catch is that the particular counterculture I examine emerges from within a conservative religious tradition—a context often perceived as antithetical to queer lives—and from a geopolitical context (Israel/Palestine) that does not align with (and actively contradicts) queer visions of solidarity and social justice.[5] Thus, the article makes an empirically informed case for a queer worldmaking project that is grounded in everyday religious practice, ritual, and scriptural interpretations.

The article draws from a larger project on the activism, identities, communities, and lived experiences of Orthodox LGBT Jews in Israel.[6] Focusing specifically on Orthodox gays and lesbians, and building on the idea that religion is both performative and generative, the article makes the deceptively simple observation that some religious LGBTQ+ persons resolve the pain of living in/between religious/queer worlds by creating a new set of identities, new scripts for everyday living: new "worlds." What is less obvious is that the generative raw materials to construct these queer worlds are deeply rooted in their faith tradition, community, rituals, and practices. Specifically, I examine the productive, generative potential of sacred as well as daily practices—"everyday theologies"—and how engagement with scripture and Jewish thought produces a particularly (Orthodox) Jewish way of being queer. The article contributes to the study of queer Orthodox Jews and the study of queer life in religion more generally. In addition, by analyzing a *religious* worldmaking process, this article brings in conversation fields that are often not connected conceptually due to their divergent intellectual and activist histories.

Queer Worldmaking and the Social Construction of a (New) Reality

This article is grounded in the idea that making LGBTQ+ lives livable entails the transformation of everyday spaces, practice, and discourses and applies it to the religious sphere, typically neglected in queer scholarship. To do so I bring in conversation the concept of queer worldmaking, which rests on the premise that cisheteronormativity is but one possible arrangement of the social world (with the implication that the social world can be rearranged) and the sociological insight that reality—any reality, including a religious and/or queer world—is, by definition, socially constructed.[7]

Queer worldmaking references a productive process by which an agentic minority group works from within the cracks of an oppressive dominant culture to produce counter-hegemonic practices, ideologies, rhetoric, and identities: a productive refusal of cisheteronormativity. Queer worldmaking has generally been associated with rhetorical, textual, and performative strategies that remake "secular" worlds, but these foci are a product of queer theory and activism's history, interests, and biases; there is nothing inherent about the concept that would preclude it from being used as a lens on other types of practices or in religious contexts.

Queer worldmaking is most often associated with Lauren Berlant and Michael Warner's 1998 essay "Sex in Public," but José Esteban Muñoz used the concept in an earlier essay, "Ephemera as Evidence."[8] Muñoz later defined queer worldmaking as a process that involves the undoing ("disassembling") of the majoritarian public sphere and use of its parts to make a new world from within.[9] Muñoz saw queer worldmaking as a process that requires "an active kernel of utopian possibility,"[10] a process that can be located in attempts to fashion a new world via "spectacles, performances, and willful enactments of the self for other."[11] Muñoz focused on public performances but acknowledged that everyday practices could qualify as queer worldmaking performances.[12]

Berlant and Warner shifted the emphasis from performance, utopia, and minorities' ability to work from within dominant structures to the creation of counter-publics that "support forms of affective, erotic, and personal living that are public in the sense of accessible, available to memory, and sustained collective activity."[13] Their worldmaking project was "constructed and reconstructed through the circulation of texts."[14]

Subsequent scholarship documented instances of decomposition and recomposition of dominant paradigms by minoritized groups, with a focus on deconstruction of cultural practices, artistic endeavors, and sexual cultures.[15] Berlant and Warner named as examples "sites of drag, youth culture, music, dance, parades, flaunting, and cruising,"[16] while Muñoz extolled the worldmaking potential of poetry, visual art, theatrical performances, and reality TV, as well as performances that often go unmarked as cultural productions, such as anonymous sex.[17] Few have drawn on the concept to interrogate activism and its intersections with everyday life as pathways of queer worldmaking, despite the fact that activists frequently use the "majoritarian culture as raw material to make a new world."[18] Likewise, there is little scholarship on the making of *religious* queer worlds.[19] This article ponders both possibilities.

Can queer worldmaking practices transcend the realm of the textual, performative, and rhetorical? If "queer world-making is rooted in the premises that cisheteronormativity is but one possible arrangement of the social world,"[20] and that worldmaking performances do not strive to merely entertain but also to demonstrate to spectators that a different future is possible, it follows that cultural productions are not the only paths to disrupt cisheteronormativity. Recent overviews of the concept's trajectory in communication studies[21] and education[22] suggest such a broadening. Likewise, a recent consideration of the production of networks of sociability, parenting practices, and narratives of everyday life demonstrates how queer worldmaking can be operationalized outside the realm of cultural practices and public performances.[23] Drawing on the experiences of Orthodox Jewish gays and lesbians, this article suggests that the creative process of making queer worlds can also include more traditional subjects of inquiry in the social sciences: religious ritual, cultural scripts, activism, and everyday life—the social building blocks that amount to the construction, or, to use Muñoz's terms, the disassembling and reassembling, of social realities. Building on Muñoz's emphasis on the queer worldmaking potential of transformation of everyday spaces, I argue that creating new identity categories and social scripts and advancing new scriptural readings and theological innovations can be routes of queer worldmaking.

This reading hinges on defining what qualifies as a queer world. In the context of queer theory and practice, religious queer worldmaking may seem as much of an oxymoron as a religious queer person seemed to Rabbi Aviner and other rabbis. The religious subject occupies an ambivalent space in the queer imaginary,[24] resulting in the erasure of such subjects from queer worlds or their designation as paradoxical queer subjects. But religion is a particularly potent arena to think about worldmaking: "religion"—just like "cisheteronormativity"—is a socially constructed world. In this world—one that prescribes scripts for everyday living, interacting, making families, and so on (this is especially true of the Jewish tradition, where elaborate rules of conduct regulate both religious observance and everyday conduct)—Others (including, especially, gender and sexual Others) are by definition disruptive. Likewise, religious practices, rituals, spaces, and ideas are considered to be generative and productive. Indeed, as I show in this article, disruptions emerge from the cracks within the system's own logics.

Thus, while queer worldmaking has predominantly been theorized as a performative, rhetorical, and secular process, it is also a quintessentially sociological process that references transformative unmaking and remaking of the social world. This article considers how religious LGBT subjects reshape hegemonic institutions, discourses, practices, and identities through a bottom-up engagement with the everyday: places, spaces, people, dominant communal narratives about sacred texts. Like textual, rhetorical, and performative strategies, these too can be sites of a "mode of being in the world that is also inventing the world":[25] actions that simultaneously inhabit and reinvent dominant social, cultural, and political structures, thereby providing a lens for making sense of the creation, negotiation, and expansion of queer worlds.

Background and Methodology

This article focuses on Israeli "religious nationalists," or religious Zionists (*dati-leumi*). Religiously, this group is a loose corollary to modern Orthodoxy in the United States. Religious nationalists also constitute a demographic category that amounts to around 20 percent of the Israeli population and that is associated not only with religious observance and spiritual belonging but also with a way of life and political identification with expansionist, nationalist visions of the state. Sociologically, then, "religious Zionists" refers to a loose category, a group whose members are engaged in political, cultural, and ideological negotiations with a range of Others, both Jewish (secular, traditionalist, ultra-Orthodox, Reform, Conservative) and non-Jewish.[26] I use the term "Orthodox" to refer to this group because "religious" in English does not have the same register as the Hebrew term.[27] For my purposes, Orthodox also includes disaffiliated persons who were raised in Orthodox homes.

From 2016–21, I worked with Orthodox LGBT persons, most of them gay, lesbians, or bisexual, and studied the Proud Religious Community, or *Kadag*, a loose coalition of organizations and initiatives launched in the mid-2000s by LGBT activists from Orthodox backgrounds. My data includes interviews, physical and digital ethnography, archival research, and analysis of media content. I conducted over 120 interviews with Orthodox LGBT persons, activists, allies, educators, therapists, family members, and rabbis. To preserve privacy, I provide little contextual background on participants; the field is so small that attempts to mask one participant might inadvertently implicate others who did not partake in this study (I do name activists when referencing publicly available information). The ethnographic component includes conventional objects of ethnographic inquiry—ritual spaces, political activism, social gatherings, and community engagement as well as digital ethnography on the Facebook pages of Orthodox LGBT persons and allies who invited me to join their networks and those of Kadag organizations and high-profile organizations and religious authorities. I supplemented interviews and fieldwork with archival research into Kadag organizations' documents and media accounts.[28] The analysis I present in this article emerges from a triangulation across this data.

The focus on Orthodox gays, lesbians, and bisexual persons is a product of careful deliberation and reflection; I concluded that one project could not do justice to all the categories under the LGBTQ+ umbrella given divergent histories, contemporary politics, and the intricacies of Jewish jurisprudence, coupled with the demands of ethnographic fieldwork and my subject position as a cisgender straight non-Orthodox Jew. I chose to focus primarily on sexual diversity, and specifically on Orthodox gays and lesbians, who were most visible and accessible at the time I conducted my research. I am cautious not to extrapolate from their experiences,[29] though when I speak of activism or generalize I do use "LGBT," mirroring my interlocutor's own terms.

Unlivable Lives

One key finding in the broader project is that Orthodox Jewish contexts—communities, religious traditions, educational institutions, cultural practices, and the very definitions of what it means to be a full-fledged, authentic member of this particular society—prescribe an overwhelming cis and heteronormative social order that renders Orthodox LGBT lives, to use Judith Butler's term, unlivable.[30]

My informants spoke of shame, secrecy, denial, repression, spiritual harms, theological angst, and family dramas that resulted in shattered life plans, social deaths, crises of faith, and a yearning to be "normal." Many fell into a depression, experienced suicidal ideation, and sought harmful interventions such as reparative therapy. Most of all, they mourned the loss of a normative (and, many believe, singular) path to Orthodox adulthood; informants spoke of a torn, shredded, broken picture, image, vision—a life plan of adulthood composed of "a normal family" that fell apart with no alternative to take its place. One gay participant reflected how "in twelfth grade, the rabbi starts talking about relationships, home, family. And I realized, to be religious means to marry a woman. To build a normative family. But I knew that I can't be there." This participant concluded that "I have no future." A thirty-two-year-old lesbian had to rethink every aspect of adult life:

> Growing up I had this idea of what Shabbat, holidays, religious rituals, and celebrations were going to look like in my home. And then there is that point where you understand. . . . It was not going to happen, I would have to let go of that dream. The home that I had been seeing in front of my eyes all these years, a learned, *halachic* [*halacha* is Jewish law] home, where religion is at the center, where children *of course* attend single-sex schools [Orthodox schools are sex segregated]. All gone. I wasn't going to have that wedding. I wasn't going to have that Shabbat table. That school. I mourned the loss of that home.

In these ways, communal messages, expectations, and structures that offered only one path to Jewish adulthood rendered Orthodox LGBT lives unlivable. (Orthodox LGBT Jews are far from outliers, and their experiences echo those of LGBT persons from other religious traditions.[31]) For the time being, most LGBT Orthodox persons still inhabit this realm of "unlivability," but a growing number have figured out what it means to be an *Orthodox* LGBT person: working from the ground up, alone in their everyday lives and together in community, they are creating new blueprints for living: queer/religious worlds.

Religious Queer Worldmaking

How does a marginalized group, especially one that is hidden and whose very existence is denied, disassemble and reassemble a cisheteronormative social world? In what follows I consider some of the ways that my respondents created a queer/Orthodox world, in the process reshaping Orthodox hegemonic institutions, discourses, practices, and identities. As we will see, the antidote to harmful Orthodox messages about same-sex attraction and LGBT identities draws on a variety of resources, suggesting the unique flavor of local projects of queer worldmaking. Given the goals of this article, my main focus is on how Orthodox LGBT persons engage with mainstream Orthodoxy, but I note that this is far from an internal Orthodox dialogue. Orthodox LGBT persons' attempts to remake material culture and practices also draw on, and involve negotiations with, the largely secular Israeli LGBT community, other demographic groups in Israel (e.g., secular, traditionalist, and ultra-Orthodox Jews), non-Orthodox Judaism (e.g., the Reform and Conservative movements, both marginalized and demonized by Orthodox Jews in Israel), and the expectations of the global queer community.

Articulating and Normalizing New Identity Categories

The making of new identity categories, normalizing them and infusing them with positive meanings and with joy,[32] has been central to Orthodox LGBT Jews' efforts to remake Orthodoxy's cisheteronormative social order—a vehicle for imagining a queered Orthodox world.

Interviewees who came of age prior to the era of Orthodox LGBT public visibility that began in the early 2010s almost uniformly said that they could not imagine "being" Orthodox and gay or lesbian: this was not a plausible social category. Their neighborhoods, families, texts, and cultural images were exclusively populated by cisheteronormative persons, families, and communities. One interviewee could not identify with the term "lesbian" despite being familiar with the term, explaining that as a "normative Orthodox girl from the yishuv [village]" the term seemed inapplicable; LGBT people were secular, characters on TV and in the movies, foreign and detached from Orthodox reality. Having never met a lesbian who was religious, this participant could not identify with the concept nor fathom living as one: "It seemed unrealistic." Many located this impossibility in utopic ideas about normative Orthodox families, a "scenery in a play: When you grow up in such a home [cishetero], in such a community, there is this scenery all around you. What the home is supposed to look like, the family. And that rubs off on you."

For many study participants, the key that unlocked access to envisioning (and enacting) alternative sceneries and stories was finding a community of like-minded people. Early communities were virtual (anonymous chatrooms that were later replaced by publicly visible social media groups), but in the late aughts, trailblazing Orthodox LGBT activists, some of whom met online, founded affirming ritual and social spaces. In the early days these spaces were largely hidden and insular. Such safe spaces, where stigmatized persons can let down their guard, have long been documented as key arenas of political mobilization: while providing respite and access to mentors, role models, and a peer group, these spaces also serve as fertile grounds for generating new rituals, symbols, rhetoric, and ideas about shared history, destiny, and needs. Hidden from prying and judging eyes, marginalized persons work together to reframe traits that distinguish them from the majority as a social positive, articulate legible social and political categories (Orthodox gay, Orthodox trans), and mobilize on behalf of the collective. In queer theory parlance, these safe spaces are sites of queer worldmaking, a point of departure for building affirming new worlds. A couple of examples illustrate this process.

Interviewees who came of age prior to the 2000s said, almost uniformly, that the internet "changed everything." In the early days, they flocked to anonymous (and, by today's standards, archaic) chat rooms. One participant said that before finding such a chat room, "there wasn't another lesbian in the world." Nati Epstein, an early Kadag activist, published an anonymous letter in a popular daily newspaper in response to an Orthodox journalist's claim that homosexuality did not exist in Orthodox circles. Nati, who frequented a chat room populated by Orthodox gays and lesbians, knew full well that they existed; they just feared exposure.

> We do have gays. They are more numerous than you can imagine. . . . I invite you to our post-Shabbat chat in our room, religious gays. My name there is Dan. I invite you to hear the heartbreaking confusion of seventeen-, eighteen-year-olds who don't understand where God abandoned them. Listen to soldiers who seek an outlet with those like them. . . . And listen to bachelors like myself who wonder what kind of future they have. . . . You can also join a conversation of the married . . . some of whom have come to terms with the lies they tell their wives, others less so. They're all looking for someone who will understand.

Another interviewee described the activity in this chatroom: "People wrote poems, told painful stories; we debated religion, what it means to be religious gay person." The catch was that initially, forum participants did not identify as Orthodox gays and lesbians; many were heterosexually married and had planned on remaining so. But bit by bit, conversations, debates, and cultural outpouring began to give shape to a new—now plausible—identity category: Orthodox gay, Orthodox lesbian. "One day, after spending hours in a chat, it suddenly hit me: I was a religious gay man. That's all there was to it. I did not need to justify my existence, I was not a rare bird—there were dozens like me! I just did not know exactly what that meant."

Finding community is a necessary but insufficient step in the journey toward making sense of oneself. Identities do not emerge nor exist in a vacuum—to figure out what it means to "be," Orthodox LGBT persons needed to also expand their community's horizons—to remake their worlds and change society. Shoval, an Israeli Orthodox LGBT outreach organization founded in the late aughts, attempts to do this via two-hour workshops. Trained volunteers meet with staff at Orthodox schools, with mental health professionals who work with Orthodox persons, or with members of an Orthodox community (neighborhood, synagogue) to educate them about sexual and gender diversity (generally in Jewish contexts). These workshops begin with volunteers telling their Orthodox LGBT story—a narrative arc revolving around a normative Orthodox childhood interrupted by a painful realization that the protagonist was "different." The Shoval story relays a period of reckoning that often includes violent ruptures on the path to normative Orthodox adulthood and culminates with the volunteer's declaration, "My name is ____ and I am a lesbian/gay/trans Orthodox person." This performance is intended to shatter audiences' allegiance to a singular vision of Orthodox authenticity. It also reaffirms the speaker's claim to Orthodoxy. Interviews with Shoval volunteers revealed that their work with the organization, and especially the opportunity to make these claims repeatedly, were key nodes on their identity journeys: "Learning to say—out loud!—I'm a lesbian. Wow!" "Writing out my story, going through the training, and now doing these workshops has helped me figure out where I stand on issues, my identity."

There is much more to be said about Orthodox Jews' journey from chat rooms and backrooms, from being fearful, anonymous, and closeted, to crafting and disseminating personal and collective narratives through viral Facebook posts that proudly feature their faces, names, families, and stories.[33] But for our purposes, the main point is this: queer worldmaking—that productive, creative, and ongoing process of rejecting cisheteronormativity by enlisting a range of social practices, cultural productions, and political activities to create new social contexts, scripts, and rituals—*also* includes the making and performing of new identity categories that stake LGBT persons' rightful place in a previously monolithic cisheteronormative world. Importantly, in this case, this new world certainly drew on well-established queer activist practices (e.g., curating and narrating one's story) but also emerged from within the cracks of Jewish Orthodoxy: study participants drew on Jewish traditions, symbols, sensibilities, language, and mythologies to reframe, reimagine, and rewrite stories of self and community.

Rescripting Orthodox Family Life

Participants who figured out how to make Orthodox LGBT lives livable were not so much plagued by the question whether "one can be" Orthodox and LGBT (though this question drives much research on religious queer life in the social sciences[34]) but rather how to pour substantive meaning into their reality. One interviewee never contemplated not being religious—though before this gay man got to know other religious gays, it "was not clear to me what life would be like." Participants figured this out on the fly as they made conscious decisions such as where to live, how to get married, whether and how to start a family, how to interact with their religious family members, choosing schools for their children, and how to adapt Jewish rituals. Such decisions involved negotiating with Judaism's heteronormative life scripts, and can thus be read as productive processes of rescripting. Same-sex weddings and family formation illustrate these queer worldmaking practices.

In queer activist and scholarly circles, family formation, monogamy, and, especially, marriage, are often critiqued as capitulation to heteronormativity.[35] But weddings—and the institution of marriage—are also creative arenas of queer rescripting. For Orthodox LGBT persons, marriage—and therefore weddings—represent a point of (re)entry to an authentic Jewish life course. Many thus ponder how to render their monogamous relationships, family units, and weddings Jewishly legible (and therefore legitimate).

Same-sex marriages in Israel are legally ambiguous. Per a 2006 Supreme Court ruling, same-sex couples who were married in jurisdictions where such marriages are legal can register as married in Israel, but this registration is of little consequence since registration serves predominantly statistical purposes. Marriage, along with other matters regarding personal status (i.e., divorce), are under the exclusive purview of religious authorities. The Chief Rabbinate, which authorizes Jewish weddings, does not recognize same-sex marriages, rendering such ceremonies symbolic. Same-sex couples' legal status is regulated by the state's cohabitation case law, which offers considerable legal protections, predominantly economic, but cannot confer same-sex couples and families the cultural and religious legitimacy they seek. Many Orthodox same-sex couples thus grapple with aligning their weddings with the Jewish tradition.

Traditional Jewish weddings are gendered and structured, involving ritual gender-coded clothing; a male wedding officiator (rabbi);[36] a Jewish wedding contract, *ketubah*, which outlines the groom's rights and responsibilities toward the bride (but not vice versa); and other practices that are performed by the groom: blessing with a ring, the ritualistic shattering of the glass. Orthodox LGBT persons are effectively shut out of this ritual domain altogether: per Orthodox religious elites, Jewish law and tradition preclude the possibility of Jewish same-sex weddings.[37] But many Orthodox gays and lesbians are determined to prove otherwise.

One couple realized that whereas heterosexual couples had to just accept the Jewish wedding ritual as is ("Ok, with slight pushback, you know, on the margins—the woman too can bless him with a ring"), they were in a position to put together a ceremony that would, in their words, be a *real* Jewish wedding, by breaking the ceremony down to its components and making decisions about each of its parts: "Can we stand under a huppah [the Jewish wedding canopy]? Which of the traditional blessings can we include? Who would bless us? Do we just tweak the language [Hebrew is highly gendered] or are there some blessings that simply don't make sense for two women? Shattering the glass was very important to us. . . . But can a woman do this?" To find answers, they turned to the Jewish tradition. Both had postgraduate training in Jewish thought,[38] and they dove into Jewish archives and sources as they asked: "What makes a wedding 'Jewish'?" They decided that the huppah could be easily incorporated into a same-sex wedding but arrived at a different conclusion regarding the shattering of the glass (other couples concluded otherwise). Nevertheless, they wove the ritual's symbolism into the ceremony. This couple easily did away with the traditional Jewish marriage contract because it was a relic of a patriarchal culture (many heterosexual couples and Orthodox feminist organizations share these concerns), and replaced it with their own tradition-inspired wedding vows. The resulting ceremony was personally meaningful and, they said, authentically Jewish, adding, only half-jokingly, that their heterosexual friends were jealous that they were "forced" to construct their own ceremony.

As in the case of identity formation, successful rescripting—or undoing, disassembling, and reassembling of dominant (heteronormative) social scripts—is an interactive, iterative, and performative process. In recent years, photos and videos of Orthodox same-sex engagement parties and wedding ceremonies have gone viral by design: couples often encourage guests (or shall we say audiences?) to post photos, videos, and reflections. One such instance is the June 2017 wedding of Kadag activists Moshe Grossman (now Argaman) and Eran Ashkenazi (now Argaman). The men exchanged vows before hundreds of family members, friends, and Orthodox LGBT peers in a wedding that many in attendance said looked and "felt" Jewish: although the ceremony was officiated by a yeshiva-trained transgender woman, not an ordained male rabbi, and did not include a bride, it featured the Jewish wedding canopy, a broken glass (two, one for each groom to crush), customary blessings with requisite queer adjustments, and both grooms—and many of their guests—presented as Orthodox (or Orthodox adjacent) in their choice of clothing and ritual garments. Social media posts celebrated the occasion as an authentic Jewish wedding because not only did the grooms identify as Orthodox, but because their community recognized them as such. A queer world was being made right before their eyes—and then shared (performed?) for the world to see.

While many couples refrain from turning their private ceremonies into public spectacles, they, too, participate in queer worldmaking in the sense that such recognizably Jewish wedding ceremonies are a product of elaborate consultations and negotiations with a large circle of family, friends, other LGBT persons, and religious leaders. These deliberations often have a public facing component, as same-sex couples routinely share information on "best practices" for Orthodox (or Orthodox adjacent) same-sex weddings on social media. Thus, as rewritten scripts, which may begin as private creative endeavors, begin to circulate, these new, queer scripts are made public. Investigations into the essence of "real Jewish weddings" that sought to modify, not duplicate or replace, traditional weddings thus resulted in creative remaking of gendered rituals and ceremonial chants, prayers, and blessings. It is notable that this iterative, deliberative process represents a new way of "doing" Orthodoxy, one that does not take the word of the religious expert (a male rabbi) or the weight of tradition as having the final, authoritative word. For those committed to conventional forms of Orthodox communities, this is the key, ultimate threat to the existing Jewish world order.[39] To be clear, LGBT persons are far from being the first constituency to articulate and act on these alternative visions of Orthodoxy.[40] But for our purposes, their interventions do amount to a form of a queer worldmaking project.

Another arena of creative rescripting is family formation. Having children is a central waystation on one's path to normative Jewish adulthood and is considered a key mitzvah, a commandment (having children is such a central principle in Jewish life that some rabbinic authorities use it to justify monogamous same-sex unions[41]). But Orthodox family and ritual life are highly gendered, rendering the same-sex family not only a cultural anomaly but also ritually deficient. One interviewee thus pondered: "Who will bless the Sabbath? Who will do kiddush, take the children to synagogue? Who will do all these tasks that in the halacha and in the Orthodox community are the tasks of the man?" Campaigns that castigate families that deviate from the cisheteronormative script as non-Orthodox, non-Jewish, foreign, and menacing capitalize on these fears (e.g., the ultranationalist, anti-feminist, transphobic, and homophobic Noam political party[42]). But Orthodox LGBT persons are undeterred.

Orthodox LGBT persons' paths to parenthood are varied, and include shared custody of children born during a previous, heterosexual marriage (at times involving a new, same-sex partner); mothers using sperm from anonymous or known donors; single gay men and couples who have children via surrogacy; and a range of alternative family structures. Orthodox communities and Jewish law trail far behind this vibrant reality, but Orthodox LGBT persons are adamant that their families, communities, and religious leaders will just have to catch up. As new realities demand that rituals and traditions be adjusted, new ones are made, sometimes on the fly. One respondent's synagogue was initially at a loss regarding the marking of a lesbian couple's birth because the ceremony typically involves the father in a set of rituals (a brother stood in); in the process of negotiating the ceremony, the mothers told me, they noticed a palatable shift in some of their co-congregants, and now thought of their synagogue not only as "a typical accepting space" but also as a truly affirming one. Another interviewee described conversations with the principal of an Orthodox school who initially balked at accepting a child with two moms. The deliberation itself was moot, since this was a public school and the principal knew that the child would be admitted: "He was just trying to scare us off, but I am not here to make people comfortable." Zehorit Sorek, a prominent Kadag activist, told a more uplifting story at a public event in 2020 while discussing a daughter's Bat Mitzvah at the inclusive Tel Aviv Orthodox synagogue Yachad. It is customary for the prayer leader to bless the child on this occasion, a ritual that includes naming the child's parents. Without missing a beat, the prayer leader named three parents—Zehorit, the child's father (Zehorit's ex-husband), and Zehorit's longtime wife who raised the Bat Mitzvah celebrant—thereby challenging seemingly intractable foundational categories in Jewish thought: Who is a parent? What constitutes a family?

In a different public event, another activist said that their family's presence in Orthodox spaces such as the synagogue, school, and the very streets of their mostly Orthodox neighborhood was an activist intervention: "They see us. We're a normal family. And they have to make space for us." Likewise, the Facebook feeds of many Orthodox LGBT persons are often filled with the unceremonious stuff of everyday life: photos of children on the first day of school; complaints about teacher strikes, which are common in Israel; home renovations; holiday celebrations; and, occasionally, a photo from a Pride event. Much like wedding photos that go viral, these depictions of conventional everyday lives serve as a vehicle of both rescripting and reassembling Orthodoxy and communicating, to a broader audience, what these new, queer worlds look like (in this case, not very different than the cisheteronormative world, except that the two proud parents accompanying an excited child to their first day or the partners showing off their new bedroom happen to be same-sex).

By creating new stories and circulating new images of Orthodox Jewish life, both religious and secular, ritual and mundane, Orthodox LGBT persons render their lives both legible and livable within a cisheteronormative tradition. Inevitably, this is a subversive process, one that rests on first challenging, and then remaking, taken-for-granted practices, rituals, categories, and definitions. What distinguishes this mode of queer worldmaking is the fact that it engages—and sometimes explicitly enlists—religious sensibilities.

Innovating Theology, Scripture, and Jewish Thought

For many queer persons who grow up in religious communities, negative messages, one interviewee told me, "are deeply entrenched. You are bad, sinful, deviant. There's no place for you." It is well documented that many LGBTQ+ persons leave their faith communities as a result of such negative messages and related hostile practices, but for some queer persons, disaffiliation is not an option. Many Orthodox gays and lesbians I talked to pursued an alternative—affirming and potentially queer-worldmaking—strategy as they ask: "How do you rewrite that narrative?" The answer, in many cases, was to mine the tradition and construct alternative theologies and scriptural interpretations that helped Orthodox LGBT persons make sense of—and celebrate—religious queer lives, though with a twist: whereas Jewish thought and theologies are often gleaned from scripture and Jewish tradition by learned religious elites, my respondents drew on their own lived experiences, everyday theologies, and interpretations born out of the scars of human existence. As noted above, this process, in and of itself, was simultaneously transgressive and a generative, constructive move.

Many queer people of faith seek answers to existential questions: Why did God create them "this" way? Did he[43] intend for them to suffer? And if so, why? My study respondents were angry and wanted answers. Lea's relationship with God had known ups and downs. Approaching thirty when we met, Lea was "pretty upset with him." Others sought to assuage their anger by reimagining their deity. Effi, a thirty-something gay man, had delved into the Jewish sources and concluded that "God is good and has your best interest in mind and doesn't want to screw you over." Effi's God did not intend for his followers to suffer and therefore must have had reasons for creating human variation.

Effi's logic may make sense, but it belies a key Jewish theological principle that associates religious commitment with sublimation. The theology of binding, or *Aqedah*, holds that accepting Jewish law, scripture, and tradition as a way of life comes down to one's willingness to subordinate oneself to a higher normative order; people who submit to God's way sublimate all sorts desires, needs, and values, and same-sex attraction is not a special challenge: doing as God instructed means that one will at times endure trials and make sacrifices.[44]

But many Orthodox LGBT persons have come to resent—and reject—this logic, claiming that it made no sense that God would create entire categories of people with the expectation that they, alone, carry an unresolvable burden: forever single, celibate, and childless. How to explain gender and sexual diversity then? Effi landed on this explanation: God created gender and sexual variance not in order to punish LGBT persons or challenge them with sublimation—making them the poster children for religious commitment (as rabbis, some of them LGBT allies, frequently claim). Rather, the challenge was to embrace and "to be how God made me." Effi reasoned that in creating gender and sexual variance, God was challenging *society* to deal with difference, rendering LGBT persons a vessel for positive social change. Effi accepted the challenge: "He created you in a way that you cannot change and gave you a social challenge that you will be different and the Other, that you will force society to deal with you. It's not easy and it's not fun. But if you choose faith, you choose this job." Not only was this social role not inferior to that fulfilled by heterosexual Jews, but it was also imbued with perhaps the ultimate mitzvah that Jews take upon themselves: practicing world repair, which, Effi said, was much more meaningful than suffering. LGBT Jews, in this reading, were no lesser than their cisheteronormative counterparts: while the latter fulfill the command to repair the world by having children, LGBT persons can fulfill this mitzvah by helping create a more tolerant and loving society. Effi's reasoning here not only turns a central Jewish principle on its head but also casts queer life as a positive social force, a net social good that is legitimated—indeed, necessitated—by Jewish ethics. There is an additional theological move here. For many Jews, observance is rooted in pious compliance with Jewish laws, scripture, and tradition. But the logic here instead grounds a committed Jewish life in a personal commitment to God and the ethics of world repair.

Such deliberations reference another theological discussion in Jewish thought: What renders a Jewish life fulfilled? Does Jewish cosmology care for individual happiness and self-fulfillment? Lea's upbringing emphasized that choosing one's own happiness defied a collectively oriented Jewish ethics. Lea was taught that fulfilling one's dreams and chasing happiness is an egoistical pursuit—un-Orthodox. But others drew on the Jewish tradition to insist that not only did God not intend for them suffer, but also that self-fulfillment and self-realization were compatible with Jewish ethics because, as one man explained, "A happy and content person who lives to their full potential can contribute much more to others." Happiness, in other words, was essential to living a Jewish life.

The moves described here challenge hegemonic theologies, but they are firmly grounded in established theological and ethical traditions within Jewish thought, albeit from less-known minority voices.[45] The point, however, is that like other queer worldmaking practices, these theological and scriptural interpretive moves represent a productive, creative, and ongoing process of rejecting cisheteronormativity by a minority group that works from within the cracks of an oppressive dominant culture to produce counter-hegemonic practices, ideologies, rhetoric, and identities. Given the intimate connection between Jewish thought, theology, and philosophy and everyday lives, these rhetorical moves literally open up livable spaces. Numerous participants mentioned in their interviews longtime Kadag ally Rabbi Benny Lau's refrain that "the closet is death, and you should choose life." "Choosing life" is a key principle in Jewish law and ethics. Elevating this principle and placing it on the same plane as scripturally derived principles that produce spiritual harm literally makes LGBT lives livable. One interviewee had come perilously close to committing suicide out of despair a few years before we met. Hearing Rabbi Lau speak persuaded this woman to decide that "I was just going to live," even without fully abiding by Jewish law. According to this participant, Jewish law, as promulgated by "generations of hetero-cis male rabbis," represented just one way to live a normative and authentic Jewish life. Orthodox conservatives would beg to differ, but the point is that innovative theologies and scriptural interpretations—ones that emerged from the Jewish tradition itself, from the bottom up—were the key to constructing meaningful queer worlds for these people of faith.

In sum, same-sex attracted Orthodox Jews engage with, rather than reject, Jewish theologies, interpretive traditions, concepts, and values. They ask foundational theological questions: What does it mean to believe? Who is this God that I believe in? What does it mean to be a religious/Orthodox/observant Jew? As they reach into the Jewish archives to seek answers, they construct new theologies of God and religious life, new modes of interpreting Jewish scripture and sources.[46] While they are fully aware that such innovations are potentially subversive, they insist that they are not out to start a revolution: "My intention," one activist said in a public outreach event, was never to start a movement. All I wanted was to make space for my family." But making space for a queer Other in an otherwise cisheteronormative community, developing an affirming and inclusive stance that is grounded in Jewish scripture, thought, philosophy, and theology is, in and of itself, a performance of difference, both utterly mundane and spectacularly outlandish, one that serves to not only enable individual survival but also to use the stuff of the real world to remake a collective sense of the world.

Conclusion

The "queer worldmaking" framework emerged in the 1990s as part of theoretical explorations into how gender and sexual difference could be channeled into not only subverting and resisting cisheteronormativity, but also creatively deployed to ensure queer thriving. Politically, worldmaking points to a strategy of building up—and, crucially, from within, rather than tearing down the existing world. Muñoz, especially, recognized the power of working from within dominant structures and hegemonic cultures, imagining worldmaking as a cultural recycling of sorts, where cisheteronormative and antiqueer cultural norms would serve as raw material that could be repurposed: "A disempowered politics of positionality that has been rendered unthinkable by the dominant culture."[47] The performances—not only theatrical ones, but also those on everyday stages such as synagogues, schools, event halls, the streets, and Facebook—that make queer worlds neither assimilate into existing cultures and structures nor completely oppose them; the key, for Muñoz, was a process of disidentification which worked from within "on, with, and against a cultural form."[48]

This article argues that the processes described here—and their consequences—are a case study of worldmaking through everyday practice and spaces that draw on antiqueer cultural material to actively imagine a new world. Politics here works from within an existing social system and draws on its logics and sensibilities as well as negotiations with its cultural Others. As we have seen, Orthodox LGBT persons' demands that they be seen, heard, acknowledged, and legitimated from within the system have been both transgressive and constructive. To arrive at new cultural scripts and identities, to rewrite stories and conjure new images, to redefine families and weddings, to invigorate ritual and study spaces, and to rethink their relationship with their creator, Orthodox LGBT persons have actively mined, leaned into, and mobilized the Jewish tradition—a Jewish tradition that they have insisted is rightfully theirs. Like other religious practitioners (Jewish and otherwise) who innovate (and queer) religious ritual, practice, and theology, sometimes inadvertently, the performances discussed here have opened up a previously unimaginable space that makes Orthodox LGBT lives livable. Livable, in the literal sense: LGBT persons raised in Orthodox homes and communities attribute public visibility and newfound plausibility to their decisions to not disaffiliate (disaffiliation was routinely the case before the turn of the twenty-first century) or, in more extreme cases, to overcome suicidal ideation. And livable in a metaphoric sense, for public performances such as same-sex weddings that legibly read as Jewish, LGBT Jewish study spaces, and well-developed Orthodox LGBT narrative arcs communicate to others: there is a blueprint and there is space for you.

The empirical sociological process I have been discussing is without a doubt one of worldmaking, but whether it can be labeled as a process of "queer" worldmaking depends on one's stance vis-à-vis a number of theoretical—and political—questions. One issue is whether queer worlds can be religious. Queer worldmaking scholarship seems to have taken for granted that queer worldmaking projects are inherently secular. This would make sense: religion has been a key (though hardly exclusive) source of trans-, queer-, and homophobia; exclusion; and violence. But, as we have seen, and as numerous other studies have shown, religious lives and LGBT ones are not inherently incompatible.[49] In fact, rejecting this compatibility lends support to conservative religious factions' claims to exclusive hold on their faith traditions and accepts queer theory's secularist bias as inevitable rather than a product of intellectual and political histories.[50]

Thus, from a theoretical perspective, the idea that a remade, queer world could be a religious one is not preposterous. Indeed, a careful reading suggests that Muñoz did not discount religion from queer futurity. Groups of people make worlds (i.e., construct reality) from the cultural raw materials at their disposal; for persons of faith, these cultural raw materials include things like religious symbols, rituals, language, and sensibilities. And if these worlds are inherently cis and heteronormative, religious queer worldmaking amounts to a productive rejection of these worlds *from within their own paradigms*. That the antidote to harmful Orthodox messages about same-sex attraction or trans experiences draws from the same fount of Orthodox scripture, wisdom, tradition, and philosophy does not inherently make this a non-queer project but rather a thoroughly *local* project of queer worldmaking. Because it emphasizes performances from the ground up, queer worldmaking helps see how ordinary people go about their lives in the context of social systems and institutions outside of their control, and how they create new forms from within the cracks. This is one sense of "unlikely queer worlds" that the title of this article alludes to.

The second issue—of whether a worldmaking project predicated on complicity, assimilation, and deradicalized politics can qualify as a queer project—may be impossible to resolve. My respondents were not merely working from within religious logics; their religious system's values (monogamous, natalist) and the larger political context (nationalist, nativist) resulted in deradicalized, homonormative, and homo-nationalist politics. "We're not seeking to destroy the institution of the straight family. . . . All we want is a room of our own within the Jewish home," a prominent Kadag activist told an audience at the Orthodox-affiliated Bar Ilan University in May 2018.[51] The Jewish Home is not only a metaphor; the Jewish Home had also been the name of a nationalist, right-wing political party. That party dissolved, but its vision lives on in other nationalist parties, including the Religious Zionist and Jewish Empowerment parties that are part of the current ruling coalition in Israel.

Early queer worldmaking theorists were critical of assimilative practices associated with homonormativity, including (especially) the reproductive, monogamous family. Even more unforgivable is affinity with homonationalist stances (the association between LGBTQ+ rights and nationalism).[52] Desiring a room in "the Jewish home" telegraphs support for a particular mode of expansive nationalism; most Orthodox LGBT persons subscribe to right-of-center nationalist visions, and while there are certainly many dissenters, activist organizations are as a general rule mum about Israel's geopolitical conflict. This is hardly a queer utopia of the sort that Muñoz envisioned. Can a project that refuses to interrogate larger social structures that do not guarantee safety and justice for all be a bona fide queer one?

Perhaps here, too, Muñoz's theorizing can offer direction. Muñoz's model of political action was grounded in "disidentification," a strategy that recognizes the importance of local context, locates resistance in everyday lives, works on and against dominant ideology, and seeks to transform cultural logics from within.[53] Rather than assessing queer lives and activism through the radical-queer-versus-complicit-sellout binary,[54] we might extrapolate that seemingly complicit practices and movements can pose a threat to heteronormativity and normalization by virtue of their very being. Everyday performances that rewrite social scripts and normalize LGBT persons' Orthodox legibility is both worldmaking and transgressive, with the heart of transgression residing in claims to Orthodox authenticity. One interviewee surmised that they were queer Orthodox, "queer" referring not to gender or sexual categories but rather to religious ones. And what is queerer than blowing up categories? This is the second sense in which my title references an "unlikely" queer world. I recognize, however, that this world belies—perhaps irrevocably—the boundaries of "queer." My goal is thus humble: to provide an opening to expand the uses of queer worldmaking while providing a conceptual framework for students of religious queer lives to discuss a number of phenomena that are often separated across research agendas, disciplinary frameworks, and epistemologies.

Orit Avishai is a professor of sociology at Fordham University and the author of *Queer Judaism: LGBT Activism and the Remaking of Jewish Orthodoxy in Israel* (2023).

Acknowledgments
QTR editors Joseph Marchal and Melissa M. Wilcox's encouragement and sage advice, as well as two anonymous reviewers' comments, helped refine the arguments I develop in this article.

Notes
1. "Conservative" here refers to those who hold traditional values and are averse to change or innovation—conservative Orthodoxy is *not* synonymous with Conservative Judaism.

2. I use "LGBT" in the context of Jewish Orthodoxy since most of my respondents use a Hebrew acronym that does not include queer; I use LGBTQ+ to refer to gender and sexual variance in other contexts in line with scholarly linguistic norms. However, a shift is underway among the youngest Orthodox LGBT persons, some of whom do identify as queer. I expect that in a few years, "Q" will become more central to the communal narrative.

3. I deploy these various frameworks in Avishai, *Queer Judaism*.

4. Berlant and Warner, "Sex in Public."

5. Puar, *Terrorist Assemblages*.

6. See also Avishai, "Religious Queer People beyond Identity Conflict"; Avishai, *Queer Judaism*.

7. Berger and Luckmann, *Social Construction of Reality*.

8. For discussion of the term's development and legacy, see Otis and Dunn, "Queer Worldmaking."

9. Muñoz, *Disidentifications*.

10. Muñoz, *Disidentifications*, 25.

11. Muñoz, *Disidentifications*, 200.

12. Muñoz, *Disidentifications*, 195.

13. Berlant and Warner, "Sex in Public," 562.

14. Otis and Dunn, "Queer Worldmaking," 5.

15. Indeed, the vast majority of articles published by the peer-reviewed journal *QED: A Journal in GLBTQ Worldmaking* operate within this framework.

16. Berlant and Warner, "Sex in Public," 561.

17. Zaino, "Queer Worldmaking."

18. Muñoz, *Disidentifications*, 196. A reader pointed out, and I concur, that in plain English, activists are engaged in a worldmaking project, and, given their agendas, one that is by definition queer. The issue is that queer worldmaking scholarship has not viewed activism through this lens, and one of the goals of this article is to expand the reaches of this scholarship to be inclusive of religion and religious practices and paradigms.

19. It is worthwhile to note that Muñoz's *Cruising Utopia* does provide an opening to consider religion as a worldmaking site.

20. Zaino, "Queer Worldmaking," 580.

21. Otis and Dunn, "Queer Worldmaking."

22. Zaino, "Queer Worldmaking."

23. Holland-Muter, "Making Place, Making Home" and "Negotiating Normativities."

24. Wilcox, *Queer Religiosities*.

25. Muñoz, *Cruising Utopia*, 121.

26. For general background on religious Zionism and some of the key processes that characterize it, see Caplan, "Studying the Orthodox Jewish Community in Israel"; Ettinger, *Undone*; Ferziger, "Israelization and Lived Religion"; Sheleg, *From Kosher Inspector to the Driver's Seat?* Note that the overlap between religious, and cultural, political, and ideological categories is not unique to the Israeli context, and students of American political culture are now observing a similar process in the United States: "Evangelical" is increasingly becoming a political rather than a religious label, with some non-Protestant and non-Christians self-identifying as Evangelical. See Burge, "Why 'Evangelical' Is Becoming Another Word for 'Republican.'"

27. Zion-Waldoks, "'Family Resemblance' and Its Discontents."

28. The data is mostly in Hebrew: I am a native speaker and translated all excerpts. All data was evaluated according to methods of grounded qualitative analysis. For more information on this study, see Avishai, *Queer Judaism*, introduction.

29. I draw here on ethical considerations offered by essays in Compton, Meadow, and Schilt, *Other, Please Specify*.

30. Butler, *Precarious Life*.

31. For recent ethnographic work on LGBT lives in other religious traditions, see Coley, *Gay on God's Campus*; Golriz, "'I Am Enough'"; Moon and Tobin, "Sunsets and Solidarity"; Moon, Tobin, and Sumerau, "Alpha, Omega, and the Letters in Between"; Shah, *Making of a Gay Muslim*; Thompson, *Muslims on the Margins*.

32. On the notion of "joy" as a perspective on the lives of marginalized communities in general, and queer and trans life in particular, see Shuster and Westbrook, "Reducing the Joy Deficit in Sociology."

33. See Avishai, *Queer Judaism*, chap. 1.

34. See critique of this line of inquiry in Avishai, "Religious Queer People beyond Identity Conflict."

35. Duggan, "New Homonormativity."

36. The Orthodox feminist revolution has resulted in a new class of learned women who fulfill many rabbinic functions, and a handful of rabbinic authorities now ordain women. However, mainstream Orthodoxy does not yet recognize women's ordination, and Orthodox conservatives maintain that Jewish scripture and tradition preclude such developments. See Raucher, "Rabbis with Skirts."

37. Recently some progressive Orthodox religious leaders have argued—at considerable risk to their own reputations—that same-sex couples should not only be "tolerated" by Orthodox communities (the position of the progressive rabbinic organization Beit Hillel, "The Congregation and People with Homosexual Tendencies"), but that in some circumstances such unions are compatible with the Jewish tradition (e.g., Lau, "On Same-Sex Couples in the Orthodox Jewish Community").

38. Jewish literacy used to be the sole purview of Jewish men. The movement promoting Orthodox women's Jewish literacy, viewed as radical a generation ago, was an early harbinger of the massive disruptions to traditional Orthodoxy's gendered world order; the practice has moved from the progressive fringes into the Orthodox mainstream. For further discussion of the history of Orthodox Jewish women's literacy, see El-Or, *Next Year I Will Know More*; Raucher, "Rabbis with Skirts."

39. See Avishai, *Queer Judaism*, 235–43.

40. Ettinger, *Undone*.

41. Mevorach, "LGBT and the Institution of the Family."

42. Avishai, *Queer Judaism*, esp. chap. 6.

43. That God was male was not a point of contention (or reflection) among my respondents.

44. Irshai, "Homosexuality and the 'Aqedah Theology.'" This view is not unique to Judaism; see Moon, "Beyond the Dichotomy."

45. For a parallel process of developing affirmative theologies in the Christian context, see Althaus-Reid, *Queer God* and *Indecent Theology*; Cheng, *Radical Love*.

46. Though I have emphasized here the intra-Orthodox dialogue, this dialogue does not happen in a vacuum. As noted, "Orthodox" in Israel denotes not only a religious affiliation but also a demographic category, a political camp, and a cultural identity whose membership rules are drawn up through negotiation and dialogue with a host of Jewish (ranging from secular to ultra-Orthodox to traditional) and non-Jewish Others. The theological and ritual innovations discussed here speak to a long history of theological and interpretive Jewish queer innovations (see, for example, Ben-Lulu, "'Who Will Say Kaddish for Me?'"; Drinkwater, "AIDS Was Our Earthquake"; Crasnow, "On Transition"). What is new, and worthy of further investigation, is that these

innovations are borrowed and adapted from more egalitarian and inclusive streams within Jewish thought and practice, even if such borrowing is not articulated or acknowledged.

47. Muñoz, *Disidentifications*, 31.

48. Muñoz, *Disidentifications*, 12.

49. For an excellent overview, see Wilcox, *Queer Religiosities*.

50. This bias is out of step with empirical realities: in the past two decades, organizations that advocate on behalf of LGBTQ+ persons of faith have proliferated across religious traditions and geographical locations.

51. Elbaum, "Orthodox LGBT Battle."

52. On the concept of homonationalism, see Puar, *Terrorist Assemblages*.

53. Muñoz, *Disidentifications*, 11–12.

54. For thinking beyond these binaries, see Oswin, "Critical Geographies and the Uses of Sexuality."

References

Althaus-Reid, Marcella. *Indecent Theology: Theological Perversions in Sex, Gender, and Politics*. London: Routledge, 2000.

Althaus-Reid, Marcella. *The Queer God*. London: Routledge, 2003.

Avishai, Orit. *Queer Judaism: LGBT Activism and the Remaking of Jewish Orthodoxy in Israel*. New York: New York University Press, 2023.

Avishai, Orit. "Religious Queer People beyond Identity Conflict: Lessons from Orthodox LGBT Jews in Israel." *Journal for the Scientific Study of Religion* 59, no. 2 (2020): 360–78. https://doi.org/10.1111/jssr.12650.

Beit Hillel. "Responsum: The Congregation and People with Homosexual Tendencies: Halachic Position Paper." April 9, 2016. https://eng.beithillel.org.il/responsa/the-congregation-and-people-with-homosexual-tendencies/.

Ben-Lulu, Elazar. "'Who Will Say Kaddish for Me?' The American Reform Jewish Response to HIV/AIDS." *Journal of Modern Jewish Studies* 20, no. 1 (2021): 70–94. https://doi.org/10.1080/14725886.2020.1763070.

Berger, Peter L., and Thomas Luckmann. *The Social Construction of Reality: A Treatise in the Sociology of Knowledge*. New York: Anchor Books, 1990.

Berlant, Lauren, and Michael Warner. "Sex in Public." *Critical Inquiry* 24, no. 2 (1998): 547–66.

Burge, Ryan. "Why 'Evangelical' Is Becoming Another Word for 'Republican.'" *New York Times*, October 26, 2021.

Butler, Judith. *Precarious Life: The Powers of Mourning and Violence*. New York: Verso, 2006.

Caplan, Kimmy. "חקר החברה היהודית הדתית בישראל: הישגים, החמצות, ואתגרים" ("Studying the Orthodox Jewish Community in Israel: Achievements, Missed Opportunities, and Challenges"). *Megamot*, no. 17 (2017): 267–90.

Cheng, Patrick S. *Radical Love: An Introduction to Queer Theology*. New York: Seabury Books, 2011.

Coley, Jonathan S. *Gay on God's Campus: Mobilizing for LGBT Equality at Christian Colleges and Universities*. Chapel Hill: University of North Carolina Press, 2018.

Compton, D'Lane R., Tey Meadow, and Kristen Schilt, eds. *Other, Please Specify: Queer Methods in Sociology*. Oakland: University of California Press, 2018.

Crasnow, S. J. "On Transition: Normative Judaism and Trans Innovation." *Journal of Contemporary Religion* 32, no. 3 (2017): 403–15. https://doi.org/10.1080/13537903.2017.1362880.

Drinkwater, Gregg. "AIDS Was Our Earthquake: American Jewish Responses to the AIDS Crisis, 1985–92." *Jewish Social Studies* 26, no. 1 (2020): 122–42. https://doi.org/10.2979/jewisocistud.26.1.11.

Duggan, Lisa. "The New Homonormativity: The Sexual Politics of Neoliberalism." In *Materializing Democracy*, edited by Russ Castronovo and Dana D. Nelson, 175–94. Durham, NC: Duke University Press, 2002.

Elbaum, Chaim. "The Orthodox LGBT Battle." Facebook, May 2, 2018. https://www.facebook.com/chaimme/posts/pfbid0N67KjGEcqaSwWafTgiLF2sqNM2fdmkVtR5ZSZ85FzvUcdwbkQwBsARgZXxkLu5Aml.

El-Or, Tamar. *Next Year I Will Know More: Literacy and Identity among Young Orthodox Women in Israel*. Detroit: Wayne State University Press, 2002.

Ettinger, Yair. פרומים: המחלוקות שמפצלות את הציונות הדתית (*Undone: The Controversies Tearing Religious-Zionism Apart*). Jerusalem: Zemorah Bittan, 2019.

Ferziger, Adam S. "Israelization and Lived Religion: Conflicting Accounts of Contemporary Judaism." *Contemporary Jewry* 40, no. 3 (2020): 403–30. https://doi.org/10.1007/s12397-020-09324-4.

Golriz, Golshan. "'I Am Enough': Why LGBTQ Muslim Groups Resist Mainstreaming." *Sexuality and Culture* 25, no. 2 (2021): 355–76. https://doi.org/10.1007/s12119-020-09773-x.

Halperin, David M. "The Normalization of Queer Theory." *Journal of Homosexuality* 45, nos. 2–4 (2003): 339–43. https://doi.org/10.1300/J082v45n02_17.

Holland-Muter, Susan. "Making Place, Making Home: Lesbian Queer World-Making in Cape Town." *Estudos Feministas* 27, no. 3 (2019): 1–14.

Holland-Muter, Susan. "Negotiating Normativities: Counter Narratives of Lesbian Queer World Making in Cape Town." PhD diss., University of Cape Town, 2018.

Irshai, Ronit. "Homosexuality and the 'Aqedah Theology': A Comparison of Modern Orthodoxy and the Conservative Movement." *Journal of Jewish Ethics* 4, no. 1 (2018): 19–46. https://doi.org/10.5325/jjewiethi.4.1.0019.

Lau, Benny. "On Same-Sex Couples in the Orthodox Jewish Community." *Times of Israel*, December 11, 2020. https://blogs.timesofisrael.com/guidelines-for-same-sex-couples-in-the-orthodox-jewish-community/.

Mevorach, Oria. "LGBT and the Institution of the Family." *Deot*, no. 75 (2016). https://toravoda.org.il/כתבה/ההומואים-הדתיים-אינם-איום-אוריה-מבורך/.

Moon, Dawne. "Beyond the Dichotomy: Six Religious Views of Homosexuality." *Journal of Homosexuality* 61, no. 9 (2014): 1215–41. https://doi.org/10.1080/00918369.2014.926762.

Moon, Dawne, and Theresa W. Tobin. "Sunsets and Solidarity: Overcoming Sacramental Shame in Conservative Christian Churches to Forge a Queer Vision of Love and Justice." *Hypatia* 33, no. 3 (2018): 451–68. https://doi.org/10.1111/hypa.12413.

Moon, Dawne, Theresa W. Tobin, and J. E. Sumerau. "Alpha, Omega, and the Letters in between: LGBTQI Conservative Christians Undoing Gender." *Gender and Society* 33, no. 4 (2019): 583–606. https://doi.org/10.1177/0891243219846592.

Muñoz, José Esteban. *Cruising Utopia: The Then and There of Queer Futurity*. New York: New York University Press, 2009.

Muñoz, José Esteban. *Disidentifications: Queers of Color and the Performance of Politics*. Minneapolis: University of Minnesota Press, 1999.

Muñoz, José Esteban. "Ephemera as Evidence: Introductory Notes to Queer Acts." *Women and Performance* 8, no. 2 (1996): 5–16. https://doi.org/10.1080/07407096096 8571228.

Oswin, Natalie. "Critical Geographies and the Uses of Sexuality: Deconstructing Queer Space." *Progress in Human Geography* 32, no. 1 (2008): 89–103. https://doi.org/10.1177/0309132507085213.

Otis, Hailey N., and Thomas R. Dunn. "Queer Worldmaking." In *Oxford Research Encyclopedia of Communication*, edited by Isaac West, E. Cram, Frederik Dhaenens, Pamela Lannutti, and Gust Yep. New York: Oxford University Press, 2021. https://doi.org/10.1093/acrefore/9780190228613.013.1235.

Puar, Jasbir K. *Terrorist Assemblages: Homonationalism in Queer Times*. Durham, NC: Duke University Press, 2007.

Raucher, Michal. "Rabbis with Skirts: Orthodox Female Clergy Embodying Religious Authority." *AJS Perspectives* (Fall 2019): 48–50.

Shah, Shanon. *The Making of a Gay Muslim: Religion, Sexuality, and Identity in Malaysia and Britain*. London: Palgrave Macmillan, 2018.

Sheleg, Yair. ממשגיח הכשרות לנהג הקטר? הציונות הדתית והחברה הישראלית (*From Kosher Inspector to the Driver's Seat? Religious Zionism and Israeli Society*). Jerusalem: The Israel Democracy Institute, 2019.

Shuster, Stef M., and Laurel Westbrook. "Reducing the Joy Deficit in Sociology: A Study of Transgender Joy." *Social Problems* (2022): spac034. https://doi.org/10.1093/socpro/spac034.

Thompson, Katrina Daly. *Muslims on the Margins: Creating Queer Religious Community in North America*. North American Religions. New York: New York University Press, 2023.

Wilcox, Melissa M. *Queer Religiosities: An Introduction to Queer and Transgender Studies in Religion*. Lanham, MD: Rowman and Littlefield, 2021.

Zaino, Karen. "Queer Worldmaking." In *Encyclopedia of Queer Studies in Education*, edited by Kamden K. Strunk and Stephanie Anne Shelton, 578–82. Leiden, Netherlands: Brill, 2022. https://doi.org/10.1163/9789004506725.

Zion-Waldoks, Tanya. "'Family Resemblance' and Its Discontents: Towards the Study of Orthodoxy's Politics of Belonging and Lived Orthodoxies in Israel." *AJS Review* 46, no. 1 (2022): 12–37. https://doi.org/10.1017/S0364009421000076.

Street Evangelists and Transgender Saints

Sylvia Rivera, Marsha P. Johnson, and the Religions of the Afro-Americas

AHMAD GREENE-HAYES

ABSTRACT This article historicizes the religious fervor of the 1969 Stonewall riots—multiple direct actions against the anti-Black and homo- and transphobic NYPD and white-owned bars in Greenwich Village—by examining the political organizing of Marsha P. Johnson and Sylvia Rivera, cofounders of Street Transvestite Action Revolutionaries. This article queries and queers the field's preoccupation with the cisgender and heterosexual regarding religious affiliation and the formation of liberation theologies, and probes at the heart of Johnson's and Rivera's critical absences in religious studies on the one hand, and the critical absence of their religious sensibilities in narrations of queer and trans politics on the other.

KEYWORDS Marsha P. Johnson, Sylvia Rivera, trans religion, Black religion, Stonewall

In a conversation with a deputy inspector, or "pig," named Seymour Pine, Sylvia Rivera—one of the heralded champions of the Stonewall Rebellion of 1969—recounted, "We used to sit around, just try to figure out when this harassment would come to an end. And we would always dream that one day it would come to an end. And we prayed, and we looked for it. We wanted to be human beings."[1] Rivera, a Latine transgender woman with familial roots in Venezuela and Puerto Rico, reflected on "the gay bashings on the drag queens by heterosexual men, women, and the police" prior to Stonewall.[2] The irony, however, was that Rivera was in conversation with a man whose professional identification was the literal antithesis of her queer-affirming, Black- and Brown-centered, antipolice political organizing. Their conversation was just one of many included in a 1989 Sound Portraits recording of Rivera, other activists, and the New York Police Department reflecting on Stonewall, twenty years later, to supposedly bridge connections between the police and persons of color—one of many "community policing" initiatives in the last term of Mayor Ed Koch.

Reflecting on how the Stonewall Rebellion started, Rivera stated to Pine, "I remember someone throwing a Molotov cocktail. I don't know who the

QTR • A Journal of Trans and Queer Studies in Religion • 1:1 • May 2024
DOI: 10.1215/29944724-11208911 © 2024 Ahmad Greene-Hayes

person was, but I mean I saw that and I just said to myself in Spanish, I said. "Oh my God, the revolution is finally here! And I just like started screaming, 'Freedom! We're free at last!'"[3] Echoing the now historic words from the charismatic man who is often shortsightedly cast by the public as the Black male hero of the civil rights movement—the Reverend Dr. Martin Luther King Jr.—Rivera tapped into an African American jeremiad and effectively queered King's 1963 "I Have a Dream" speech.[4] "Free at last! Free at last! Thank God Almighty, we are free at last!" became "Freedom! We're free at last!," thus disrupting the cisheterosexist freedom dreams of the era and calling into focus how LBGTQ political organizers like Rivera "had done so much for other movements," and now "it was [their] time."[5]

Marsha P. Johnson, a Black transgender woman who cofounded Street Transvestite Action Revolutionaries (STAR) with Rivera in 1970, also engaged in queer organizing amidst the civil rights and Black Power movements.[6] Her desire to "save" lesbian, gay, and transgender youth from the streets of New York City, where homelessness, poverty, and the threat of murder were quotidian conditions, is aptly depicted by sociologists Zandria F. Robinson and Marcus Anthony Hunter. They describe her as both political organizer and evangelist, complicating long-standing secularized narratives about radical activism.

> Johnson walked and talked with Jesus, prayed to Jesus for strength, knew Jesus heard her pleas and prayers, and had the spirit of Jesus on earth. Adorned with masterfully crafted crowns of flowers, she could be found prostrate in churches, worshipping and meditating at the altar. Out in the streets she spread the gospel of humanity not through a heavy-handed evangelism but through acts of kindness and miracles of survival only queens of color from the Stonewall era know. She greeted folks with that familiar glow and wide smile, gave people her last penny, hustled, and nursed the sick. People called her a saint and knew she was a queen, and they saw her works near the Hudson River like the works of Jesus near Jordan.[7]

Johnson's religious convictions were not secondary to her political convictions, but indeed her politics were religious, and her religion was political. This might seem like a rudimentary claim, but how often are Black trans women regarded as political strategists, religious thinkers, or theologians in popular remembrances of civil rights activism? Further to this point, trans women like Rivera and Johnson shed light on the inextricable relationship between the religious and the political—two categories that have for a long time worked in the service of their extermination. In this vein, notwithstanding Robinson and Hunter's Christocentric characterization of Johnson—a practitioner of Santeria and other alternative religious orientations and esotericisms—it is perhaps more fitting to describe Johnson and Rivera in the parlance of feminist theologian Marcella Althaus-Reid's notion of the "indecent theologian" or "a theologian who has learned to survive with several passports. She is a Christian and a Queer theologian or a minister and a Queer lover who cannot be shown in public and she is a woman and a worker: the list of the game of multiple representations extends."[8] Indeed, as I will show, Johnson and Rivera drew upon a host of diasporic, spiritual modalities both within and beyond Christian churches in their cultivation of their own religious and political commitments in the service of "drag queens, transvestites, transsexuals and other gender variant people."[9] Relatedly, Althaus-Reid's contention that "a Queer theologian has many passports because she is a theologian in diaspora, that is, a theologian who explores at the crossroads of Christianity issues of self-identity and the identity of her community, which are related to sexuality, race, culture, and poverty," more astutely captures the survivalisms of queer and transgender religionists and practitioners.[10] Both Rivera and Johnson—like the Hebrew midwives Shiphra and Puah, perhaps, who disobeyed Pharaoh's command and did not kill the male newborns[11]—used their religious convictions, their lived experiences, and their alignment with a global decolonial ethos to save, house, and nurture a dying generation of queer and transgender youth prior to the AIDS epidemic of the 1980s and 1990s and amidst a worldwide struggle for human and civil rights, and in so doing, they cultivated their own transed liberation theologies and ritual practices.

While the historiography on gender and the civil rights movement has rightly uncovered and reoriented our shared attention to the critical role of Black and non-Black cisgender women of color in the fight for civil and human rights during the twentieth century, much, if not all, of the literature excludes Black and non-Black transgender women of color, despite their presence, political organizing, and institution-building (with the exception of the literature on gender nonconforming Episcopalian priest, the Reverend Pauli Murray).[12] In addition, while both Rivera and Johnson are remembered in contemporary recollections and commemorations of queer and transgender activism in the twentieth century, there is still not an exhaustive monograph or biography that explores their work and lives beyond the Stonewall Rebellion, and many accounts of Stonewall, its tributaries, and its aftermaths tend to ignore religious people and practices altogether, which I argue are untetherable from trans religious innovation.[13] More to this point, archival collections across the nation mention Rivera's and Johnson's names and prize photographs of them, but their written beliefs and ideas have not been uniformly housed or preserved.[14] Thus, this article is not the definitive account on either Rivera and Johnson. It cannot be, given the ways society and the academy have stifled their voices. Nor is it an attempt to comprehensively analyze their connections to the field of religious studies. Rather, this article is about their critical absence in American religious history, and it is about exhuming their stories—or what fragments we can recover—to insert them into discourses in religious studies where queer and transgender people are hidden in plain sight or are erased by the privileging of cisgender, heterosexual, straight-presenting and cis-assumed religious actors.[15] In addition, this article stages a revisitation of these now widely acclaimed (and indeed, mythologized and idolized) trans activist figures—with a focus primarily on Marsha P. Johnson—in order to challenge secularized narratives of trans history. Questions at the helm of my revisitation—yes, in the way of ancestral veneration—involve probing into the core of what they believed and why they believed it. Moreover, this article takes seriously the historian Heather R. White's brilliant observation about Stonewall that "professional historians . . . have proved to be a poor match against the history-making power of commemoration,"[16] and seeks to uncover, to the best of my ability, what lies beneath the surface and beyond the veil of fanfare, celebritizing, and the mythologizing of these now prominent activist figures.

To do so, I blend some semblance of an "archival collection" for Johnson and Rivera using interview clips included in the many documentaries on them, along with the anthologizing work of activist Tourmaline on her blog, "The Spirit Was." She writes, "I unearthed this material thru hustling my way into spaces that are historically inaccessible to black trans women. . . . Most recently when I went to the New York Public Library to try and find STAR's statement I was accosted coming out the bathroom and scrutinized by security. This isn't something new, just part of living for me. But that's also part of the story of how the statement landed on the internet."[17] Tourmaline's blog—itself a site of Black trans scripturalizing and theological inquiry— serves as a portal to taking seriously Rivera, Johnson, and other trans religious practitioners and their complex politics. Bearing in mind Tourmaline's words, this article testifies to the difficulties that plague historical scholarship—especially in religious studies—on Black and Latino transgender activists before the era of social media, and it is an act of solidarity with the struggles of Tourmaline working to recover and to re/member lives lost to transantagonism.[18] In this regard, I think with Abram J. Lewis, who has argued that "the transgender archive demands a hauntological reading in order to reckon with its contents [and to] name the archive as opaque to historicization insofar as a haunting is a diagnostic of knowledges and experiences that are disavowed within rationalist, positivist, and disciplinary epistemes—the founding epistemes of history."[19] In short, mainstream history has both invisibilized transgender persons and relied on the hauntings of transgender violence as a historiographical device and hermeneutic, rarely thinking about or considering the realities of transgender living, theologizing, and worlding—central features of the archiving that Tourmaline has done on her blog and in her public work.

Similarly, religious studies scholars often assume that transgender people do not experience or practice religion on their own terms. Yet Melissa M. Wilcox has written about "religion and the sacred [that] are already transed," even as "religious studies needs to be transed" due to the exclusion of transgender people in religious studies scholarship.[20] In this article, I follow Wilcox and the lead of historians of American religion who encourage scholars to read histories of sexuality and histories of American religion as co-constitutive elements. In *Devotions and Desires: Histories of Sexuality and Religion in the Twentieth-Century United States,* editors Gillian Frank, Bethany Moreton, and Heather R. White contend that racialization, the evolution of science and technology, and state formation shaped a "modern terminology" of race, gender, sexuality, and religion. "Conceptions of 'true religion' and 'good sex' connected to broader preoccupations about the social order: what countered as 'true religion'—that is, practices and beliefs perceived to be spiritually authentic and socially beneficial," they write, "was that which also supported and encouraged 'good sex,' or forms of erotic expression and kinship structures that were socially valued."[21] In this way, in order to locate the transed religions of Rivera and Johnson, this article attends to the sites where both Rivera and Johnson lived out their religions: in the streets, on the altars of city churches, in bars, and at the Christopher Street pier. While this article largely focuses on Marsha P. Johnson due to the quantity of ephemeral archival materials available that showcase her religious sensibilities in comparison to the number of materials available relating to Rivera, it nonetheless takes seriously how religion also shaped Rivera's political organizing. Next, the article examines the interconnectedness of various resistance movements and liberationist struggles during the twentieth century, endeavoring to insert Rivera and Johnson into a historiographical accounting of civil rights literature, and it ends with an analysis of the fluidity between Johnson's myriad religious practices. Throughout the article, I use the terms "saint," "evangelist," and "prophet" interchangeably to describe Johnson and Rivera to demonstrate how they have been revered by their contemporaries and by younger generations of queer and trans activists, and also to mark how their political organizing relied on a multiplicity of religious grammars to represent their beliefs and their varied modes of political protest. While it is becoming increasingly difficult to find new things to say about these mythologized trans figures, I hope to demonstrate how attention to their religious innovation—or what fragments we come to know through archival snippets—illuminates how trans women who are not only deemed "deviant" but also inept at the project of theologized world-making ultimately counter the terms of Western theology in robust ways. This bears saying especially because their neurodivergence, mental illnesses, suicidality, and drug use have often been wielded against them as weapons or as proof of their supposed inability to lucidly articulate the core of what they believed.[22]

Sylvia Rivera, the Church, and the Forgotten Ones

Yet Sylvia Rivera's engagement with institutional churches in New York City is a revelatory illustration of the rich theological intellectualisms at the core of her political project. Rivera, who was an active member of the Metropolitan Community Church of New York for many years in which she directed the church's food pantry, explained in an undated piece, "Queens in Exile, the Forgotten Ones": "Many of us have to live by night, because of the lack of laws or protections. A lot of trans women are standing out on street corners and working clubs. And many of them are highly educated, with college degrees. Many of us have to survive by selling our bodies. If you can't get a job, you have to do whatever it takes to live."[23] The streets were where Rivera and Johnson performed miracles in which they embodied what the historian Robert Orsi has described as a "theology of the streets"; they understood the significance of religion in shaping radical activism and regarded the Divine—broadly construed—as co-laborer in the struggle for justice.[24] Indeed, "the Spirit was upon [them], anointing [them] to proclaim good news to the poor, to bind up the brokenhearted, to proclaim freedom for the captives and release from darkness for the prisoners."[25] Rivera, like Johnson, testified about being "tired of seeing [her] children," namely "homeless, transgender children [and] young, gay children . . . sleeping on the steps of [the] church." She "went [into the church] with an attitude. [She] raised hell."[26] Like "Jesus [who] went into the temple of God, and cast out all them that sold and bought in the temple, and overthrew the tables of the moneychangers," condemning them for turning "the house of prayer" into a "den of thieves,"[27] Rivera, too, "tried to destroy the front desk [of the church] but did not attack anybody."[28] She was frustrated with the new buildings and renovations across New York City for the wealthy, which many would later describe as "urban renewal" or, more appropriately, as gentrification. She then staged a clear critique, grounded in righteous indignation, about how "[the city could] afford to renovate a building for millions and millions of dollars and buy another building across the street and still not worry about [its] homeless children from [their] community." In response to her organizing against the city and nonprofit organizations that exploited queer and transgender youth and the homeless, Rivera claimed, "they had me arrested and put in Bellevue!"[29] Like other queer prophets, street evangelists, and transgender saints of her generation, Rivera was institutionalized for "crying aloud and sparing not, lifting up her voice as a trumpet, and showing the people their transgressions."[30]

Following the dynamic leadership of Rivera and Johnson and in line with the ethos of liberation theology during the twentieth century, STAR drew connections between transmisogynistic violence in New York City with the brutalities of imperialism. Rivera, while describing the grief that consumed queer and transgender activists following the tragic death of Judy Garland, an actress and singer known as "the Elvis of homosexuals" who died in 1969 due to a drug overdose, once reflected on the conditions that she believed led to the Stonewall riot. "I guess there was tension in the air. It was a hot, muggy night, in the eighties or nineties, like when most riots happen," she stated. "I don't know how many other patrons in the bar were activists, but many of the people were involved in some struggle. I had been doing work in the civil rights movement, against the war in Vietnam, and for the women's movement."[31] On another occasion, while protesting for "gay rights" (which at the time also included transgender rights), Rivera observed,

There was a "Stop the War in Vietnam" demo and people started coming. The cops had dispersed the demo, and I'm standing out there collecting signatures, and two cops come by, and they say, "You have to move." And I'm like, "Why? All I'm doing is collecting signatures. I'm petitioning for gay rights." "It's against the law." I said, "What? I thought it said in the Constitution we have the right to acquire signatures . . ." "You don't have an American flag." "What does an American flag have to do with my collecting signatures?" "You have to have an American flag." I said, "It wouldn't make a difference. I've been to jail with poor Rosie over there, who is always being arrested with her American flag and her Bible for preaching the gospel." Rosie was a right-wing Bible-thumper. Well, I got arrested for petitioning for gay rights.[32]

Rivera compared her political organizing for gay rights to "right-wing Bible-thumper" Rosie, "arrested with her American flag and her Bible for preaching the gospel." Despite Rosie's embodied American religious nationalism—with flag and Bible in hand—she was arrested, like Rivera, for not following demonstration regulations in alignment with the First Amendment. Unlike Rivera, however, Rosie's right-wing, conservative theological perspective militated against Rivera's existence and her petitioning of heaven and the courts for gay rights. In effect, as Rivera stood her ground declaring a liberation theology for gay and transgender people along with those victimized, maimed, and brutalized by the Vietnam War's inhumane and devastating impact on Southeast Asians, soldiers, and the families of all involved, Rosie declared a fire and brimstone gospel seeking to destroy the nonwhite, nonheterosexual, and non-American.

During these struggles, STAR began as a caucus of the Gay Liberation Front (GLF) in 1970, which modeled itself after Algeria's and North Vietnam's National Liberation Fronts as well as other anticolonial and unashamedly communist movements. GLF developed an antiracist and anticapitalist political platform and stood in solidarity with the Black Panther Party and various third world struggles. "We are a revolutionary group of men and women formed with the realization that complete sexual liberation for all people cannot come about unless existing social institutions are abolished," they declared in their manifesto. "We reject society's attempt to impose sexual roles and definitions of our nature."[33] GLF, which began following the Stonewall Rebellion, spread like wildfire throughout American cities and onto a global stage in such places as Canada, Australia, and London. Rivera noted that she "enjoyed [GLF] because [they] concentrated on many issues for many different struggles." She continued, "We're all in the same boat as long as we're being oppressed one way or the other, whether we are gay, straight, trans, Black, yellow, green, purple, or whatever. If we don't fight for each other, we'll be put down. And after all these years, the trans community is still at the back of the bus."[34] In this vein, the historian Justin David Suran has written about the intersection of antimilitarism and homosexuality during the 1960s and has contended, "If a civil-rights ethos and the example of the Civil Rights Movement informed homosexual politics between 1961 and 1966, the late 1960s were dominated by the Vietnam War: after 1966, military service and antiwar protest emerged as the pivotal issues in homosexual politics."[35] Although Suran's focus is primarily on gay men or men who sleep with men and their subsequent removal and criminalization by the United States military, his insistence on an expressed antimilitarism by gay men and lesbian women during the Vietnam War as a self-described pronouncement of antihomophobic politics is especially prescient. In his discussion of San Francisco's "homophile" groups in the late 1960s, for example, he observes, "For Gay Liberationists, homosexual acts were revolutionary acts: to claim a gay identity meant to rebel against the very system waging war in Vietnam. Almost universally, 'liberated' gays denounced the American intervention as an effect of the same repressive apparatus that alienated homosexuals from their own desires."[36]

Indeed, as Marsha P. Johnson and Sylvia Rivera, like so many other gay and transgender activists at the time, spoke out against the war in Vietnam, they were also demanding an end to the quotidian violence of homophobia and transphobia. As sex workers and survivors of sexual violence, Johnson and Rivera certainly understood the threat of murder for walking down the street as transgender women brutalized by men and the police, so they most certainly could sympathize with their gay brothers who had been victimized, raped, or kicked out of the military for being "found out" or "outed" as gay. Johnson, for example, often spoke of being raped as she performed sex work to pay her bills and feed her chosen kin. In effect, STAR's commitment to housing queer youth, with its critique of hegemonic Christian institutions, suggests that these efforts were not only rooted in a race, gender, and anticapitalist consciousness, but also in the spirit of antirape activism.[37] Focusing on the first three decades of the twentieth century, historian LaShawn Harris tells the story of a long-standing history of sex work in New York City, which I argue set the stage for the underground economy that would later fund STAR in the 1970s, and as Harris shows, was especially dangerous for Black and other working-class women.[38] While Harris's focus is exclusively on Black cisgender women of the working class, her attention to the threat of violence for all Black working-class women provides a base to consider how transantagonisms exacerbated the effects of anti-Blackness, poverty, and racial-sexual terrorisms such as police brutality, sexual assault, street harassment, and murder. In 1971, for instance, Rivera observed, "Transvestites are homosexual men and women who dress in clothes of the opposite sex. . . . Transvestites are the most oppressed people in the homosexual community. My half sisters and brothers are being raped and murdered by pigs, straights, and even sometimes by other uptight homosexuals who consider us the scum of the gay community."[39] Notwithstanding the everydayness of the violence that transgender people experienced, Rivera and Johnson "had the guts to stand up and fight on the front lines for many years" for both "Black Power" and "Gay Power," and they did so alongside a host of others whose names escape the historical record and commemorative narrations of this rich history.[40]

Marsha P. Johnson and Black Religious Fluidity

For many transgender people during this period, Afro-Caribbean and Latin American religions, which derived from the continent of Africa, allowed them to reimagine their own theologically and socially gendered understandings of themselves and of these global movements altogether, and their transed religious practices also augmented their political sensibilities and organizing. For instance, based on reflections from her contemporaries and her own thoughts on race, religion, and politics, Marsha P. Johnson was undoubtedly a practitioner of African American religious fluidity. In *Pay It No Mind: The Life and Times of Marsha P. Johnson* (2012), Johnson is described as "Saint Marsha" by several of her friends from Christopher Street. One person remembered how Marsha, who was reared in the Mount Teman African Methodist Episcopal Church in Elizabeth, New Jersey, as a child, would lie prostrate in front of the statue of the Virgin Mary in Catholic churches throughout New York City, never facing the altar but facing the street, engaging in dramatic embodied action like the biblical prophets of old. In her reverent critique of the church's relics, her true posture of prayer—toward the street—served as an indication of where her heart and moral vision truly lay. Johnson's ministry, beyond the bounds of ordination or clerical institutionalization, was one that centered "the least of these,"[41] or those discarded by family, the church, the civil rights and Black Power movements, and the state for being queer, gender nonconforming, transgender, poor, HIV-positive, formerly incarcerated, an immigrant, non-Christian, or simply for being Black or Latino. Her politics were also reflected in her spiritual practice. "I practice the Catholic religion because it is part of the Santeria religion," Johnson confessed. "It says that we are all brothers and sisters. We are all the same."[42]

Having been raised in the African Methodist Episcopal Church—the first independent denomination founded by Africans in the Americas in 1816, which grew out of the Free African Society in Philadelphia—Johnson's willful shift to the Catholic and Santeria religions should not be overlooked or diminished, especially by scholars of Africana religions interested in the paradoxes of religio-racial boundaries; gender, sexuality, and deviance; and the queering and transing of theoretical categories.[43] As anthropologist Aisha M. Beliso-De Jesús contends in *Electric Santería*, "Globally, Santería is a practice associated with racialized criminals and social deviants who practice a putatively backward superstition."[44] Beliso-De Jesús further contends, "Santería is a religion that has historically emerged as a solution to problems for marginalized subjects. As an epistemology, Santería is about finding solution through copresences," which she defines earlier as, "energies of nature and spirit, divinity and body entangled in diffracted waves of knowledge and power."[45] An Afro-Cuban transnational religion, with roots in West Africa prior to colonization and the enslavement of Africans in the Americas, Santería (otherwise known as *regla ocha* by practitioners) was concretized in Cuba in the late nineteenth and early twentieth centuries. Its tenets and belief systems are influenced by "a pantheon of Yoruba-inspired oricha";[46] and the historical and contemporaneous usage of the term *Santería* has been used to differentiate "improper worship of Catholic saints" from a more authentic, real, and orthodox Catholicism, which proliferated in the Caribbean and in Latin America due to the religious efforts—notwithstanding their entanglements with racial-sexual terrorisms—of Portuguese and Spanish missionaries in the colonial period.[47] However, to date, scholars of Catholicism and of religion in the Americas more broadly, continue to debate the question of what constitutes an "authentic" Catholicism, and as is often the case, African peoples distort, queer, trouble, disrupt, and Blacken religious norms.[48] However, for the purposes of this article, it is worth thinking about the ways twentieth-century African-descended people in the United States, such as Marsha P. Johnson, continued to embody what Nora Jaffary describes as "deviant orthodoxy" in their religious practices, African rituals, and religiously motivated political organizing.[49] Indeed, Johnson's religious practice was "deviant" in the context of her African American Protestant upbringing given the demonization of African-derived religions in such denominations as the African Methodist Episcopal Church.[50] Historian Yvonne P. Chireau, who in her usage of the term "vernacular religion" draws a distinction "between the official doctrines of institutional religions such as Protestant Christianity and the vast territory of behaviors that human beings may invest with religious meaning."[51] She later deploys the term "magico-religious" to describe what Jaffary conceptualizes as "deviant orthodoxy" in order to amplify African and African American religions that defy sharp, and often, contrarian demarcations. "Many African people of the past, as now, drew few distinctions between the substance of their beliefs and the other aspects of the world in which they participated," Chireau writes. "A spiritual reality governed human life, within belief systems that were not elaborated as philosophical or speculative knowledge but rather enfolded ways of being and living."[52] Johnson's self-constructed spiritual practice, which included aspects of her Black Protestant upbringing and an intentional engagement with Catholicism and Santería, was rooted in a larger cultural history of the religious innovations of everyday African-descended people in the afterlife of chattel slavery.

While Johnson confessed in 1992, "I practice the Catholic religion because it is part of the Santeria religion," it is necessary to differentiate between these two religions, as one is rooted in Eurocentric, colonial logics and a history of Christianization and the coerced conversions of the enslaved, and the second is founded in a history of Afro-Cuban resistance to those processes in the Americas. To this end, it is perhaps essential to invert Johnson's construction of the relationality between the two, and to consider how Afro-Cubans embodied what the historian Albert Raboteau described as a process of adapting to the demands of the plantocracy and Christianization using the blending of African religious practices and Christianity, thus forming "slave religion." He writes, "The most immediately apparent innovation that *Santeria, Shango,* and *Candomble* have brought to African theological perspectives is the identification of African gods with Catholic saints. Initially the veneration of saints must have provided the slaves with a convenient disguise for secret worship of African gods."[53] Indeed, in following the work of scholars of Africana religions, Catholicism is part of Santería, even as Catholic authorities have traditionally demonized and policed Santería, other non-Christian African diasporic religions, and the religiosity of both Johnson and Rivera.

While the archive shows no record of Johnson traveling to Cuba or of her being initiated into Santería, or even how exactly she personally encountered the religion in New York City, the historian Tracey E. Hucks, while citing Steven Gregory, has observed, "From 1960 to 1970, incidents of convergence as well as of conflict emerged between African American and Cuban orisa communities in New York City."[54] In this vein, Johnson's practicing of Santería as a Black transgender woman, sex worker, and political organizer who had critiques of the African Methodist Episcopal Church of her upbringing also substantiates Dianne M. Stewart's contention that the "spirituality [of women who practice African-derived religions] directly challenges prevailing Christian beliefs that oppress women of African descent while institutionalizing praxes of [women's] empowerment and authority within the structures of African-derived religions."[55] Scholars have also written about the preservation of Santería and other Africana religions in New York City by Cuban and Puerto Rican practitioners, and as historians have pointed out, there was much convergence in political organizing among gay and transgender activists, the Young Lords (a Puerto Rican leftist organization based in Spanish Harlem, with which Rivera was also involved), and the Black Panther Party.[56] Given these details, it is possible that Johnson may have learned about Santería from her Latina comrade Rivera or from one of the many youths she housed. It is also probable that Johnson, like so many queer and transgender individuals, found in Santería what sociologist Salvador Vidal-Ortiz characterizes as religious and sexual negotiation, especially with regard to traditional Afro-Cuban linguistics for queer gender performance—despite the prevalence of anti-Blackness, what Beliso-De Jesús terms "heteronationalisms," and legalized homo- and transantagonisms in both Cuba and the United States.[57] Similarly, Susana Peña observes that the 1970s Transsexual Action Organization based in Miami, Florida, utilized the Afro-Cuban religion Santería "to articulate a transsexual identity."[58] Carolyn Watson contends that gender fluidity emerged in Afro-Cuban religious organization during the late nineteenth and early twentieth centuries, following Cuba's 1898 independence from Spain, as a strategic response to the legal prosecution of cross-dressing and deviant and queer gendered performances. Watson argues, "Rather than discarding Yoruba gender metaphors for social organization, practitioners wove them into religious praxis so that the *orisha*, not the medium, contravened certain comportments, thereby subverting Cuban gender identities that were believed to follow naturally from anatomical sex."[59] While sources do not substantiate these inclinations as Johnson's personal truth, her shift from a Black Protestant church to Santería does evidence the sorts of gendered and sexual freedoms gained by disavowing hegemonic Christianity, further confirming the observations of other scholars on this subject.

In effect, Johnson's commitment to the Afro-Cuban religion Santería had meaningful influence on her self-formation, political sensibilities, and her transvestite, drag, and sex-work identities in an ever-changing 1960s to early 1990s New York City where racialized violence, gendered brutalities, poverty, the War on Drugs, the AIDS epidemic, and the incessant murders of Black and Latina transgender women in the streets with impunity were quotidian practices. Beliso-De Jesús contends, "Santería does not offer a utopia. Rather, it assumes the terrors of violence and negotiations with negativities as part and parcel of the everyday. Copresences are haunting conjurings of seething imperfections, partialities that link injustice and marginality."[60] In this way, for Johnson, as her friends from Christopher Street observed, making offerings of clothes and coins to "King Neptune, to her father, and to the spirits in the water at Christopher Pier"[61] was a means of recognizing, honoring, and calling upon the protective guidance of copresences, or what writers and Africana practitioners such as Toni Morrison have described as "ancestors [who] are not just parents, they are sort of timeless people whose relationships to the [living] are benevolent, instructive, and protective, and they provide a certain kind of wisdom."[62] Those ancestors were conjured by Johnson—using what Elizabeth Pérez describes as "religious micropractices," or ritual experiences that "can be broken down into more minute units of activity"—in order to survive transmisogynoiristic, anti-Black violence in her twentieth-century world; and to also receive spiritual power from those rebellious Africans and maroons in Cuba and across the Americas who resisted colonial rule by the Spanish and other European powers during the arduous eighteenth and nineteenth centuries.[63] Johnson's attentiveness to copresences is also indicative of an evidence of joint struggle with the oppressed peoples of Cuba, many of whom faced immense queer and transantagonistic violence and incarceration under the tenure of Communist revolutionary Fidel Castro, despite his professed radicalisms.[64] For Johnson, a Black transgender woman, Santería was African and non-Christocentric in its orientation and thus capable of providing her with strength and direction for her ministry as street evangelist and transgender saint to the many Black and Latino queer and transgender youth she and Rivera pastored, nursed, mothered, protected, served, led, loved, and housed. By turning our attention to Johnson and Rivera's religious sensibilities, specifically their relationships to Afro-Caribbean and Latin American religions in their radical activism, it is evident that the religious is political, and the political is religious. Using a queer Africana religious studies approach also allows scholars of queer and transgender experiences to understand how religion and politics are inextricably linked along raced, classed, and gendered lines.[65] It also allows for critical analysis of alternative liberation theologies in the streets, where LGBTQ persons consistently organize, save the homeless, and speak back to churches that have shut their doors.

Conclusion: "Transed" Afro-Latin Religions in the Americas

Liberation theologies emerged alongside and in conversation with the queer- and trans-led, antipolice actions of the Stonewall Rebellion and the organizing work of the Street Transvestite Action Revolutionaries. Rivera saw her political praxis in direct opposition to white supremacist, heterosexist, imperialist, and right-wing Bible fundamentalism, and Johnson intentionally merged her Black Protestant upbringing with Catholicism and the Afro-Cuban religion Santería to enliven her commitments to global, diasporic social movements. As Rivera once observed about her colaborer, "Marsha lived in her own realm, and she saw things through different eyes. She liked to stay in that world." In another moment, following the death of Marsha's partner, Rivera recounted how "Marsha came over to [her] house dressed like the Virgin Mary, in white and blue, and she was carrying a wooden cross and a Bible. She came in and started preaching the Bible to [her] and [they] had a few words."[66] Saint Marsha and evangelist Rivera, in tandem, with hearts with the dispossessed and with an espoused politics of refusal to white supremacy and cisheteropatriarchy, rescued homeless queer and transgender youth off church steps. In effect, they embodied what the historian Lilian Calles Barger describes as "intellectual siblings born of a shared revolutionary history," such that "[the] Black and feminist theologies that US thinkers developed were not an import of Latin American theology," but rather, in concert with each other as a practice of joint struggle."[67] Their Afro-Latin-informed liberation theology and Africana religious sensibilities allowed them to transgress orthodox religious formations, cisheterosexist theo-cultural boundaries, and a rigid gender binary, such that their own personal, lived religion was already transed. It was a transed liberation theology, rooted in the fluidity of Africana religions, which made living the unlivable possible. Yet, though physically dead, Rivera and Johnson—and their work—continue to live through such organizations as the Marsha P. Johnson Institute and the Sylvia Rivera Law Project, in which they, as copresences, continue to guide a new generation of organizers in housing queer, transgender, gender nonconforming, nonbinary, two-spirit, bisexual, gay, and homeless youth.[68]

As a copresence, one of Johnson's questions from 1992 continues to haunt religious studies and social movements more broadly. In *Pay It No Mind*, the only documentary to date which includes footage of an interview conducted by Larry Mitchell with Marsha P. Johnson just three days before she disappeared in New York City, Johnson reflects on a recently erected monument in her honor in the West Village's Sheridan Square Park. With pure astonishment she asked, "How many people have died for these two little statues to be put in the park to recognize gay people?"[69] Such a query is a beckoning call, too, to religious studies to take seriously the ways we do or do not historicize and commemorate queer and transgender people in discourses about religion, even when the lives and experiences of queer and transgender people are sacred. By invoking the language of "sacred," and by extension "sainthood," I draw again upon Althaus-Reid's prophetic insight that "the signs of sainthood—decency and the legal sexual order of T-Theology—have become equivalent to the real lives of saints, eliminating gestures of defiance and the contradiction of colonial geographies of sainthood. The purpose of these manoeuvres into sainthood is clear: by de-queering saints, the church has supported social and politico-economic contracts."[70] Yet Rivera and Johnson and so many other street evangelists and transgender saints remind us of the import of queering and transing sainthood by calling into question the very foundations upon which the church's social and politico-economic contracts have been constructed. Sainthood, then, is less about a normative elocution of "purity" and thus a recapitulation of what Black feminist bell hooks long described as "imperialist white supremacist capitalist patriarchy" with its cis-heteronormative structuring apparatus.[71] Rather, "sainthood" is a reclamation of what Althaus-Reid describes as "demonology,"[72] the inchoate space of the rebellious, the dissident, the prophets, the queers, and the stone throwers who raise hell and expose the true *white, cis, het devils* and systems of domination at work in the world as we know it.

Ahmad Greene-Hayes is assistant professor of African American religious studies at Harvard Divinity School. His book *Underworld Work: Black Atlantic Religion-Making in Jim Crow New Orleans* is forthcoming.

Acknowledgments
Portions of this article previously appeared in *Religion Compass* and have been reprinted with permission. See Greene-Hayes, "'Queering' African American Religious History."

Notes

1. Tourmaline, "Sylvia Rivera and NYPD Reflect on Stonewall Rebellion."
2. Tourmaline, "Sylvia Rivera and NYPD Reflect on Stonewall Rebellion."
3. Tourmaline, "Sylvia Rivera and NYPD Reflect on Stonewall Rebellion."
4. On the African American jeremiad, see Pitney, *African American Jeremiad*.
5. Feinberg, *Trans Liberation*, 107.
6. For a comprehensive history of STAR, please see Cohen, *Gay Liberation Youth Movement in New York*, 89–163. In this article, I follow the lead of transgender persons, scholars, thinkers, and activists in using *transgender* when referring to the historical term *transvestite*, which has since been rendered pejorative. As a historian and queer theorist, however, I use *transvestite* when citing Sylvia Rivera and Marsha P. Johnson's words, especially their self-descriptions about their own gender identities and performances in the twentieth century.

7. Hunter and Robinson, *Chocolate Cities*, 68.

8. Althaus-Reid, *Queer God*, 7.

9. Metropolitan Community Church of New York, "Obituary for Sylvia Rae Rivera."

10. Althaus-Reid, *Queer God*, 7.

11. See Exodus 1:15–21.

12. See, for example, Ransby, *Ella Baker and the Black Freedom Movement*; Lee, *For Freedom's Sake*; Bell, *Lighting the Fires of Freedom*; Robnett, *How Long? How Long?*; Holsaert et al., *Hands on the Freedom Plow*; Olson, *Freedom's Daughters*; Theoharis, *Rebellious Life of Mrs. Rosa Parks*; McGuire, *At the Dark End of the Street*; Garrow, *Montgomery Bus Boycott*. For work on Pauli Murray and other attempts at "queering" civil rights movement history, please see, for example, Cooper, *Beyond Respectability*, 87–114; Rosenberg, *Jane Crow*; Murray, *Song in a Weary Throat*; Rustin, *Time on Two Crosses*; Mumford, *Not Straight, Not White*.

13. See, for example, Carter, *Stonewall*; Rutledge, *Gay Decades*; Duberman, *Stonewall*.

14. For a recent collection of documents including Johnson and Rivera, please see Baumann, *Stonewall Reader*.

15. Please see, for example, Greene-Hayes, "'Queering' African American Religious History"; Pennington, "Willmer Broadnax."

16. White, *Reforming Sodom*, 139.

17. Tourmaline has accused David Francis, the white gay cisgender director of *The Death and Life of Marsha P. Johnson* (2017), of stealing her ideas and plagiarizing her archival labor from *Happy Birthday, Marsha!* (2018). For an examination of this controversy, see Calafell, "Narrative Authority." Much of Tourmaline's archival material first appeared in Untorelli Press's book, *Street Transvestite Action Revolutionaries: Survival, Revolt, and Queer Antagonist Struggle* (2013), without Tourmaline's consent. For more on that, see Tourmaline, "On Untorelli's 'New' Book." Upon the advice of this article's reviewers, I have decided against privileging citations of the Untorelli Press anthology and have prioritized Tourmaline's blog, *The Spirit Was*. This controversy raises a host of questions about the ethics of archival excavation and the politics of citation. A question for queer and trans studies in religion: What do we do with sources, produced unethically or in questionable ways, that offer us insights otherwise unknown about figures too-often overlooked and discarded?

18. I use "re/member" here as a nod to Wells-Oghoghomeh, *The Souls of Womenfolk*, in which "re/membrance was [enslaved] women's response to dismemberment" (6).

19. Lewis, "'I Am Sixty-Four,'" 27.

20. Melissa M. Wilcox, "Religion Is Already Transed," 86. See also Sumerau, Mathers, and Cragun, "Incorporating Transgender Experience"; Strassfeld and Henderson-Espinoza, "Trans*/Religion"; and Wilcox, "Theory in the Interstices."

21. Frank, Moreton, and White, *Devotions and Desires*, 6.

22. For a powerful critique of these assumptive logics, see Piepzna-Samarasinha, "Disability Justice/Stonewall's Legacy."

23. Rivera, "Queens in Exile," 84. See also Metropolitan Community Church of New York, "Obituary for Sylvia Rae Rivera."

24. Orsi, *Madonna of 115th Street*, 219–31.

25. See Isaiah 61:1.

26. Rivera, "Bitch on Wheels."

27. Matthew 21:12–13.

28. Rivera and Johnson, *Street Transvestite Action Revolutionaries*, 34.

29. Rivera, "Bitch on Wheels."

30. Isaiah 58:1.

31. Rivera, "Queens in Exile, the Forgotten Ones," 77.

32. Rivera, "Queens in Exile, the Forgotten Ones," 79.

33. Bateman, "Gay Liberation Front."

34. Rivera, "Queens in Exile, the Forgotten Ones," 80.

35. Suran, "Coming Out against the War," 458.

36. Suran, "Coming Out against the War," 469–70.

37. For a history of antirape activism in Black communities, see McGuire, *At the Dark End of the Street*.

38. Harris, *Sex Workers, Psychics, and Numbers Runners*, 53.

39. Rivera and Johnson, *Street Transvestite Action Revolutionaries*, 19. While I prefer to follow Tourmaline's lead by not engaging this source due to its problematic production, it is the only source in which I find these words from Rivera.

40. Rivera and Johnson, *Street Transvestite Action Revolutionaries*, 19.

41. Matthew 25:40.

42. Kasino and Morrison, *Pay It No Mind*.

43. For more on the African Methodist Episcopal Church, please see George, *Segregated Sabbaths*; Campbell, *Songs of Zion*; J. Melton, *Will to Choose*; Newman, *Freedom's Prophet*; and Bailey, *Race Patriotism*.

44. Beliso-De Jesús, *Electric Santería*, 112.

45. Beliso-De Jesús, *Electric Santería*, 104, 77.

46. Although Santeria has been primarily linked to Yoruba-inspired religions, there are other African religious traditions from which the religion has historically drawn influence, such as the Ibo of Nigeria, the Akan of Ghana, and the Fon-wew of Venin. For more on "African origins," please see Palmié, *Cooking of History*.

47. Beliso-De Jesús, *Electric Santería*, 82. See also, for example, Desmangles, *Faces of the Gods*; and Johnson, *Diaspora Conversions*.

48. See, for example, Cressler, "Black Catholic Conversion" and *Authentically Black and Truly Catholic*; Orsi, *Between Heaven And Earth*; Appleby and Cummings, *Catholics and the American Century*; and O'Toole, *Habits of Devotion*. See also Tinsley, "Black Atlantic, Queer Atlantic."

49. See Jaffary, *False Mystics*.

50. Dickerson, *African Methodist Episcopal Church*, 73–74.

51. Chireau, *Black Magic*, 3–4.

52. Chireau, *Black Magic*, 38, 48–49.

53. Raboteau, *Slave Religion*, 22.

54. Hucks, *Yoruba Traditions and African American Religious Nationalism*, 143.

55. Stewart, "Womanist Theology in the Caribbean Context," 81.

56. On STAR and the Young Lords working together, see Cohen, *Gay Liberation Youth Movement in New York*, 134–35; on the work of the Young Lords, see Wanzer-Serrano, *New York Young Lords*; on Santería, see Schmidt, *Caribbean Diaspora in the USA*; Gregory, *Santería in New York City*; Brandon, *Santeria from Africa to the New World*; Murphy, *Santeria*; and Beliso-De Jesús, *Electric Santería*; on Cuban immigrants and African Americans, see Hucks, *Yoruba Traditions and African American Religious Nationalism*, 83–87, 153–54.

57. Vidal-Ortiz, "Sexuality Discussions in Santería"; Vidal-Ortiz, "'Maricón,' 'Pájaro,' and 'Loca'"; and Vidal-Ortiz, "'Puerto Rican Way.'" For more on "heteronationalisms," please see Beliso-De Jesús, "Contentious Diasporas." For more on the complicated web of racial, religious, gendered, and sexual politics in Cuba, please see Allen, ¡*Venceremos?*; and in Lucumí/Santería specifically, please see Peréz, *Religion in the Kitchen*.

58. Peña, "Gender and Sexuality in Latina/o Miami," 758. See also Sparks and Conner, *Queering Creole Spiritual Traditions*; Alexander, *Pedagogies of Crossing*; and Tinsley, "Black Atlantic, Queer Atlantic" and *Ezili's Mirrors*.

59. Watson, "Witches," 426.

60. Beliso-De Jesús, *Electric Santería*, 102.

61. Kasino and Morrison, *Pay It No Mind*.

62. Morrison, "Rootedness," 343.

63. Beliso-De Jesús, *Electric Santería*, 119–20; Pérez, *Religion in the Kitchen*, 9.

64. See Epps, "Proper Conduct"; Lumsden, *Machos Maricones and Gays*; and Beliso-De Jesús, *Electric Santería*, 151–54.

65. Strongman, *Queering Black Atlantic Religions*; Greene-Hayes, "'Queering' African American Religious History."

66. Rivera and Johnson, *Street Transvestite Action Revolutionaries*, 44–45.

67. Barger, *World Come of Age*, 9.

68. Scholars interested in supporting queer and transgender organizing and survival work can make donations to the Marsha P. Johnson Institute (https://marshap.org/) and the Sylvia Rivera Law Project (https://srlp.org/), along with the Audre Lorde Project (https://alp.org/).

69. Kasino and Morrison, *Pay It No Mind*.

70. Althaus-Reid, *Queer God*, 141.

71. hooks, *Writing Beyond Race*, 4.

72. Althaus-Reid, *Queer God*, 133–53.

References

Alexander, M. Jacqui. *Pedagogies of Crossing: Meditations on Feminism, Sexual Politics, Memory, and the Sacred*. Durham, NC: Duke University Press, 2005.

Allen, Jafari S. *¡Venceremos? The Erotics of Black Self-Making in Cuba*. Durham, NC: Duke University Press, 2011.

Althaus-Reid, Marcella. *The Queer God*. London: Routledge, 2003.

Appleby, R. Scott, and Katherine Sprows Cummings, eds. *Catholics and the American Century: Recasting Narratives of US History*. Ithaca, NY: Cornell University Press, 2012.

Bailey, Julius H. *Race Patriotism: Protest and Print Culture in the AME Church*. Knoxville: University of Tennessee Press, 2012.

Barger, Lilian Calles. *The World Come of Age: An Intellectual History of Liberation Theology*. New York: Oxford University Press, 2018.

Bateman, Geoffrey W. "Gay Liberation Front." *glbtq: An Encyclopedia of Gay, Lesbian, Bisexual, Transgender, and Queer Culture*. Chicago: glbtq, 2004. https://web.archive .org/web/20150222025202/http://www.glbtq.com/social-sciences/gay_liberation _front.html.

Baumann, Jason, ed. *The Stonewall Reader*. New York: Penguin Books, 2019.

Beliso-De Jesús, Aisha M. "Contentious Diasporas: Gender, Sexuality, and Hetero-nationalisms in the Cuban Iyanifa Debate." *Signs* 40, no. 4 (2015): 817–40.

Beliso-De Jesús, Aisha M. *Electric Santería: Racial and Sexual Assemblages of Transnational Religion*. New York: Columbia University Press, 2015.

Bell, Janet Dewart. *Lighting the Fires of Freedom: African American Women in the Civil Rights Movement*. New York: New Press, 2018.

Brandon, George. *Santeria from Africa to the New World: The Dead Sell Memories*. Bloomington: Indiana University Press, 1997.

Calafell, Bernadette Marie. "Narrative Authority, Theory in the Flesh, and the Fight over *The Death and Life of Marsha P. Johnson*." *QED* 6, no. 2 (2019): 26–39. https://doi.org /10.14321/qed.6.2.0026.

Campbell, James T. *Songs of Zion: The African Methodist Episcopal Church in the United States and South Africa*. New York: Oxford University Press, 1995.

Carter, David. *Stonewall: The Riots That Sparked the Gay Revolution*. New York: St. Martin's, 2004.

Chireau, Yvonne P. *Black Magic: Religion and the African American Conjuring Tradition*. Berkeley: University of California Press, 2003.

Cohen, Stephan L. *The Gay Liberation Youth Movement in New York: "An Army of Lovers Cannot Fail."* New York: Routledge, 2008.

Cooper, Brittney C. *Beyond Respectability: The Intellectual Thought of Race Women*. Urbana: University of Illinois Press, 2017.

Cressler, Matthew J. *Authentically Black and Truly Catholic: The Rise of Black Catholicism in the Great Migration*. New York: New York University Press, 2017.

Cressler, Matthew J. "Black Catholic Conversion and the Burden of Black Religion." *Journal of Africana Religions* 2, no. 2 (2014): 280–87.

Desmangles, Leslie Gérald. *The Faces of the Gods: Vodou and Roman Catholicism in Haiti*. Chapel Hill: University of North Carolina Press, 1992.

Dickerson, Dennis. *The African Methodist Episcopal Church: A History*. Cambridge: Cambridge University Press, 2020.

Duberman, Martin B. *Stonewall*. New York: Dutton, 1993.

Epps, Brad. "Proper Conduct: Reinaldo Arenas, Fidel Castro, and the Politics of Homosexuality." *Journal of the History of Sexuality* 6, no. 2 (1995): 231–83.

Feinberg, Leslie. *Trans Liberation: Beyond Pink or Blue*. Boston: Beacon, 1998.

Frank, Gillian, Bethany Moreton, and Heather R. White, eds. *Devotions and Desires: Histories of Sexuality and Religion in the Twentieth-Century United States*. Chapel Hill: University of North Carolina Press, 2018.

Garrow, David, ed. *The Montgomery Bus Boycott and the Women Who Started It: The Memoir of Jo Ann Gibson Robinson*. Knoxville: University of Tennessee Press, 1987.

George, Carol V. R. *Segregated Sabbaths: Richard Allen and the Emergence of Independent Black Churches, 1760–1840*. New York: Oxford University Press, 1975.

Greene-Hayes, Ahmad. "'Queering' African American Religious History." *Religion Compass* 13, no. 7 (2019): e12319. https://doi.org/10.1111/rec3.12319.

Gregory, Steven. *Santería in New York City: A Study in Cultural Resistance*. New York: Taylor and Francis, 1999.

Harris, LaShawn. *Sex Workers, Psychics, and Numbers Runners: Black Women in New York City's Underground Economy*. Urbana: University of Illinois Press, 2016.

Holsaert, Faith S., Martha Prescod Norman Noonan, Judy Richardson, Betty Garman Robinson, Jean Smith Young, and Dorothy M. Zellner, eds. *Hands on the Freedom Plow: Personal Accounts by Women in SNCC*. Urbana: University of Illinois Press, 2010.

hooks, bell. *Writing Beyond Race: Living Theory and Practice*. New York: Routledge, 2013.

Hucks, Tracey E. *Yoruba Traditions and African American Religious Nationalism*. Albuquerque: University of New Mexico Press, 2012.

Hunter, Marus Anthony, and Zandria F. Robinson. *Chocolate Cities: The Black Map of American Life*. Oakland: University of California Press, 2018.

Jaffary, Nora E. *False Mystics: Deviant Orthodoxy in Colonial Mexico*. Lincoln: University of Nebraska Press, 2004.

Johnson, Paul Christopher. *Diaspora Conversions: Black Carib Religion and the Recovery of Africa*. Berkeley: University of California Press, 2007.

Kasino, Michael, and Richard Morrison, dirs. 2012. *Pay It No Mind: Marsha P. Johnson*. Redux Pictures. https://www.youtube.com/watch?v=rjN9W2KstqE.

Lee, Chana Kai. *For Freedom's Sake: The Life of Fanny Lou Hamer*. Urbana: University of Illinois Press, 1999.

Lewis, Abram J. "'I Am Sixty-Four and Paul McCartney Doesn't Care': The Haunting of the Transgender Archive and the Challenges of Queer History." *Radical History Review*, no. 120 (2014): 13–34.

Lumsden, Ian. *Machos Maricones and Gays: Cuba and Homosexuality*. Philadelphia: Temple University Press, 2010.

McGuire, Danielle. *At the Dark End of the Street: Black Women, Rape, and Resistance—A New History of the Civil Rights Movement from Rosa Parks to the Rise of Black Power*. New York: Alfred A. Knopf, 2010.

Melton, J. Gordon. *A Will to Choose: The Origins of African Methodism*. Lanham, MD: Rowman and Littlefield, 2007.

Metropolitan Community Church of New York. "Obituary for Sylvia Rae Rivera." *Sylvia's Place*. https://web.archive.org/web/20060619122836/http://www.sylviasplace.org/sylvia_obituary.htm.

Morrison, Joseph M. *Santeria: African Spirits in America*. Boston: Beacon, 2011.

Morrison, Toni. "Rootedness: The Ancestor as Foundation." In *Black Women Writers (1950–1980): A Critical Evaluation*, edited by Mari Evans, 339–45. New York: Anchor Books, 1984.

Mumford, Kevin. *Not Straight, Not White: Black Gay Men from the March on Washington to the AIDS Crisis*. Chapel Hill: University of North Carolina Press, 2016.

Murphy, Joseph M. *Santeria: African Spirits in America*. Boston: Beacon, 2011.

Murray, Pauli. *Song in a Weary Throat: Memoir of an American Pilgrimage*. Edited by Patricia Bell-Scott. New York: W. W. Norton, 2018.

Newman, Richard S. *Freedom's Prophet: Bishop Richard Allen, the AME Church, and the Black Founding Fathers*. New York: New York University Press, 2008.

Olson, Lynne. *Freedom's Daughters: The Unsung Heroines of the Civil Rights Movement from 1830–1970*. New York: Scribner, 2001.

Orsi, Robert A. *Between Heaven and Earth: The Religious Worlds People Make and the Scholars Who Study Them*. Princeton, NJ: Princeton University Press, 2013.

Orsi, Robert A. *The Madonna of 115th Street: Faith and Community in Italian Harlem, 1880–1950*. New Haven, CT: Yale University Press, 2010.

O'Toole, James M., ed. *Habits of Devotion: Catholic Religious Practice in Twentieth-Century America*. Ithaca, NY: Cornell University Press, 2005.

Palmié, Stephan. *The Cooking of History: How Not to Study Afro-Cuban Religion*. Chicago: University of Chicago Press, 2013.

Peña, Susana. "Gender and Sexuality in Latina/o Miami: Documenting Latina Transsexual Activists." In *Historicizing Gender and Sexuality*, edited by Kevin P. Murphy and Jennifer M. Spear. Special issue, *Gender and History* 22, no. 3 (2011): 229–46.

Pennington, Stephan. "Willmer Broadnax, Midcentury Gospel, and Black Trans/Masculinities." *Women and Music*, no. 22 (2018): 117–25.

Pérez, Elizabeth. *Religion in the Kitchen: Cooking, Talking, and the Making of Black Atlantic Traditions*. New York: New York University Press, 2016.

Piepzna-Samarasinha, Leah Lakshmi. "Disability Justice/Stonewall's Legacy, or: Love Mad Trans Black Women When They Are Alive and Dead, Let Their Revolutions Teach Your Resistance All the Time." *QED* 6, no. 2 (2019): 54–62.

Pitney, David Howard. *The African American Jeremiad: Appeals for Justice in America*. Philadelphia: Temple University Press, 2005.

Raboteau, Albert. *Slave Religion: The "Invisible Institution" in the Antebellum South*. Oxford: Oxford University Press, 2004.

Ransby, Barbara. *Ella Baker and the Black Freedom Movement: A Radical Democratic Vision*. Chapel Hill: University of North Carolina Press, 2003.

Rivera, Sylvia. "Bitch on Wheels." https://lambdaliterary.org/2021/01/bitch-on-wheels/.

Rivera, Sylvia. "Queens in Exile, the Forgotten Ones." In *Genderqueer: Voices beyond the Sexual Binary*, edited by Joan Nestle, Clare Howell, and Riki Wilchins, 67–85. Los Angeles: Alyson Books, 2002.

Rivera, Sylvia, and Marsha P. Johnson. *Street Transvestite Action Revolutionaries (STAR): Survival, Revolt, and Queer Antagonist Struggle*. Edited by Ehn Nothing. Untorelli, 2013. https://untorellipress.noblogs.org/post/2013/03/12/street-transvestite-action-revolutionaries-survival-revolt-and-queer-antagonist-struggle/.

Robnett, Belinda. *How Long? How Long? African-American Women in the Struggle for Civil Rights*. New York: Oxford University Press, 1997.

Rosenberg, Rosalind. *Jane Crow: The Life of Pauli Murray*. New York: Oxford University Press, 2017.

Rustin, Bayard. *Time on Two Crosses: The Collected Writings of Bayard Rustin*. Edited by Devon W. Carbado and Donald Weise. San Francisco: Cleis, 2003.

Rutledge, Leigh W. *The Gay Decades: From Stonewall to the Present—The People and Events That Shaped Gay Lives*. New York: Plume, 1992.

Schmidt, Bettina. *Caribbean Diaspora in the USA: Diversity of Caribbean Religions in New York City*. New York: Routledge, 2016.

Sparks, David Hatfield, and Randy P. Conner. *Queering Creole Spiritual Traditions: Lesbian, Gay, Bisexual, and Transgender Participation in African-Inspired Traditions in the Americas*. New York: Harrington, 2004.

Stewart, Dianne M. "Womanist Theology in the Caribbean Context: Critiquing Culture, Rethinking Doctrine, and Expanding Boundaries." *Journal of Feminist Studies in Religion* 20, no. 1 (2004): 61–82.

Strassfeld, Max, and Robyn Henderson-Espinoza, eds. "Trans*/Religion." Special Issue, *TSQ* 6, no. 3 (2019).

Strongman, Roberto. *Queering Black Atlantic Religions: Transcorporeality in Candomblé, Santería, and Vodou*. Durham, NC: Duke University Press, 2019.

Sumerau, J. E., Lain A. B. Mathers, and Ryan T. Cragun. "Incorporating Transgender Experience toward a More Inclusive Gender Lens in the Sociology of Religion." *Sociology of Religion* 79, no. 4 (2018): 425–48.

Suran, Justin David. "Coming Out against the War: Antimilitarism and the Politicization of Homosexuality in the Era of Vietnam." *American Quarterly* 53, no. 3 (2001): 452–88.

Theoharis, Jeanne. *The Rebellious Life of Mrs. Rosa Parks*. Boston: Beacon, 2013.

Tinsley, Omise'eke Natasha. "Black Atlantic, Queer Atlantic: Queer Imaginings of the Middle Passage." *GLQ* 14, nos. 2–3 (2008): 191–215.

Tinsley, Omise'eke Natasha. *Ezili's Mirrors: Imagining Black Queer Genders*. Durham, NC: Duke University Press, 2018.

Tourmaline. "On Untorelli's 'New' Book." *The Spirit Was* (blog), March 13, 2013. https://thespiritwas.tumblr.com/post/45275076521/on-untorellis-new-book.

Tourmaline. "Sylvia Rivera and NYPD Reflect on Stonewall Rebellion." *The Spirit Was* (blog), February 23, 2012. https://www.tumblr.com/thespiritwas/18108920192/sylvia-rivera-nypd-reflect-on-stonewall.

Vidal-Ortiz, Salvador. "'Maricón,' 'Pájaro,' and 'Loca': Cuban and Puerto Rican Linguistic Practices, and Sexual Minority Participation, in US Santería." *Journal of Homosexuality* 58, nos. 6–7 (2011): 901–18.

Vidal-Ortiz, Salvador. "'The Puerto Rican Way Is More Tolerant': Constructions and Uses of Homophobia among Santería Practitioners across Ethno-Racial and National Identification." *Sexualities* 11, no. 4 (2008): 476–95.

Vidal-Ortiz, Salvador. "Sexuality Discussions in Santería: A Case Study of Religion and Sexuality Negotiation." *Sexuality Research and Social Policy* 3, no. 3 (2006): 52–66.

Wanzer-Serrano, Darrel. *New York Young Lords and the Struggle for Liberation.* Philadelphia: Temple University Press, 2015.

Watson, Carolyn E. "Witches, Female Priests, and Sacred Manoeuvres: (De)Stabilising Gender and Sexuality in a Cuban Religion of African Origin." *Gender and History* 25, no. 3 (2013): 425–44.

Wells-Oghoghomeh, Alexis. *The Souls of Womenfolk: The Religious Cultures of Enslaved Women in the Lower South.* Chapel Hill: University of North Carolina Press, 2021.

White, Heather R. *Reforming Sodom: Protestants and the Rise of Gay Rights.* Chapel Hill: University of North Carolina Press, 2015.

Wilcox, Melissa M. "Religion Is Already Transed; Religious Studies Is Not (Yet) Listening." *Journal of Feminist Studies in Religion* 34, no. 1 (2018): 84–88.

Wilcox, Melissa M. "Theory in the Interstices: Queering and Transing Religious Studies, Religioning Trans and Queer Studies." *Temenos* 56, no. 1 (2020): 119–46. https://doi.org/10.33356/temenos.91485.

Social Fabric or Glitter Bombs?
Questions on Trans and Queer Methods in Religious Studies

JANET R. JAKOBSEN

ABSTRACT This essay raises the question of how to understand social differences, including those indexed by trans, queer, antiracist, and feminist studies, as both intersectional and incommensurable. Through an analysis of how oscillation between the poles of binary oppositions works to reinforce hegemony and weave different issues into a hegemonic social fabric, the essay considers how methods and metaphors for trans and queer studies in religion can create counter-hegemonic possibilities. Specifically, in moving from coherent ideas of "the social" as represented by different social relations woven into a hegemonic social fabric to queer and trans ideas of moving and shimmering social relations that might touch across disjunctions, can trans and queer studies in religion contribute to social possibilities in a revolutionary hue?

KEYWORDS hegemony, intersectionality, incommensurability, justice, revolution

In "Transing Religious Studies," Max Strassfeld provides a reading of antitrans legislation passed in 2016 (Mississippi HB 1523) that has proven all too accurate well beyond its specific focus on a single antitrans bill.[1] While there were some relatively successful efforts to push back against the antitrans bills passed in 2016, as shown in the (partial) reversal of an antitrans bill in North Carolina in 2017, what we have witnessed in the last few years is a rapid-fire passage of state legislation targeting LGBTQIA+ rights, reproductive justice, the teaching of the history of racism in the United States, and books of many types, including those that speak to religious diversity. This legislative hurricane really began to intensify in 2021 after the appointment in 2020 of a third Supreme Court justice during the Trump presidency. Once Trump had appointed a full third of the Court, the new solidly conservative majority soon showed its willingness to undo precedent and opened the boundaries of what might conceivably be upheld as constitutional. Conservative state legislatures were more than willing to step through that opening. And, indeed, the *Dobbs* decision striking down *Roe v. Wade* in a case that was originally about a ban on abortion at fifteen weeks in Mississippi shows that conservative state legislators can expect their claims to be upheld and even exceeded by US Supreme Court rulings. The continuing passage of a series of antitrans, antifeminist,

QTR • A Journal of Trans and Queer Studies in Religion • 1:1 • May 2024
DOI: 10.1215/29944724-11208920 © 2024 Janet R. Jakobsen

and racist state bills that cater to a politicized right-wing Christianity shows the ongoing relevance of Strassfeld's analysis. Most significantly, these events show the increasing import of Strassfeld's argument for transfeminist religious studies in conjunction with an active politics to challenge racist, antisemitic, and anti-Muslim governmental actions.

Conservative governors and state legislatures continue to try to outdo each other in a situation where it appears there are few guardrails to protect democracy in states that are heavily gerrymandered and have enacted policies of voter suppression.[2] While it is impossible to keep up with this legislative action while writing for academic publication, the series of antitrans legislative efforts in 2016 provides a useful starting point, in part, because this antitrans focus followed rapidly on the footsteps of the 2015 Supreme Court *Obergefell* decision that legalized gay marriage nationally. The shift from antigay to antitrans legislation sustained the focus of conservative Christian politics in the United States in terms of what Mary Ann Case has called the "seamless garment" of gender and sexual conservatism that also ties together much Catholic and Protestant conservatism.[3]

For Case, the fact that the threads of both Catholic jurisprudence, Protestant secular presumption, and US case law are woven together into this single garment shows the need, as Strassfeld suggests, to combine feminist, queer, and trans political action and also to recognize the intertwining of secular and religious politics with the history of racism in the United States. Strassfeld has made clear that the different strands of misogynist, homophobic, racist, antitrans, antisemitic, and anti-Muslim politics are not the same. For example, antitrans bills can position queer and trans people differently in relation to US law.[4] But one major question of contemporary work for justice is how to respond to the ways in which these different strands are so often woven together.

In the United States, this garment might be named as the hegemonic social fabric of a white Christian nationalist polity and its accompanying dedication to racial capitalism. It weaves together multiple strands of domination and exploitation, including, but not exclusively, ongoing coloniality, racism, misogyny, transphobia, homophobia, ableism, antisemitism, and anti-Muslim politics. As Strassfeld has shown about Mississippi HB 1523 and as is borne out by the current situation, the intertwining of these different strands demands a politics that makes connections across issues lest the forces of oppression simply move from one issue to the next as a shuttle moves across a loom, creating a fabric that may be woven from very thin threads (including outright lies) and yet prove very strong and impervious to attempts to unravel it.

In my recent book *The Sex Obsession*, I call this movement among issues "mobility-for-stasis," in which movement among issues of focus in US public discourse creates kaleidoscopically shifting patterns that nonetheless maintain hegemonic relations of domination and exploitation.[5] The metaphor of the kaleidoscope allows analysis of a dynamic intersectionality in which many issues are interrelated in patterns that may shift without undoing the frame of the kaleidoscope itself: mobility-for-stasis.[6] So, for example, when conservative politics moves among attacks on reproductive justice, voting rights, immigration, critical race theory, trans athletes, and drag queen story hour, the issues target different constituencies even as the various political strands are also intersecting. The conservative focus may bring one issue or another to the fore and move others temporarily to the background, but the overall effect of the shifting-but-repeated patterns is to reinforce hegemony.[7]

I am completely convinced by both Strassfeld's and Case's arguments and have committed much of my scholarship and activism to realizing a vision of interconnected, intersectional politics. And yet, in thinking about the subject of this new journal, *QTR: A Journal of Trans and Queer Studies in Religion*, and about the shape of the field to which it contributes, I have also been reminded of queer- and trans-theorist Kadji Amin's admonition to attend to disjunctions as well as connections across issues, identities, and politics:

> If Queer Studies is to become a genuinely interdisciplinary field, it is critical to multiply its theoretical genealogies. However, this process of multiplication will inevitably give rise to both dissonances and resonances with the habits of thought and feeling that had previously shaped the field. Investigating the source of these dissonances and amplifying the resonances should be part of the work of claiming alternate theoretical genealogies for queer scholarship.[8]

Amin is here talking about the different theoretical traditions, formed in and through different material genealogies, that have constituted contemporary queer thinking, but his point also applies to politics. What are the dissonances and resonances of the multiple genealogies for queer and trans politics in relation to religion? To what should those who seek justice attend? What are the frameworks for such attention? And how do these frameworks relate to each other? For example, in the widely read essay "Decolonization Is Not a Metaphor," Eve Tuck and K. Wayne Yang argue that the colonial theft of land from indigenous peoples and its ongoing effects is *incommensurable* with other forms of oppression and that the repatriation of these lands demanded by decoloniality is similarly incommensurable with other forms of social justice, including reparations for the violence of enslavement during the colonial period.[9] Tuck and Yang ask for two responses that could allow for a politics embracing both repatriation and reparations: (1) the recognition of the specificity of different oppressions such that social justice accountability would include accounting for these differences, and (2) the active questioning of *how* different forms of social justice might be brought together in light of incommensurability, rather than assuming connections across difference.

One of my questions, then, is how to build queer and trans studies in religion while keeping in mind both the resonances *and* the dissonances within different genealogies, which include a range of critical approaches to social and cultural analysis: queer, trans, antiracist, decolonial, feminist, materialist (old and new), and many more.[10] As someone who has taken as helpful Case's metaphor of the seamless garment of gender and sexual conservatism, the question becomes: Is the social fabric seamless? And if it is not seamless, how are we to understand the relations among sexism, homophobia, transphobia, colonialism, racial capitalism, and many more interrelations?

Hegemonic Social Fabric

A first step in conceptualizing the hegemonic social fabric is to include dynamism among social relations. Fabric might seem less dynamic than a kaleidoscope, but, as I consider in more detail below, fabric is reversible, and I also find it helpful to think of how the threads of social relations are woven into patterns that may shift from one pattern to the next but that may also reinforce existing norms. There are many fashionable variations on a military jacket that still materialize the original referent. I also sometimes think of *The Unicorn Tapestries* at the Metropolitan Museum of Art in which different scenes of a magical forest are depicted, but in the centerpiece, the unicorn is chained and fenced even as the forest remains magical. In one part of the series, unicorn hunters are at the fore; in another, a group of youths play a game; in a third, the unicorn is surrounded but may also be magically "purifying" the water of the fountain. In one scene, the unicorn meets with a "maiden," sometimes interpreted as a virgin, who subdues the unicorn. In one scene, the unicorn is killed and brought to the castle; but the most well-known tapestry is that of the unicorn "resting" encircled by fencing.[11] Interpretations vary. Perhaps it is not a single series. But nowhere among the different scenes is there any sense that the unicorn will escape captivity.

Movement among scenes in the tapestry or among different issues in political discussions may allow single issues to provide the leading edge of debate while also weaving an overall sense that civilization will always subdue unicorn magic in one way or another. In this way, for many years it seemed that antigay politics provided the wedge for broader conservative action as the federal government and state after state passed some form of "defense of marriage" act.[12] These bills not only targeted "gay marriage," they also brought conversative voters to the polls. Yet when this leading issue became less sustainable, movement among associated political topics has allowed new issues, like transphobia, book banning, and antiabortion politics, to come to the fore. These issues were part of the pattern of mainstream politics and so, even if the interaction between the maiden and the unicorn is the focus of one scene, the unicorn hunt could be forcefully pulled back into political discourse as part of an overall onslaught.

Knotting the Threads

While any rundown of current legislative efforts will necessarily fall behind the frenzied pace of current activity, it is still helpful to trace just some of the threads as they are knotted together. The *Dobbs* decision ending any right to access abortion and leaving reproductive access to the political whims of different states is a central strand of these efforts, showing the US Supreme Court's willingness to overturn precedent, and it is woven together with many strands of state-based legislation to muster the force of law on behalf of racial, sexual, and gender conservatism in response to a Republican base understood as primarily white, Christian, and nationalist. These efforts include state-based abortion bans that have taken many forms, among which Texas SB 8 is particularly important because it allows private citizens to act as enforcers of antiabortion politics, enabling a type of vigilante misogyny. The attorney general of Texas has also declared that support for trans children should be understood as "child abuse," and the governor ordered that state authorities investigate the provision of medical care to trans children.[13] An appeals court has currently halted this action, but given the state of the US judiciary, it is unknown how long it will last. Florida's "Don't Say Gay" bill not only limits speech about LGBTQIA+ people, but also would require counselors or teachers to inform the parents of any statements about identity that queer and trans children might make, effectively removing schools as any kind of safe space for queer and trans children to find adult support if it is not available—or if they face outright hostility or abuse—at home. In April 2022 the state of Alabama passed legislation to ban medical care for trans children; Oklahoma passed a near-total ban on abortion, while legislators in Missouri have suggested they may have the right to control the actions of citizens of Missouri who cross state lines to obtain an abortion.[14] The bans on health care for trans children also expanded to laws preventing full participation by trans students in school activities, particularly in sports.[15]

These laws are closely associated with other lines of attack meant to shore up white Christian nationalism, including efforts to ban the teaching of critical race theory in schools. For example, the current line of attack against trans people focuses on trans children, not with concern for the lives of those children but to promote "parents' rights," even as white Christian hegemony conceived as individual liberty is built into parental claims to individual control over their children's schooling.[16] The attacks on trans children and education also position transness as somehow associated with "child abuse" and "grooming" for sexual violence. This discourse, which draws on the long history of associating homosexuality and pedophilia, was also used in right-wing attacks on Supreme Court nominee Ketanji Brown Jackson, who is the first African American woman to serve as a Supreme Court justice. Senator Josh Hawley charged on Twitter that Judge Jackson "has a pattern of letting child porn offenders off the hook" despite the fact that this claim runs counter to the empirical record.[17] This line of attack is particularly important because it weaves together a series of associations that are quite active in right-wing political formations, in part due to the focus in QAnon discourse on child abuse as the fundamental sin of the political Left. The focus on children also ties in a set of issues about schooling currently animating both right-wing and mainstream Republicans, like Virginia governor Glenn Youngkin, and extending to responses to the COVID-19 pandemic and the power of teachers' unions. These issues include the teaching of the history of racism in the United States and the banning of books such as those related to critical race theory, or those like *Maus*, which represents historical antisemitism and its attendant violence. As columnist Charles Blow has noted in the *New York Times*, the GOP is framing critical race theory as an enemy of white, Christian governance in the same way it positioned Sharia law earlier in the twenty-first century.[18] This association is articulated as several new court cases reraise the centuries-long question of whether religious liberty in the United States is applicable beyond conservative Christian claims. From the Supreme Court's upholding of the anti-Muslim framework of both the Trump administration's "travel ban" and 2019's *Dunn v. Ray*, to cases focused on gender and sexuality, "religion" and "Christianity" have been re-sutured as synonymous in US law and policy.[19]

Locating this associative discourse in hearings to confirm a justice to the Supreme Court who was nominated by the Democratic president who (in Trumpian and QAnon fantasy) "stole" the 2020 election also ties this set of issues (homophobia, transphobia, critique of critical race theory, antisemitic book banning, and anti-Muslim legislation) to the central issues of concern facing the Supreme Court (voting rights, affirmative action, immigration, religious freedom, and the status of democracy in the United States).[20] And, while the mainstream press often presented accusations against Justice Brown as "playing to the right," we have to admit that this play was put on by a set of sitting US Senators on the Senate Judiciary Committee. In other words, it was part of a process that is as mainstream as mainstream gets when it comes to politics in the United States.

Associations like these tie knots in the social fabric that are hard to break (homosexuals are child molesters, Democrats like homosexuals, therefore Democrats are child molesters and any issue associated with Democrats is leading to child abuse). In other words, the associations are woven together exceptionally tightly, forming a garment seamless enough that almost any social justice issue can currently be positioned as equivalent to child abuse.

Reversing the Fabric

Thus far, I've provided some illustration of how movement among issues can knot together a hegemonic social fabric. How can social analysis also track incommensurability among issues? Here, I will focus on oscillation.[21] One way to think of interrelation and incommensurability together is to imagine them as two sides of a social fabric. Political discussions often focus on one side or the other. This singular focus elides the fact that hegemonic relations are constructed through issues that are both disjunctive and interconnected, both dissonant and resonant. This elision is maintained in part through oscillation back and forth so that only one side of the fabric is visible at any time.

Flipping back and forth between one side and the other of such oppositional pairs can narrow the allowable parameters of debate while also blocking discussion of the conditions that produced the supposed pair of opposites. Thus, oscillation is one mechanism by which binary pairs that are supposedly in opposition to each other can work together in support of hegemonic relations. For example, flipping back and forth between what Lisa Duggan and Lauren Berlant have noted as the overvaluing and undervaluing of issues related to gender and sexuality sustains the moralism of contemporary culture wars while also allowing conservatives to slough off any ethical import that sexual violence might have.[22] In a typical back-and-forth between those who would take sex—and sexual violence—seriously as a political issue and those who would dismiss it, Newt Gingrich accused the media of being obsessed with sex for focusing on the story of Donald Trump and sexual assault. Of course, Gingrich was also Speaker of the House during the Clinton administration and acted as one of the drivers of the impeachment of President Clinton in response to his sexual relations with Monica Lewinsky.[23] But oscillation allows each side of the pairing (sex is unimportant and should not be discussed, or sex is so important a president should be impeached) to appear as if its reverse does not exist or is not relevant. This oscillation was also enacted in the Senate hearings to confirm Brett Kavanaugh to the Supreme Court, in which defenders of Kavanaugh sometimes configured sexual violence as merely high school hijinks, while the discussion of Kavanaugh's behavior was also declared to be so denigrating to him personally that Lindsay Graham could raise it as the justification for badgering Justice Jackson. Or, in another example of this kind of oscillation, debate over sex in US public life is configured as a binary choice between a regulatory Christian conservatism that produces state regulation and a popular culture permeated by sexual violence. The debate oscillates back and forth between the two as if there are no other choices, even as both of the apparent options tend to reinforce hegemonic power relations in which sex and gender nonnormativity are marginalized.[24]

To understand the import of oscillation, let us continue with the metaphor of a hegemonic social fabric and consider the ways in which this fabric might be reversible so that it can be flipped back and forth as the two sides remain part of a single tapestry. The flipping back and forth of various pieces of social fabric can also become a series of tapestries—all different, but all supportive of the overarching hegemonic narrative.

Currently, mainstream politics is understood as a struggle between a right-wing authoritarian movement and defenders of democracy. This is an important fight that includes the battle for voting rights and defense of the rule of law itself. But this oscillating struggle between mainstream political parties also covers over the ways in which US democracy is itself part of hegemonic relations constructed through racial capitalism and dedicated to sustaining the largest military in the world. When mainstream public discourse focuses only on the back-and-forth between these two "sides" of US politics, the deeper relations that knot the two sides together are hidden by each side of the fabric.

One way to name the current right-wing formation is as "white Christian nationalism," a designation that is increasingly recognized in academic analyses beyond religious studies, like the one offered by sociologists Phillip Gorski and Samuel Perry.[25] Just as legal and extralegal action combined to create white supremacist culture in the Jim Crow era, the new spate of antidemocratic legislation in state capitols around the country combines with extralegal action to deny freedom to those not associated with the current version of white, Christian nationalism. The tendency of this right-wing formation toward an authoritarian understanding of US nationalism was expressed directly and dramatically on January 6, 2021. In a conference call with organizers, for example, right-wing operative Jason Sullivan distinguished between US "patriots" who he urged should descend on the capitol building and simple "citizens" of the United States who should not be trusted to govern. The "patriots" were the true heirs of US nationalism and should go to any lengths to secure the nation, including either "martial law" or the extralegal "pressure" enacted during the riot itself. And, as testimony in the January 6 cases has shown, many participants in the riot saw themselves as simply fulfilling instructions from Donald Trump as part of the Make America Great Again movement.

That said—and this is the part that makes analysis complex—it is also the case that those who support constitutional democracy in the current moment may well be dedicated to something that could be accurately named as "white Christian nationalism," albeit in a less virulent form. Certainly, the Constitution is a nationalist document—its main function being to establish a new nation, how could it be otherwise? Yet it can also be valuable to resist naturalizing this nationalism. In particular, the current political economy in which virtually the entire earth is covered by nation-states makes it seem as if nationalism is a natural (perhaps inevitable) political formation rather than a historically specific and contingent formation produced out of colonialism. When Ramón Grosfoguel talks about ongoing coloniality, he means, in part, the ways in which contemporary nationalism carries forward colonial imperatives, with the concomitant implication that decoloniality might well require a different political formation than that of the nation-state system.[26]

There is, similarly, strong evidence that the Constitution is steeped in white supremacy from the number of its signatories who themselves enslaved people through the infamous Three-Fifths Compromise, to the very structure of the federation, states' rights, and the Electoral College. While it is true that historians argue about just how deeply white supremacy is embedded in the Constitution, as with ongoing coloniality, its continuing effects are readily found in US political processes—from the overrepresentation of less-populous, predominantly white states in the Senate and the Electoral College to the ability of states to abrogate fundamental rights, including that of Equal

Protection, allowing for the current spate of legislation against voting rights, trans rights, and reproductive justice.[27]

One of the more complex challenges in understanding the way in which the constitutional democracy of the United States is also organized by white, Christian nationalism is when it comes to the "Christian" part. Historian Jon Butler has convincingly argued that many of the Constitution's framers were not—as contemporary right-wing advocates claim—Christian, but rather, as Butler once said to me in conversation, "some other odd thing."[28] But as the subtitle of Butler's book *Awash in a Sea of Faith: Christianizing the American People* names quite clearly, despite the fact that many of the framers understood themselves as deists or oddly (queerly?) non-Christian, Christianity became predominant in the United States. Deist and other Enlightenment understandings of religion opened the door to a form of religious freedom that did not establish religion yet was also structured so as to enable the institutionalization of the "extraordinary power of Christianity" in the United States.[29] And, as Ann Pellegrini and I, among others, have argued, particularly when it comes to gender and sexuality, appeals to Christian history, norms, and assumptions remain central to US legislation and jurisprudence.[30] Pellegrini and I have termed this connection between Christian presumption and secular law "Christian secularism," which names not just the history of constitutional interpretation but also the reason why it is so easy for "religious liberty" to revert back to Christian hegemony. Liberals may actively challenge the Christian Right, but this challenge is often mounted on the basis of defending (Christian) secularism rather than through engagement with the multiplicity of religion. In defending only secularism (and often refusing even to talk about religion), the conflation of "religion" and "Christianity" goes unchallenged, even as the predominant version of secularism also has deep historical ties to Christian norms.

Part of the problem in US politics, then, is that Republican attacks on people, knowledge, and democracy are grounded in much longer traditions in the United States, traditions that are shared by Democrats and Republicans, even if Democrats oppose the specific attacks. These connections are obscured, however, by a structure of political debate that tends to oscillate between the supposed "two sides" of American politics, represented by the two-party political system and a clichéd understanding that there are two sides to every story. The two-sides approach has become increasingly untenable because of the contemporary asymmetry between the two political parties as the Republican Party becomes unconnected from any agreement on empirical reality and is instead tethered to a "big lie" in support of authoritarianism.[31] And yet the two sides approach is maintained by the legacy media outlets in surprising ways.[32]

The "two sides" version of debate hides the shared positions between "sides" (such as support for donor interests shared by both political parties), focusing instead on an oscillation between political differences and thereby eliding underlying agreement—agreement that constitutes the (hegemonic) common sense of democracy in the United States. This mechanism is enacted over and over again in mainstream politics and media discourse.[33] Oscillation works in part because both sides play into the existing power structure—the right-wing version of white Christian nationalism is, indeed, powerful, but it is also minority movement made powerful by its connections to the long-standing hegemony shared by both Democrats and Republicans and their cultural and social (economic) interests: coloniality, patriarchy, racial capitalism, limited democracy, and most recently neoliberalism: in other words, white, Christian nationalism.

Oscillation thus produces a hegemonic common sense in which challenging racism or Christian hegemony or the nationalism of "strong borders" is to be treated with trepidation by Democrats as well as Republicans. The repeatedly muted response on the part of both the Democratic Party and the mainstream media to increasingly egregious statements and actions on the part of right-wing white Christian nationalists is in part due to the fact that mainstream Democrats share the sense that the United States is a majority white nation that sustains its Christian secularist heritage. White Christian nationalism thus serves as a singular social fabric holding together US political discourse, even as that discourse flips back and forth between its more mainstream and its more authoritarian "sides."

The Democratic Party is slow to take up social justice issues, including trans rights and reproductive justice, even when public opinion polling shows that the majority of people in the United States support social justice. Only after *Roe* was overturned and voters consistently supported abortion rights were Democrats willing to take on the issue with any enthusiasm. Because the underlying connection between the "sides" so often represents "common sense" (even if not a majority view), many mainstream politicians are not willing to vigorously defend social justice issues that they perceive as separated from that common sense. Strangely, as with abortion rights, this leaves the majority position to be adjudicated as if it is a minoritized claim within a court system that has now been effectively captured by the political Right. When the courts reject these reproductive rights *as rights*, conservative legislative processes also move to keep the majority position from being instituted through voting. The broad gerrymandering and voter suppression of conservative states is well documented, and the Right has similarly tried to prevent ballot initiatives that would allow direct voting on abortion rights.[34]

The hegemonic political formation in the United States has produced a starkly divided polity with consequential differences that is nonetheless also held together by a common sense of white Christian nationalism. In the current moment, the differences between the "two sides" of American politics are desperately consequential—for voting rights, for reproductive justice, for trans people, for whether some of the worst effects of neoliberal economics will be ameliorated, and for whether authoritarianism succeeds in the United States and elsewhere. Unfortunately, the differences are also less consequential than they might be in that both parties remain committed to some form of white supremacy, whether that of outright racism or the dominative control of tokenism and representational politics.[35] Both parties remain dedicated to US nationalism in the form of supporting the US military budget, draining funds from other possible budget initiatives, and supporting military action throughout the world (both directly by the United States and through US military aid to other armies). And both parties remain committed to Christian norms in US politics (whether in religious or secular form). These norms include understanding the world in terms of Christian familialism that limits queer politics to the question of whether queer people are allowed to have families and that allows "religious liberty" to mean only Christian conservatism.[36]

As a result, major political differences in the United States are both highly consequential *and* do not challenge the country's fundamental structure of exploitation and domination. These two realities are both meaningful even as they are disjunctive (they cannot simply be reconciled), and they lead to different understandings of political action.[37] In one part of the disjunctive reality, the fight against the Right is hugely consequential, and in the other, the fight against the Right is a massive struggle to hold power for already dominant political forces and ensure that not much changes.

Given these bifurcated realities, any singular focus can be misleading for both analysis and action. For example, a focus only on fighting the Right and its white Christian nationalism ignores what makes the Right so powerful—its being stitched into the centerpiece of the hegemonic US social fabric. A focus only on changing mainstream investments in white Christian nationalism, however, risks failing to produce any bulwark against rising and renewed authoritarianism. Political fights move back and forth between one form of white Christian nationalism and another. And this oscillation also sets up an oscillation in response, between those who think that electoral politics matter greatly (they do) and those who think that electoral politics will never get at the root problems and make fundamental change (they won't). And so the oscillation goes.[38]

The political disjunction between different forms of white Christian nationalism that allows oscillation between the two supports hegemony through its incoherence.[39] These two political formations are held apart—they are even talked about as opposites—and they are tied together by a variety of threads that are both loose enough to allow for this motion and at other points knotted so tightly as to make them hard to break. As the fabric is flipped back and forth to show one side and then the other of mainstream politics, the colors may appear distinct—red on one side, blue on the other. It may even appear as though these two sides are separate layers of fabric that could be torn apart. And yet the space between the layers, making it seem as if they could exist free from one another, can hide the knots deep within the fabric that hold the two sides together and that may grow tighter with each oscillating twist. Holes may develop, the fabric may unravel at points, become tattered even, and at the same time the difference between the two sides allows for a movement that twists the fabric together again, snarling the threads.

The dynamics between the disjunctive parts of the hegemonic social fabric can be thought of as one part of the kinetic struggle that twentieth-century social theorist Antonio Gramsci called a "war of position" (in contrast to a direct revolution). Shifts in social power are created by moves to tear apart the fabric so as to make room for social change, to create openings, to unravel threads and pull them out from the blanketing effect of hegemony. These efforts are critical, but over decades of struggle one also learns that they are also most efficacious when they recognize the ways in which individual threads can be pulled back into hegemonic knots at different points.[40]

One way to counteract the reweaving of social relations into the current patterns of hegemony is to connect the threads to each other in a different way—to thread together a new pattern, pull the fabric into a different shape, or weave a new social fabric altogether. For Gramsci, hegemony itself is not the source of domination and exploitation. Hegemony is the necessary common sense of any social relations—sociality requires some ability to make sense to one another. But the capitalist hegemony for Gramsci in Italy in the 1920s, or the capitalist and white Christian nationalist hegemony of the United States in the 2020s, means that the current common sense repeatedly reinforces domination and exploitation. In the hegemonic version of the social fabric, the eminent potentiality of simultaneous difference is denied and effectively smothered—hidden, elided, and obfuscated; refused material expression and elaboration.

Seams

If trans, queer, and feminist studies hope to address the issues underlying the contemporary back-and-forth between mainstream and authoritarian nationalism, can we also avoid the concomitant oscillation between electoral and radical politics, or reform and revolution? And, to return to my original question, can queer and trans social analysis avoid an oscillation between intersectionality and incommensurability, between disjunction and resonance? Can we attend to substantive differences while also recognizing interconnection?

In the Gramscian tradition, a new social fabric has been imagined as being held together by a sense of equivalence among the threads. As Ernesto Laclau and Chantal Mouffe argue in building on this tradition in the now classic *Hegemony and Socialist Strategy*, equivalence across struggles for the "rights of man" that were developed in the French Revolution are expanded as women claim rights equivalent to those of men and colonized people claim rights equivalent to those of citizens of the metropole.[41] In this way, equivalence pulls together a set of threads that stretch toward a new horizon of meaning, shifting the social fabric away from its dominative covering of social possibility and toward a radically democratic future. This approach, in which different struggles are made equivalent in order to expand the horizon of meaning to a new common sense, still requires the concordance of difference—in which differences must be made equivalent, concorded—so as to produce a coherent social world. In attempting to create a new social fabric, movements organized by equivalence suppress incommensurable difference under that very fabric so as to create a whole cloth that may be pulled in more radically democratic directions but nonetheless covers all those whose lives might not be equivalent to the normative "man" whose rights are democratically enshrined. These differences in people's material realities are covered with the social fabric of an even newer hegemony and lined up together as different threads, running in the same new direction (that of linear progress) and in the same new pattern (even if the linear pattern forms a rainbow).

Alternatively, I hope to imagine a queer and trans studies in religion that embraces both incommensurability among social differences and practices that thread connections between and across these differences. Queer and trans studies are often recognized as refusing the coherence of a concordant social world and instead challenging the boundaries that are supposed to contain any category of social analysis or social life. Trans and queer studies are concerned with the ways in which social differences are too-often rejected, obscured, or excluded because they cannot be wrangled into place for the sake of coherence. While debates remain lively on this point, for those who take *queer* and *trans* as verbs in which "transing" or "queering" lead to an opening of possibility rather than a foreclosing of identity, a path to social justice that is not taken to be synonymous with social equivalence remains traversable.[42]

A related valuing of difference can be found in religious studies, especially in the critique of secularism.[43] For example, in her book *Queer Faith: Reading Promiscuity and Race in the Secular Love Tradition,* Melissa Sanchez points out how the secular love tradition is often contrasted with Christian sexual morality, but even in the secular tradition "to be monogamous—whether in classical friendship, premodern brotherhood, or modern coupledom—is to aspire to the privilege that comes with a distinctly racialized sexual respectability."[44] The coherence of monogamous coupledom can become part of the dynamic that knots together Christian secularist morality, racism, and normative demands on sex and gender. Sanchez encourages a kind of queer practice, in her case a practice of reading, that refuses any clear divide between religious and secular traditions and that also refuses a singular idea of gender and sex. Reading these traditions queerly is a way of coming to understand that the hegemonic social fabric, whether in the canonical form of the literary secular love tradition or in the legislative canon of US law on gender and sexuality, is not so seamless after all. And thus, practices of solidarity in response also do not need to be seamless.

Allowing the seams to show takes account of incommensurability in both analysis and action while visibly challenging the seamless garment of conservatism. Rather than flipping back and forth between one or another side of the hegemonic social fabric, trans and queer theory in religion might sew together pieces of fabric that are not seamless but would nonetheless hold together across difference, perhaps building out from intersectional knots to broader patterns that may connect while also remaining disjunctive. This approach might produce textures and textiles that have rips and holes and whose colors might clash. This messier, perhaps more brightly colored fabric with the frayed edges might be more fun to wear and certainly would not require the concordance of difference in order to fit in at the disco.

Glitter Bombs as Method

And if differences exceed efforts at concordance, perhaps the idea hegemony that makes the image of a social fabric such a powerful metaphor also needs to change. Even when brought together on behalf of social justice, differences may not form a fabric at all. Different threads might, for example, come together in terms of something more like the game of cat's cradle, in which the action of the game, rather than the product of the weaving, is the substance of relation. The connecting points where string is tied together, where the strings cross each other, the gaps in between the threads, and the movement among different patterns are all evident.

Or perhaps it would be helpful to move metaphorically from the idea of connecting threads to that of glitter bombing the world. Can we find ways to make the social world shimmer, sometimes appearing one way and sometimes another as a result of various lights hitting trails of glitter? Could these different trails, each with their own combinations of light and magic, help to illustrate how it might be possible to recognize simultaneous incommensurability and interconnection?

As one possibility, consider the arguments from within trans studies, queer studies, and religious studies about the multiplicity of time. Many religious traditions offer fundamentally differing understandings of time—of what time (or year) it is now, of how time is to be counted (in a Gregorian solar or in a lunar calendar, for example), and even of how time moves (linearly or circularly). The change in language from *AD*, "anno Domini nostri Jesu Christi," to *CE*, the English phrase "Common Era," does not manage to dissolve the time frames of multiple religions or to make them "common," but is rather an expression of the hegemonic power of bringing all time into a single Christian secular timeline that runs financial markets and the political calendar of the international system of nation-states.

Queer studies offers a different but potentially interrelated critique of Christian secular time, specifically of the linear timelines that aim to match the course of individual lives to that of capitalist social relations in the "Common Era." Thinkers such as Elizabeth Freeman, Jack Halberstam, and José Esteban Muñoz read queer time as resistant to the straight line of linear progress. Elizabeth Freeman, for example, has argued that queer relations challenge the capitalist logic of development, insisting "that various queer social practices, especially those involving enjoyable bodily sensations, produce form(s) of time consciousness, even historical consciousness, that can intervene upon the material damage done in the name of development."[45] Decades of socialist thinking have argued for the revolutionary possibility of reclaiming leisure time as subversive of capitalism.[46] Muñoz brilliantly elaborates a version of queer communism in *Cruising Utopia: The Then and There of Queer Futurity*, that suggests queer utopian possibility is not to be found in future progress toward horizontal equivalence but in the immanent potential of a historical past created in places like the streets of New York and underground performance spaces where one might cruise for sex and possibility.[47]

Although both queer studies and religious studies provide sources for critique of Christian secular time, and in this sense their paths may cross, they certainly don't then become similar approaches that provide equivalent elements in a lineup of critique. Nor is the relation between religious studies and queer studies somehow structurally determined. As Nikki Young argues about the intersection of queerness and religion, this relation can either contribute to hegemonic relations or activate "the queer capacity of standing outside of and counter to the society for which it was dictating hegemonies."[48] Rather than a concordant lineup, the different trails of light left by each critique might be thought of as contributing to the tumult of critique—a glitter bomb, if you will.

TSQ published a special issue on "trans-historicity" that locates a distinct site of critique while also depicting how conceptualizations of time cannot be brought into a single linear relation—whether that of past, present, and future or that of equivalent "differences." The intersection of trans possibility and historical difference turns out to be a site of multiplicity rather than simple meeting. As editors Leah DeVun and Zeb Tortorici summarize, "We intend our brief engagement with historicity's past iterations . . . to demonstrate how the term might hold in productive dialogue multiple visions of epistemology and temporality, as well as competing theoretical, methodological, and historiographical modes."[49]

Illuminations and refractions are further multiplied across social relations. For example, in describing an interview with Maya Mikdashi and Carlos Motta, makers of the film *Deseos* / رغبات, DeVun and Tortorici write,

> On the one hand, *Deseos* / رغبات speaks to the legibility of historical subjects who are marked in some way as "hermaphrodites," "sodomites," or "lesbians." At least provisionally, it accepts those categories and, in doing so, it offers answers that cannot be supplied by other means, and it spurs new forms of kinship with the past. On the other hand, the film's imaginative and temporal crossings rest on a refusal to assume that we can ever fully know historical subjects. And such a refusal ultimately "rests on differences—differences that confound, disrupt, and render ambiguous the meaning of any fixed binary opposition," be it between male and female, past and present, fantasy and historical record. . . . [I]nfusing historical narration with the radical potential of the imagination enables new possibilities for the conditions of queer and trans experiences across time and place.[50]

The point, then, is not that all of these versions of time are the same—all equivalently queer or counter-hegemonic. The point is rather that they all exist, in this world, in the here and now, as well as the then and there. Such is also the case for the intersections of transness and religion or queerness and transness. Do they simply come together at a single point? And do we—as social analysts and scholars—focus only on that point, or can we also follow their incommensurable lines as they run off in multiple directions, even to infinity? If we think of these different trails of time as both intersecting and incommensurable, then time is neither seamless, nor completely disjointed.

So the question is not just one of multiplicity, but rather of how multiplicity is understood. Which moments and sites are related and how? Which remain incommensurable?

This conceptual shift implies a change in political action. Many very radical movements dedicated to revolutionary change have reiterated the need for a coherent subject of revolution. Once we break up that subject into not just a plural lineup of equivalences but an unstable display of light, what is the basis for alliances and solidarity within and across these fields? If it is not only the points at which they come together, are there alternate bases for alliances? If we move away from identity, equivalences, or identical interests in resistance to the seamless garment of oppression, where do we turn? Perhaps to desire, care, justice, and relation?

Practices and Possibilities

So, how might we understand these different times as something other than concordant differences in an expanding liberal horizon? As Zillah Eisenstein long ago pointed out, starting, rather than ending, with the liberal horizon and then turning in another direction could produce movement toward a "radical future."[51] A surprisingly good example of the liberal pluralist versions of different calendars can be found in the New York City street-cleaning regimen, even as that regimen is bemoaned in the press.[52] To clean the streets, NYC requires that all cars parked on one side or the other be moved twice a week during certain hours for the street cleaners to pass. Those who need to keep a car for whatever reason attentively watch the parking calendar for the days when street cleaning is suspended. These days include the national secular holidays and major religious holidays—but in this case, "religion" does not just mean "Christian" or even "Judeo-Christian"; it also includes Eid Al-Fitr and Eid Al-Adha, and Diwali. So, although this calendar extends beyond most mainstream understandings of "religion in America," it still follows the pluralist sense of holidays "like" those of normative religion.

One can imagine that if the concept of religion were further expanded, it would put the whole system in crisis. The city would be faced with a situation not of how to "include" many differences in the normative understanding of holidays but of how to get the work done at all. And, for radical critics of racial capitalism, this might be a social good. Not that the streets of New York shouldn't be clean, but keeping them clean and also recognizing religious calendars would imply rethinking the whole system, a project that could go in any number of directions: Fewer cars and clean streets, perhaps with more public transport and more outdoor dining? A reorganization of the idea of work itself? Should we clean in the morning and criticize after dinner (a Marxian approach that doesn't push social reproduction to the side)? Should we give up on work and reclaim our leisure time? These are all questions trans and queer studies in religion could ask.

To return to the disjunctive reality of oscillating political sides in contemporary politics—the question becomes how to hold both sides of supposed oppositions simultaneously. Is it possible to take up points that are often placed on opposite sides of various lines, like the distinction between reform and revolution, and mix them together without making them either equivalent or seamless?

One approach to this project would be to adopt "differential consciousness" as described by Chela Sandoval in *Methodology of the Oppressed* and elaborated by Dean Spade in "Methodologies of TransResistance."[53] Sandoval's idea of "differential consciousness" does not claim one side of a binary opposition over the other, a refusal that addresses the oscillations created when such binaries are embedded in complex, hegemonic social formations. Instead of trying to re-create logical coherence, Sandoval urges moving "'between and among' oppositional categories."[54] Sandoval identifies different modes of activism for social justice, and she suggests that it is possible to move among these different modes of action. Instead of being *either* revolutionary *or* reformist, social movement may be both at the same time.[55]

Dean Spade has adopted Sandoval's concept of "differential consciousness" as a method for thinking about action in the context of trans resistance, pointing out that differential consciousness provides a means of addressing the paradoxical world created by the administrative state. Spade takes as his measure of any approach the effects on those most directly affected by a particular action.[56] This approach is akin to the liberation theology version of the Catholic "preferential option for the poor" and also intersects with the disability justice conceptualization of universal access, which addresses the specific needs of different, and sometimes radically disadvantaged, disabled people. This starting point means that justice will be built not by moving toward an ever-receding horizon but by starting from the material infrastructure that enables impossible lives and building from there.[57]

So, how does one glitter bomb the current set of legislative initiatives directed against trans and queer people's basic rights, against critical race theory or any public acknowledgment of racism (particularly in schools), and against reproductive justice? One way is to emphasize the religious difference described above *as the basis of* religious freedom. So often in the United States, religious freedom has meant only the freedom to act like Christians (and conservative Christians at that).[58] Thus, when people challenge antiabortion legislation on the basis of religious freedom, as, for example, some Jewish congregations, organizations, and individuals have done, they not only challenge specific laws and the constitutional basis of the *Dobbs* decision, but they also expand the possibilities for religious freedom as a whole.[59] Similarly, Pellegrini and I argued in *Love the Sin* that sexual freedom and religious freedom are actually entwined. If the basis for legislation and court decisions supporting sexual regulation is specific religious commitment (as politicians have frequently claimed), then the constitutional basis for sexual freedom is religious freedom.[60]

One could make similar claims when thinking about the discourse around "parents' rights" in education, which have been invoked to ban the teaching of the history of racism in the United States or any support for trans children. As with sexual regulation, the history of parents' rights movements in the United States is deeply entwined with white Christian nationalism. For example, in response to the desegregation of public schools, a network of "segregation academies," was built across the Southern states.[61] These schools were often established as "Christian schools," including Jerry Falwell's Lynchburg Christian Academy, to allow white parents to avoid newly desegregated public schools.[62] The effects of this movement reverberate in Christian commitments to private "school choice," as espoused by Trump administration Secretary of Education Betsy DeVos.[63] Oftentimes, the progressive response to this history is a defense against Christian claims based on the assertion of a secular public sphere, thereby reinforcing a binary opposition between religion and secularism. Claiming religion on the side of trans rights, racial justice, sexual freedom, and reproductive justice undoes the social fabric of this opposition and scatters the pieces on the floor where their sequins can shine not just on the side of secular life but also amid religiosity and its liturgical colors.

One final question, then: Can queer and trans studies in religion contribute not just to a different social fabric but also to different (less coherent, perhaps more shimmering) kinds of revolutionary possibility?

Janet R. Jakobsen is the Claire Tow Professor of Women's, Gender, and Sexuality Studies at Barnard College, Columbia University. She is most recently author of *The Sex Obsession: Perversity and Possibility in American Politics* (2020).

Notes

1. Strassfeld, "Transing Religious Studies."

2. For a rundown on antitrans legislation, see Track Trans Legislation, "2023 Anti-Trans Legislation."; on anti-LGBTQ rights bills see: ACLU, "Mapping Attacks"; on new restrictions on voting, see Brennan Center for Justice, "Voting Laws Roundup"; on abortion policy specifically, see: Guttmacher Institute, "State Laws and Policies"; on a reproductive justice response, see: SisterSong, "Visioning New Futures for Reproductive Justice."

3. Case, "Seeing the Sex and Justice Landscape."

4. Strassfeld, *Trans Talmud*, 81–88.

5. Jakobsen, *Sex Obsession*, 18.

6. For some of the major texts developing the concept of intersectionality, see Crenshaw, "Demarginalizing the Intersection of Race and Sex"; Collins, *Intersectionality as Critical Social Theory*.

7. Jakobsen, *Sex Obsession*, 18.

8. Amin, "Genealogies of Queer Theory," 26.

9. Tuck and Yang, "Decolonization Is Not a Metaphor."

10. Any way of writing this list shows the limits of contemporary analyses in that it includes elements that are both incommensurable (and thus not accurately placed in a linear list) and overlapping (yet another reason that the list is inaccurate). Moreover, the list is never complete in its naming of social relations, not even in naming relations of domination and exploitation.

11. *Unicorn Tapestries*.

12. Pew Research Center, "Same-Sex Marriage."

13. Ghorayshi, "Texas Governor Pushes."

14. Rojas and Mzezewa, "Alabama Approves Ban."

15. As of this writing, in 2023 forty-five states in the US have proposed antitrans legislation and eighteen have signed such legislation into law (Track Trans Legislation, "2023 Anti-Trans Legislation.")

16. Anthony Hatch recently made this point about face-mask politics ("Data Will Not Save Us").

17. The judge's record in sentencing is in line with those of other sentencing judges whose appointments to higher posts in the judiciary Hawley supported (Silverman, "QAnon's Takeover").

18. Blow, "The G.O.P. is Making 'Critical Race Theory' the New 'Sharia Law.'"

19. On the travel ban, see Volp, "Role of 'Honor Killings' in the Travel Ban."; and on *Dunn v. Ray*, see *New York Times* Editorial Board, "Is Religious Freedom for Christians Only?"

20. In *Dunn v. Ray*, the court rejected a request by Domineque Ray to have his Muslim spiritual advisor present at his execution by the state of Alabama. A Christian chaplain employed by the prison could be present at the execution but not an imam because the prison staff does not have a Muslim chaplain. The court did agree that the chaplain could be excluded in this case, but the imam could not be present in the execution chamber (Liptak, "Justices Allow Execution of Muslim"). The court shifted its position in response to a similar request from a Christian in the state of Texas, approving a request by John Ramirez to have his Christian pastor present and allowed to pray audibly and lay hands on him. Some have interpreted the shift in *Ramirez v. Collier* as a recognition by the court that it had gone "too far" in denying religious liberty to Mr. Ray. See Millhiser, "Supreme Court's Latest Opinion." But one can also read the difference between the two cases as yet another instance in the long history of the US Supreme Court granting religious liberty to Christian claimants and denying liberty to all others.

21. I have been influenced by Sandra Soto's incitement for social and cultural analysis to move away from the search for the perfect concept metaphor and to engage more concepts and more metaphors. Soto declares that "race, sexuality and gender are much too complex, unsettled and porous . . . mutually constitutive, unpredictable, incommensurable, and dynamic, certainly too spatially and temporally contingent, *ever* (even if I only use that word for an instant) to travel independently of one another." She concludes, "What I want to suggest is that we be *wordy*" (Soto, *Reading Chican@ Like a Queer*, 6).

22. Berlant and Duggan, *Our Monica, Ourselves*, 5.

23. North, "Newt Gingrich's Strange Fascination with Sex."

24. See Hanna Rosin's review of Dagmar Herzog's book on conservative Christian sexual culture, in which Rosin concludes that Herzog misses the point because the "problem is not" Christian conservatism but the licentiousness of teen sexual culture ("In Bed with the Christian Right"). Jasbir Puar also traces an oscillation between

"disciplinary and control societies," that braids the two into Foucauldian "apparatuses of security" (*Right to Maim*, 21).

25. Gorski and Perry, *The Flag and the Cross*.

26. Grosfoguel, "World-Systems Analysis."

27. For an important reading on the basis for reproductive rights in the fourteenth amendment, see Goodwin, "No, Justice Alito."

28. Butler, *Awash in a Sea of Faith*, 2.

29. Butler, *Awash in a Sea of Faith*, 2.

30. Jakobsen and Pellegrini, *Secularisms*, 12.

31. On the "big lie," see Snyder, *Road to Unfreedom*.

32. As just one example, in 2022 Dean Baquet, speaking on stepping down as editor of the *New York Times*, claimed that incredibly extensive coverage of Hillary Clinton's emails was justified (Malone, "Dean Baquet").

33. For a sense of how the idea of both-sides "impartiality" reinforces existing hegemonic power, one need look no further than the recent Superior Court ruling that the *Washington Post* was justified in refusing to allow reporter Felicia Somnez to work on #MeToo-related stories because she was public about her own experiences as a survivor of sexual violence, denying the relevance of this experience to potential reporting in order to, in the judge's words, "adopt and enforce policies intended to protect public trust in its impartiality and objectivity" (Robertson, "D.C. Judge Dismisses a Discrimination Case").

34. Ollstein and Messerly, "Abortion on the Ballot?"

35. Melamed, *Represent and Destroy*, 25.

36. See two reports from the Columbia Law School's Law, Rights, and Religion project for different takes on the choice of supporting reproductive justice as one between religious freedom and reproductive freedom, as opposed to a choice in which protecting religious freedom could challenge Christian hegemonic understandings and see reproductive justice as protected by, rather than opposed to, religious freedom (Law, Rights, and Religion Project, "We the People (of Faith)"; Law, Rights, and Religion Project, "Religious Right to Abortion").

37. I analyze this type of social disjunction in *Sex Obsession*, developing an understanding of "the social body multiple" that draws on Anne Marie Mol's depiction of "the body multiple" in her ethnography of medical practice (Mol, *Body Multiple*, 105–8).

38. For a discussion of the oscillation between reform and revolution, see Ferguson, *Aberrations in Black*.

39. On the "productive incoherence" of disjunctive political projects, see Jakobsen, *Sex Obsession*, chap. 2; and Grabel, "Post-crisis Experiments."

40. Gramsci, *Prison Notebooks*, 495.

41. Laclau and Mouffe, *Hegemony and Socialist Strategy*, 154.

42. For three different approaches to the verb forms of "transing" and/or "queering," see Snorton, *Black on Both Sides*, 207; Stryker, Currah, and Moore, "Trans-, Trans, or Transgender?"; Jakobsen, "Queer Is? Queer Does?"

43. Pellegrini and I argue that modern secularism does not provide a single framework for all views, traditions, and practices, but is rather one perspective among many (Jakobsen and Pellegrini, *Secularisms*).

44. Sanchez, *Queer Faith*, 70.

45. Freeman, "Time Binds," 59.

46. Herbert Marcuse writes, "In proclaiming the 'permanent challenge' [*la contestation permanente*] . . . the Great Refusal, they recognized the mark of social repression, even in the most sublime manifestations of traditional culture, even in the most spectacular manifestations of technical progress." Marcuse, *Essay on Liberation*.

47. Muñoz, *Cruising Utopia*.

48. Young, "Queer Studies and Religion."

49. DeVun and Tortorici, "Trans, Time, and History," 534.

50. "And such a refusal ultimately 'rests on differences—differences that confound, disrupt, and render ambiguous the meaning of any fixed binary opposition,' be it between male and female, past and present, fantasy and historical record" (DeVun and Tortorici, "Trans, Time, and History," 521, quoting Scott, *Gender and the Politics of History*).

51. Eisenstein, *Radical Future of Liberal Feminism*.

52. Chang, "Talking Alternate-Side Parking."

53. See also Sandoval, "U.S. Third World Feminism," 1.

54. Sandoval, "U.S. Third World Feminism," 15.

55. Sandoval, *Methodology of the Oppressed*.

56. Spade, "Methodologies of TransResistance," 256.

57. On impossible lives, see Spade, "Impossibility Now"; and Tourmaline, "Making a Way out of No Way."

58. The history of how the courts have differentially favored Christian claims and rarely granted non-Christian claims to religious freedom is well documented, including in Feldman, *Please Don't Wish Me A Merry Christmas*; Sullivan, *Impossibility of Religious Freedom*; Wenger, *Religious Freedom*.

59. Shimron, "Jewish Women Sue."

60. Jakobsen and Pellegrini, *Love the Sin*, conclusion.

61. Rooks, *Cutting School*, 102–4.

62. Harding, *Book of Jerry Falwell*, 27.

63. Merritt, "Segregation is Still Alive."

References

American Civil Liberties Union (ACLU). "Mapping Attacks on LGBTQ Rights in U.S. State Legislatures." https://www.aclu.org/legislative-attacks-on-lgbtq-rights (accessed December 18, 2023).

Amin, Kadji. "Genealogies of Queer Theory." In *The Cambridge Companion to Queer Studies*, edited by Siobhan Sommerville, 17–29. New York: Cambridge University Press, 2020.

Berlant, Lauren, and Lisa Duggan, eds. *Our Monica, Ourselves: The Clinton Affair and the National Interest*. New York: New York University Press, 2001.

Blow, Charles M. "The G.O.P. is Making 'Critical Race Theory' the New 'Sharia Law.'" *New York Times*, January 5, 2022. https://www.nytimes.com/2022/01/05/opinion/critical-race-theory-gop.html.

Brennan Center for Justice. "Voting Laws Roundup." December 2022, https://www.brennancenter.org/our-work/research-reports/voting-laws-roundup-december-2022.

Butler, Jon. *Awash in a Sea of Faith: Christianizing the American People*. Cambridge, MA: Harvard University Press, 1992.

Case, Mary Anne. "Seeing the Sex and Justice Landscape through the Vatican's Eyes: The War on Gender and the Seamless Garment of Sexual Rights." In *The War on Sex*, edited by David Halperin and Trevor Hoppe, 211–25. Durham, NC: Duke University Press, 2017.

Chang, Clio. "Talking Alternate-Side Parking with the Queen of Securing a Spot." Interview with Mary Norris. *New York Magazine: Curbed*, April 20, 2022. https://www.curbed.com/2022/04/mary-norris-alternate-side-parking.html.

Collins, Patricia Hill. *Intersectionality as Critical Social Theory*. Durham, NC: Duke University Press, 2019.

Crenshaw, Kimberlé. "Demarginalizing the Intersection of Race and Sex: A Black Feminist Critique of Antidiscrimination Doctrine, Feminist Theory, and Antiracist Politics." *University of Chicago Legal Forum* 1989, no. 1 (1989): 139–68.

DeVun, Leah, and Zeb Tortorici. "Trans, Time, and History." *TSQ* 5, no. 4 (2018): 518–38.

Eisenstein, Zillah. *The Radical Future of Liberal Feminism*. London: Longman, 1981.

Feldman, Stephen M. *Please Don't Wish Me a Merry Christmas: A Critical History of the Separation of Church and State*. New York: New York University Press, 1998.

Ferguson, Roderick. *Aberrations in Black: Toward a Queer of Color Critique*. Minneapolis: University of Minnesota Press, 2003.

Freeman, Elizabeth. "Time Binds, or, Erotohistoriography." In "What's Queer about Queer Studies Now?," edited by David Eng, Jack Halberstam, and José Esteban Muñoz. Special issue, *Social Text*, nos. 84–85 (2005): 57–68.

Ghorayshi, Azeen. "Texas Governor Pushes to Investigate Treatments for Trans Youth as 'Child Abuse.'" *New York Times*, February 23, 2022. https://www.nytimes.com /2022/02/23/science/texas-abbott-transgender-child-abuse.html.

Goodwin, Michelle. "No, Justice Alito, Reproductive Justice is in the Constitution." *New York Times*, June 26, 2022. https://www.nytimes.com/2022/06/26/opinion/justice -alito-reproductive-justice-constitution-abortion.html.

Gorski, Philip, and Samuel Perry. *The Flag and the Cross: White Christian Nationalism and the Threat to American Democracy*. New York: Oxford University Press, 2021.

Grabel, Ilene. "Post-crisis Experiments in Development Finance Architectures: A Hirschmanian Perspective on 'Productive Incoherence.'" *Review of Social Economy* 73, no. 4 (2015): 388–414.

Gramsci, Antonio. *Selections from the Prison Notebooks*. Edited and translated by Quentin Hoare and Geoffrey Nowell Smith. London: Lawrence and Wishart, 1971.

Grosfoguel. Ramón. "World-Systems Analysis in the Context of Transmodernity, Border Thinking, and Global Coloniality." *Review* (Fernand Braudel Center) 29, no. 2 (2006): 167–87.

Guttmacher Institute. "State Laws and Policies." https://www.guttmacher.org/united -states/abortion/state-policies-abortion.

Halberstam, Jack. *In a Queer Time and Place: Transgender Bodies, Subcultural Lives*. New York: New York University Press, 2005.

Harding, Susan Friend. *The Book of Jerry Falwell: Fundamentalist Language and Politics*. Princeton, NJ: Princeton University Press, 2000.

Hatch, Anthony Ryan. "The Data Will Not Save Us: Afropessimism and Racial Antimatter in the COVID-19 Pandemic." Online lecture, Smith College, March 3, 2022. https:// drive.google.com/file/d/1zioNueYtp7qqviIR6wKGe8HynoOo9Kwp/view.

Jakobsen, Janet R. "Queer Is? Queer Does? Normativity and Resistance." *GLQ* 4, no. 4 (1998): 511–36.

Jakobsen, Janet R. *The Sex Obsession: Perversity and Possibility in American Politics*. New York: New York University Press, 2020.

Jakobsen, Janet R., and Ann Pellegrini. *Love the Sin: Sexual Regulation and the Limits of Religious Tolerance*. New York: New York University Press, 2003.

Jakobsen, Janet R., and Ann Pellegrini. *Secularisms*. Durham, NC: Duke University Press, 2008.

Laclau, Ernesto, and Chantal Mouffe. *Hegemony and Socialist Strategy*. Translated by Winston Moore and Paul Cammack. London: Verso, 1985.

Law, Rights, and Religion Project. "A Religious Right to Abortion: Legal History and Analysis." Columbia Law School, August 2022. https://lawrightsreligion.law .columbia.edu/sites/default/files/content/LRRP%20Religious%20Liberty%20 %26%20Abortion%20Rights%20memo.pdf.

Law, Rights, and Religion Project. "We the People (of Faith): The Supremacy of Religious Rights in the Shadow of a Pandemic." Columbia Law School, June 2021. https://lawrightsreligion.law.columbia.edu/sites/default/files/content/Reports/We%20The%20People%20%28of%20Faith%29%20Report.pdf.

Liptak, Adam. "Justices Allow Execution of Muslim Death Row Inmate Who Sought Imam." *New York Times*, February 7, 2019. https://www.nytimes.com/2019/02/07/us/politics/supreme-court-domineque-ray.html.

Malone, Clare. "Dean Baquet Never Wanted to Be an Editor." *New Yorker*, February 18, 2022. https://www.newyorker.com/news/the-new-yorker-interview/dean-baquet-never-wanted-to-be-an-editor.

Marcuse, Herbert. *Essay on Liberation*. 1969. https://www.marxists.org/reference/archive/marcuse/works/1969/essay-liberation.htm.

Melamed, Jodi. *Represent and Destroy: Rationalizing Violence in the New Racial Capitalism*. Minneapolis: University of Minnesota Press, 2011.

Merritt, Jonathan. "Segregation Is Still Alive at These Christian Schools." *Daily Beast*, July 12, 2017. https://www.jonathanmerritt.com/article/segregation-still-alive-christian-schools.

Millhiser, Ian. "The Supreme Court's Latest Opinion Should Reassure Religious Liberals." *Vox*, March 24, 2022. https://www.vox.com/2022/3/24/22994540/supreme-court-religion-death-penalty-ramirez-collier-john-roberts-prison.

Mol, Anne Marie. *The Body Multiple: Ontology in Medical Practice*. Durham, NC: Duke University Press, 2003.

Muñoz, José Esteban. *Cruising Utopia: The Then and There of Queer Futurity*. New York: New York University Press, 2009.

New York Times Editorial Board. "Is Religious Freedom for Christians Only?" *New York Times*, February 9, 2019. https://www.nytimes.com/2019/02/09/opinion/supreme-court-alabama-execution.html.

North, Anna. "Newt Gingrich's Strange Fascination with Sex." *New York Times*, October 26, 2016. https://www.nytimes.com/2016/10/26/opinion/newt-gingrichs-strange-fascination-with-sex.html.

Ollstein, Alice Miranda, and Megan Messerly. "Abortion on the Ballot? Not if These Republican Politicians Can Help It." *Politico*, March 19, 2023. https://www.politico.com/news/2023/03/19/abortion-on-the-ballot-not-if-these-republican-lawmakers-can-help-it-00087688.

Pew Research Center. "Same-Sex Marriage: State-by-State." June 26, 2015. https://www.pewresearch.org/religion/2015/06/26/same-sex-marriage-state-by-state-1/.

Puar, Jasbir. *The Right to Maim: Debility, Capacity, Disability*. Durham, NC: Duke University Press, 2017.

Robertson, Kate. "D.C. Judge Dismisses a Discrimination Case Against the Washington Post." *New York Times*, March 25, 2022. https://www.nytimes.com/2022/03/25/business/media/discrimination-case-washington-post.html.

Rojas, Rick, and Tariro Mzezewa. "Alabama Approves Ban on Medical Care for Transgender Youth." *New York Times*, April 7, 2022. https://www.nytimes.com/2022/04/07/us/alabama-transgender-youth-bill.html.

Rooks, Noliwe. *Cutting School: The Segrenomics of American Education*. New York: New Press, 2017.

Rosin, Hanna. "In Bed with the Christian Right." *New York Times*, August 31, 2008.

Sanchez, Melissa. *Queer Faith: Reading Promiscuity and Race in the Secular Love Tradition*. New York: NYU Press, 2019.

Sandoval, Chela. *Methodology of the Oppressed*. Minneapolis: University of Minnesota Press, 2000.

Sandoval, Chela. "U.S. Third World Feminism: The Theory and Method of Oppositional Consciousness in the Postmodern World." *Genders*, no. 10 (1991): 1–24.

Scott, Joan Wallach. *Gender and the Politics of History*. New York: Columbia University Press, 1999.

Shimron, Yonat. "Jewish Women Sue over Kentucky Abortion Laws, Citing Religious Freedom." *Washington Post*, October 10, 2022. https://www.washingtonpost.com /religion/2022/10/10/kentucky-abortion-law-2022-jewish-lawsuit/.

Silverman, Jacob. "QAnon's Takeover of the Republican Party is Virtually Complete." *New York Magazine*, March 26, 2022. https://nymag.com/intelligencer/2022/03 /qanons-takeover-of-the-gop-is-virtually-complete.html.

SisterSong. "Visioning New Futures for Reproductive Justice. 2023." https://www .sistersong.net/visioningnewfuturesforrj.

Snorton, C. Riley. *Black on Both Sides: A Racial History of Trans Identity*. Minneapolis: University of Minnesota Press, 2017.

Snyder, Timothy. *The Road to Unfreedom: Russia, Europe, America*. New York: Penguin Random House, 2018.

Soto, Sandra K. *Reading Chican@ Like a Queer: The De-mastery of Desire*. Austin: University of Texas Press, 2010.

Spade, Dean. "Impossibility Now." Video and slideshow. *Scholar and Feminist Online* 11, nos. 1–2 (2012–13). https://sfonline.barnard.edu/impossibility-now/.

Spade, Dean. "Methodologies of TransResistance." In *A Companion to Lesbian, Gay, Bisexual, Transgender, and Queer Studies*, edited by George E. Haggerty and Molly McGarry, 237–61. Oxford: Blackwell, 2007.

Strassfeld, Max. "Transing Religious Studies." *Journal of Feminist Studies in Religion* 34, no. 1 (2018): 37–53.

Strassfeld, Max. *Trans Talmud: Androgynes and Eunuchs in Rabbinic Literature*. Oakland: University of California Press, 2022.

Stryker, Susan, Paisley Currah, and Lisa Jean Moore. "Introduction: Trans-, Trans, or Transgender?" *WSQ* 36, nos. 3–4 (2008): 11–22.

Sullivan, Winnifred Fallers. *The Impossibility of Religious Freedom*. Princeton, NJ: Princeton University Press, 2005.

Tourmaline. "Making a Way out of No Way." Keynote address at the conference "Scholar and Feminist 41: Sustainabilities," Barnard College, New York, February 27, 2016. https://www.youtube.com/watch?v=li6Y9nAwmf8.

Track Trans Legislation. "2023 Anti-Trans Legislation." https://www.tracktranslegislation .com/.

Tuck, Eve, and K. Wayne Yang. "Decolonization Is Not a Metaphor." *Decolonization: Indigeneity, Education, and Society* 1, no. 1 (2012): 17–36.

The Unicorn Tapestries. Metropolitan Museum of Art, New York. https://www.metmuseum .org/search-results?q=unicorn+tapestries.

Volp, Leti. "The Role of 'Honor Killings' in the Travel Ban." In *The Cunning of Gender Violence*, edited by Lila Abu-Lughod, Rema Hammami, and Nadera Shalhoub, 122–50. Durham, NC: Duke University Press, 2023.

Wenger, Tisa. *Religious Freedom: The Contested History of an American Ideal*. Chapel Hill: University of North Carolina Press, 2017.

Young, Nikki. "Queer Studies and Religion: Methodologies of Freedom." *Scholar and Feminist Online* 14, no. 2 (2017). https://sfonline.barnard.edu/queer-studies-and -religion-methodologies-of-freedom/.

Archiving Religious Piety and Trans Identity
Notes toward a Nonsecular Transfeminism in Turkey

ŞAHİN AÇIKGÖZ

ABSTRACT This article proposes a nonsecular transfeminist critique to interrogate how labels such as *political*, *strategic*, and *activist* are deployed in ways that reproduce exclusionary transgender archives in Turkey. It analyzes the section on religion and spirituality from the South African Gabrielle Le Roux's activist documentary *Proudly Trans in Turkey* (2012) as well as Rüstem Ertuğ Altınay's article "Reconstructing the Transgendered Self as a Muslim, Nationalist, Upper-Class Woman" (2008), which focuses on the statements and performances of Bülent Ersoy, who has been a very popular trans public figure in Turkey since the eighties and who has, to the surprise of many, publicly embraced Islam in the last three decades. Through this analysis, this article demonstrates how a Western secular framework persistently disciplines and limits trans studies in a Turkish context by foregrounding trans people whose agency can be described in terms of resistance or subversion, thus excluding those pious Muslim trans people whose approaches differ.

KEYWORDS Islam, nonsecular transfeminism, Turkey, agency

On a scorching summer day in the Mediterranean city of Mersin, Turkey, in the early nineties, I remember going to the biggest mosque of the city with my grandmother for a special occasion whose details I barely recall. I was young enough to be allowed entry into the women's prayer area where I always felt both "ambivalent" and "at home" even though my official gender classification would definitively mark me as an outsider in the years to come. I felt at home since I was among other women, yet I was ambivalent since I felt that I could never fully belong in that religious space. On that day, however, I thought for the first time that I was not the only ambivalent outsider there. There was a woman praying, ignoring the inquisitive and appalled looks of other women. Soon these women's questioning gazes turned into hostile murmurs replete with interrogations as to how this woman who "clearly" looked like a man could dare to enter into a religious space exclusively allocated to women. In what other women saw as a source of anxiety and boundary violation, I found a source of affirmation for belonging. Nonetheless, I could not help thinking about why she felt the need to come to that space. I was there because my

DOI: 10.1215/29944724-11208929 © 2024 Şahin Açıkgöz

grandmother took me there (I doubted that I would go if I had a choice) but who or what took that woman there? Why did I even feel the need to question her existence in that quintessentially Islamic space? These questions haunted me for many years and eventually led to more interrogations: Can Islam accommodate trans people? Is the figure of a pious Muslim trans person an oxymoron par excellence? Last but not least, what kind of epistemic universe, political positionality, and cultural capital allow for the possibility to pose these questions regarding Islam and pious trans people?[1]

In this article, I take up these questions to interrogate how labels such as *political*, *strategic*, and *activist* are deployed in ways that reproduce exclusionary transgender archives in Turkey.[2] First, I engage the theoretical frameworks of various trans and feminist scholars who have made important contributions to the discussions on agency, embodiment, ethics, and nonsecular feminist politics. While acknowledging the significance of their contributions, I argue that the limitations of their frameworks in terms of addressing the archival politics vis-à-vis the pious trans people in the Global South point out the need to formulate a nonsecular transfeminist analysis. In light of these discussions, I move on to the close reading of Rüstem Ertuğ Altınay's article,[3] which analyzes the statements and performances of Bülent Ersoy, who has been a very popular trans public figure in Turkey since the eighties and who has, to the surprise of many, publicly embraced Islam in the last three decades. My close reading is followed by my analysis of the section on religion and spirituality from the South African Gabrielle Le Roux's activist documentary *Proudly Trans in Turkey* (2012). I show that the kind of transgender religiosity espoused by activist projects and queer scholarship risks foreclosing the possibility of engaging and rendering visible the ethical self-formation of certain pious trans people in Turkey. Hence, my examination demonstrates how a Western secular framework persistently disciplines and limits trans studies in a Turkish context by foregrounding trans people whose agency can be described in terms of resistance or subversion, thus excluding those pious Muslim trans people whose approaches differ.

Given the political and cultural stakes of this article, I should clarify three points. First, by focusing on Altınay's article and Le Roux's documentary, I do not imply that their politics of representation and ideological commitments are exceptionally emblematic of all the significant visual and textual literature published on transness, queerness, secularity, and religion within the context of Turkey. Rather, I argue that both of these works help exemplify, in their own unique ways, a larger epistemic concern regarding how the Eurocentric and secular deployment of concepts such as resistance, activism, and oppositional politics renders invisible the complex and dynamic relationship between transness and religion. Second, the trans people and their narratives analyzed in this article pertain to a specific (and predominantly Sunni) culture and discursive tradition, namely that of Turkey, and therefore are in no way intended to be representative of all trans communities from other Islamic traditions.

What one refers to as Islamic tradition is a vastly heterogeneous signifier that displays dramatically distinct characteristics depending, among others, on geography, ethnicity, culture, language, political economy, and nationality. This heterogeneity is unambiguously reflected in the multivalent ways trans people embody or distance themselves from Islam. Third, I do not intend to make the argument that pious trans people who embrace Islam and religious discourse do so necessarily with the aim of formulating a subversive interpretation within Islamic tradition or recovering the emancipatory dimensions of a nonliberal tradition. Rather, I argue that one should resist the temptation to take concepts such as subversion, emancipation, or complicity as self-evident, highlighting instead their historically and epistemically situated axioms.

A nonsecular transfeminist analysis enables one to avoid, in Max Strassfeld's words, "diminishing the possibilities of how we understand both trans and religion."[4] It also allows one to go beyond what I term "diagnostic reading," which can be described as an implicit replication of the medical discourse through secular[5] cultural critique when the subject matter is trans. As I show in this article, even antitransphobic and queer/feminist works risk perpetuating a diagnostic reading. They enact this reading praxis by either using trans people as exceptional tropes with which to analyze cultural, religious, political, and economic transformations that a nation undergoes, or by interpreting trans people's relationship to various forms of institutions and state apparatuses through a subversive-complicit dyad. I contend that adopting a nonsecular transfeminist methodology and going beyond the limitations of a diagnostic reading require one not to read certain trans people's reservations about or distance from Islam as the vindication of incommensurability between Islam and trans ontology. It also entails one to refrain from reading the pious espousal of Islam and religious discourse by trans people in Turkey as a mere masquerade driven by circumstantial survival strategies.

Secular Transgender Agency and Its Discontents

While the question of agency has been one of the central points of contention among feminist theorists, it has equally shaped the critical terrain of transgender studies since its earliest days. From the antitrans radical feminist Janice G. Raymond who, in her notorious book *The Transsexual Empire*, blamed society "for producing the conditions that create the transsexual body/spirit,"[6] to Sandy Stone, who in her groundbreaking post-transsexual manifesto asked, "How, then, can the transsexual speak?,"[7] the issue of transgender agency has defined almost every scholarship published on transgender politics. Arguably, no other scholars have made such controversial contributions to these debates as Judith Butler and Jay Prosser, who have positioned themselves on the opposite sides of the discussion. As Prosser argues, "Without doubt . . . the single text that yoked transgender most fully to queer sexuality is Judith Butler's *Gender Trouble*. . . . "[8] In *Gender Trouble*, Butler, not very "intentionally," conceptualized drag as the privileged subject of queer theory by virtue of its potential to offer subversive forms of homosexuality that can destabilize the assumed naturalness of heterosexuality.[9] Nonetheless, in the very visibility and privilege accorded to the drag and transgender body in Butler's theorization of gender performativity in their earlier work, some transsexual scholars saw the erasure of the embodied transsexual subject whose materiality, they argued, disappears under the discursive referent of "transgender."[10] In response to queer theory's reclamation of the transgender as the poster child, Prosser asked: "What are the points at which the transsexual as transgendered subject is not queer?"[11] In Prosser's reading, Butler appropriates the transsexual subject only to decontextualize its material corporeality and create out of this decontextualization a transgender subject with a potentially subversive politics. In other words, the figure of the transsexual with its materiality and literality constitutes the limits of queer politics represented through the figure of the discursively constructed and subversive transgender. This precarious position of the transsexual in Butler's theory of performativity not only leads, according to Prosser, to the erasure of the transsexual agency that is now read as potentially reinscriptive and literalizing but also serves to valorize the transgender agency as the potential catalyst of sexual and gender insubordination. However, if Butler's earlier theoretical framework erases the transsexual agency through abstraction and valorizes the subversive modalities of the transgender agency,[12] I argue that Prosser's critique is equally guilty of erasure, one that operates through the concealment of the secular and Western cultural capital that sustains the autonomous agency of the transsexual subject. In his desire to ensure that the referential transsexual subject does not disappear in queer politics, Prosser universalizes the authorial agency of the transsexual subject by locating the transsexual in the secular and sexological archives of the Global North.

When Prosser reclaims autobiography as an empowering genre central to the subjective constitution of transsexual people, he challenges the disempowering use of autobiography as the only genre through which transsexual people were allowed to speak and become intelligible to a nontranssexual audience. Prosser states that "whether s/he publishes an autobiography or not, then, every transsexual, as a transsexual, is originally an autobiographer."[13] He goes on to emphasize the centrality of the autobiographical narrative by arguing that "narrative is also a kind of second skin: the story the transsexual must weave around the body in order that this body may be 'read.'"[14] Prosser's description of the transsexual as an original authorial subject is grounded in the transsexual's discursive and material interaction with the clinician's office since, as he argues, "The autobiographical act for the transsexual begins even before the published autobiography—namely in the clinician's office where, in order to be diagnosed as transsexual, s/he must recount a transsexual autobiography."[15] I argue that it is precisely this spatial and cultural construction of transsexual agency that centers the secular trans subject of the Global North. In Prosser's framework, transsexual agency only becomes legible and intelligible when read through Western sexological archives.[16] In that sense, Prosser's valorization of the referential transsexuality in response to the transgender's theoretical popularity in queer politics conceals the role of the Western sexological and cultural capital in the formation of the secular transsexual subject. To the extent that Prosser's account of transsexual agency challenges the universality of agency-as-resistance, it does not interrogate the liberal conception of the transsexual as an autonomous being, nor does it problematize the construction of the trans subject as inherently Western. Despite his nuanced critique of the erasure of the transsexual through figuration and abstraction, Prosser creates a modern transsexual archive composed of raceless, classless, autonomous, and teleological subjects whose narratives (second skins) are engendered by the Global North's secular cultural capital.

Transgendering the Nonsecular Turn in Feminism

Prosser's erasure of the role of colonial and sexological violence in the constitution of the secular transsexual subject highlights the lack of critical frameworks to engage the epistemological challenges posed by the pious trans subject in the Global South. One very productive analytical framework to start theorizing the embodied pious trans subject, however, comes from Saba Mahmood, who draws on Judith Butler's nonvolitional and discursively constructed model of subjectivity to develop her own critique of neo-Kantian humanist conceptions of agency and subject.[17] Butler's theory of subjectivity, argues Mahmood, allows a broader understanding of norms as conventions that are not only consolidated and/or subverted but also performed, inhabited, and experienced in a variety of ways.[18] In her desire "to expand on Butler's insight that norms are not simply a social imposition on the subject but constitute the very substance of her intimate, valorized interiority,"[19] Mahmood moves away from an agonistic framework, which, she argues, characterizes Butler's framework due to its contextual constraints, and instead invests in "think[ing] about the variety of ways in which norms are lived and inhabited, aspired to, reached for, and consummated."[20] Mahmood's theoretical trajectory opens up two possibilities to reflect on the ethical self-formation of the pious subject. First, by not necessarily locating agency in the political and moral autonomy of the subject,[21] it renders intelligible and legible the ethical practices that the pious subject embodies in their self-cultivation. Second, by disarticulating oppositional consciousness from the politics of agency, it challenges the misreading of piety and docility as lack of politics and false consciousness.

Mahmood's nonsecular conception of agency finds its resonance in Rosi Braidotti's call for a postsecular turn in feminist studies where she stresses the need to challenge European feminism by theorizing subjectivity as "a process ontology of auto-poiesis or self-styling, which involves complex and continuous negotiations with dominant norms and values, and hence also multiple forms of accountability."[22] Braidotti also continues the project of dissociating agency and subjectivity from the production of counter-subjectivities by locating them in religious piety and/or various affirmative manifestations of spirituality.[23] In that sense, both Braidotti and Mahmood view technologies of self and embodied ethical praxes as alternative forms of becoming that force the secular-liberal political capital to reckon with issues of alterity and epistemic difference.[24] However, not all feminists who write on the relationship between feminist politics and religious piety feel as enthusiastic as Mahmood and Braidotti about the political implications of nonsecular agency defined as the affirmative ethics of self-formation. In "The Politics of Postsecular Feminism," Rosa Vasilaki questions "whether this particular conceptualization of [post-secular] agency, in close synergy with religion as a matrix for subject formation, can have genuine subversive, counter-hegemonic, conceptual and political effects."[25] Arguing that the postsecular turn predicated on the teleology of cultural incommensurability engenders "a reasoning which embodies 'the disavowal of history itself,'"[26] Vasilaki states that the postsecular historical moment "does not suggest a substantial turn towards alternative spiritualities but, on the contrary, towards powerful forms of hegemonic religious conservatism" and reactionary forms of subjectivation.[27]

In addition to the problematic bifurcation of religion and spirituality in her analysis, which is itself a largely colonial construct, Vasilaki's critique of the postsecular turn in feminism as disarmed vis-à-vis the historical and political ramifications of the separation between autonomy and agency[28] is also grounded in her Eurocentric epistemic universe that takes concepts such as politics, progressiveness, or reactionariness as self-evident. Nevertheless, I argue that her reductionist critique can be taken to instead think about the limitations of nonsecular feminist frameworks in terms of addressing the archival politics regarding the pious trans people in the Global South. I make this argument for two reasons. First, by prioritizing the category of cissexual/ cisgender woman to theorize the power relationships between secular and pious movements/subjects, non-secular feminism becomes vulnerable to the critiques grounded in historiography that suggests that the historical record of religious subjectivities "tends to weigh more on the side of repression and social control than creativity and openness."[29] This secular feminist critique can only be justified to the extent that it ignores the reversal of this historical record for trans politics within which the Eurocentric cultural capital and the Western medical-industrial complex have overdetermined the transsexual as a secular and modern category to the exclusion of the pious trans subject. Hence, a nonsecular transfeminist critique—that is, a nonsecular feminism that seriously engages the issues of piety and transness, particularly in the Global South—can show that the historical record of the pious trans subject situated within the intersections of geopolitical, (trans)national, and (neo) colonial discourses weighs more on the side of secular and political erasure than religious social control.

Second, by conceptualizing the feminist/queer constitution of transgender archives as a form of secular epistemic violence, a nonsecular transfeminist critique can push nonsecular feminist frameworks to go beyond their primary focus on the affirmative and ethical self-formation of subjects. This shift away from subjectival formation toward the archival formation that seriously reckons with the historically contingent and often illegible manifestations of transness can enable non-secular feminist methodologies to broaden the scope of their analyses and examine the ways in which the secular Eurocentric cultural capital saturates the language of trans politics, discourse, and activism. As I show in the following sections, labels such as *strategic*, *political*, and *activist* perform the ideological work of centering a specific trans subject in Turkey, an archival erasure that a non-secular transfeminist analysis lays bare.

Bülent Ersoy and Strategic Religiosity

In his informative article "Reconstructing the Transgendered Self as a Muslim, Nationalist, Upper-Class Woman: The Case of Bülent Ersoy" (2008), Rüstem Ertuğ Altınay, following Simone de Beauvoir, traces how Bülent Ersoy, a very popular trans public figure referred to as the diva of Turkish classical music by the mainstream media,[30] "has become a Muslim, nationalist, and an upper-class woman"[31] in light of the neoliberal, nationalist, and conservative transformations that Turkey has gone through since the fascist military coup d'état of 1980. *Performance* emerges as the key term in the article as Altınay analyzes the multivalent ways in which Ersoy has strategized and performed various hegemonic identities to carve out spaces of tolerance and acceptance in a society that defines her identity as abject. The seemingly descriptive nature of his analytical framework, however, obscures the performative politics of his queer/feminist scholarship, which, informed by secular Eurocentric cultural capital, determines the boundaries of what counts as acceptable trans religious performance in Turkey. By characterizing Ersoy's performances as emanating from her interested desire to mirror the increasingly conservative public and political climate, Altınay's secular queer analysis leaves little room for understanding the complexity of Ersoy's subjectivity outside of a subversive-complicit dyad. This becomes particularly problematic when Altınay does not discuss how Ersoy embodies Islam and religion outside of her "interested" desire to be accepted. Instead, Altınay overemphasizes the tactics, performances, and strategies that Ersoy deploys to construct an image of a pious Muslim woman.[32] This theoretical framework not only replicates a long tradition of diagnostic reading performed by critical theorists with its undertones of deceptive, complicit, and/or tropological transsexual[33] but also suggests that the figure of a pious Muslim trans person is at best a tactical masquerade.

Critiquing Ersoy's problematic silence on the atrocities committed by the military regime against trans people and sex workers in the postcoup political atmosphere on the grounds that she "was the only person who had the power to have her voice heard," Altınay states that "she [Ersoy] was clearly rejecting transgenderism as an opportunity to deny established gender codes. She desired only to be accepted as a woman. She did not have any intention to fight against heterosexism either."[34] In another instance, Altınay again critiques Ersoy for not resisting the hegemonic gender norms when he argues that "Ersoy has internalized the restrictive discourses on gender and the body rather than resisting them."[35] In Altınay's secular epistemic universe, what seems to characterize a good trans subject is ultimately their desire and radical intentionality to subvert gender norms. A subversive trans subject who resists and exercises their agency to challenge the social norms is privileged, while a complicit trans subject who embodies the norms and traditions either strategizes for personal interests or suffers from false consciousness. This characterization has been pervasive, as Prosser reminds us,[36] not only in transphobic radical feminist and constructionist analyses but also in certain strands of feminist and queer theory. As Prosser points out, whether these analyses celebrate "the transsexual" as deliteralizing and transgressive or condemn "the transsexual" as literalizing and reinscriptive, "the referential transsexual subject can frighteningly disappear in his/her very invocation."[37] In Altınay's reading, the epistemic erasure of the referential transsexual is coupled with the secular erasure of pious trans subjectivity. Ersoy's transness that manifests through her gender expression as a pious nationalist woman is reduced to a strategic and literalizing theatrical performance on the grounds that she willingly pays lip service to Turkey's heteropatriarchal gender norms. Furthermore, because her performance is characterized as her hypocritical and deceptive discourse, the authenticity and sincerity of her commitments, particularly religious commitments, become debatable.

Altınay discusses Ersoy's performance of strategic religiosity once again with the secular hermeneutics of suspicion when he analyzes her decision to recite the *adhan*, which is called out by a muezzin (who is traditionally a cisgender man) five times a day from a mosque to summon Muslims for prayer. Altınay argues that "by reciting the *adhan* in Arabic, Ersoy asserted her identity as a conservative Muslim . . . This gave Ersoy the opportunity to reaffirm her faith in Islam and also have others reaffirm her gender identity as a woman."[38] This argument implies that Altınay considers Ersoy's pious Islamic identity relevant only insofar as it enables her to gain social acceptance in Turkey's fast-changing neoliberal landscape. Ersoy's decision to recite the *adhan* in Arabic instead of Turkish and to use a vocabulary abundant in Ottoman words is read as an indication of Ersoy's strategic rejection of modernity to perform a conservative and pious Muslim identity.[39] At this juncture, one wonders why one cannot interpret Ersoy's lexical and linguistic preferences not as performances conditioned by circumstantial necessities but rather as manifestations of her desire to embody the norms of Islam and claim a religious space that has been systematically denied to cis and trans women as well as trans men? Why does Altınay read her religious and conservative performances as ironically strategic rejections of modernity and queer/transgender identity on the grounds that transsexuality and queer theory were made possible through modern epistemologies and medical technologies,[40] when one can instead read modernity and Western identity categories as an alibi for the neocolonial universalization of a particular secular Western episteme? Altınay's diagnostic reading diminishes the possibilities of understanding Ersoy's relationality to Islamic space and temporality by reducing her piety and religious praxes to self-interested strategic performances.

The idea that Ersoy's conservative Muslim identity is a contingent phenomenon is further underscored when Altınay contends that "as the importance of nationalism and Islam in Turkish public discourse has increased since 1980s, the significance of these elements in Ersoy's construction of her own identity has increased as well."[41] This argument shares a similarity with Annick Prieur's explanation of *jotas'* and *vestidas'* femininity in the ethnographic research that she conducted in Mexico City in the late eighties and early nineties. In that research, drawing on Pierre Bourdieu, Prieur theorizes the femininity of *jotas* and *vestidas* as emanating from these identities' resistance to symbolic violence.[42] However, as Vek Lewis insightfully argues, Prieur's theorization of *jotas'* and *vestidas'* femininity renders both categories "as highly contingent phenomena which in a different set of variables would not and need not exist."[43] Similarly, Altınay's discussion of Ersoy as a tropological trans figure mirroring the transformations that Turkey has gone through implies that in a different cultural context with different political, social, and economic changes, Ersoy would not and need not be pious. In other words, Ersoy's pious religiosity can only be strategic and tactical, a circumstantial necessity that can be "diagnosed" through a secular constructionist queer lens.

Proudly Activist and (Ir)religious in Turkey

Designed by the South African artist Gabrielle Le Roux in collaboration with Amnesty International Turkey and two Turkish trans organizations, Istanbul LGBTT and Pembe Hayat, *Proudly Trans in Turkey* (2012) is an activist art project that includes eighteen videos and seventeen portraits by Le Roux. The videos include interviews with trans activists in Turkey that touch on themes such as religion, hate crimes, activism, family, and work. In this section, I do a close reading of a specific portion of these video interviews where the trans activists respond to the open-ended question "What is the role of religion and spirituality in your life?" and discuss its implications within the larger framework of Le Roux's activist art project. As their responses reveal, the trans activists relate to religion, in general, and Islam, in particular, in distinct and dynamic ways. Their relationality is inflected by, among other things, their activism, family, class position, ethnicity, geography, lived experience, and political affiliation. While some respondents state that Islam or other religions are not compatible with their trans existence and Weltanschauung, others critique orthodox interpretations of Islam, challenging various forms of violence and marginalization inflicted in the name of religion. On the surface, Le Roux's activist and collective art project represents the rich diversity and multidimensional aspects of trans religiosity and activism in Turkey. However, I argue that her project raises serious issues that need to be analyzed through a non-secular transfeminist lens. First, Le Roux universalizes the secular feminist conceptualization of agency and portrays a diverse group of urban political activists who speak the global and Eurocentric language of queer and feminist politics as the true representatives of trans diversity in Turkey. Secondly, Le Roux's positionality as a white South African artist and human rights activist who created similarly engaged multimedia projects before in the Global South enables her to transform the language of resistance into the language of neoliberal consumption by tying the national trans activism to the global and universal language of human rights. Finally, by ignoring the tensions between the rural and the urban as well as the regional and the national/global, Le Roux's archival politics misreads secular cultural capital as diversity and erases the pious trans people whose lack of "subversive" politics are deemed unfit and illegible for transnational and global circulation.

Le Roux's use of strategic diversity and the collective nature of her project are praised by Cüneyt Çakırlar in his article on documentary LGBTQ narratives from Turkey.[44] Çakırlar argues that "the ethic of collaborative ethnography, the primary address aimed at activists, and strategic diversity in Le Roux's activist practice intervene in 'a politics of pity . . . [that] situates the sufferer as passive and the one who observes the suffering as obliged to act.'"[45] While Çakırlar is right in his argument that the contemporary rights-based ethnographic documentaries produced for the consumption by the Global North base their representational framework on victimhood[46] and that Le Roux's politics of representation is not driven by the savior complex, he does not analyze the ways in which the ethnographic gaze also manifests itself through the secular constitution of agency, language, and cultural capital.[47] The project's strategic diversity operates as an alibi for the simultaneous erasure of pious trans people whose politics are not legible and who refuse to/do not have the cultural capital to speak the language of resistance and subversion. In this context, the label "political," as Evren Savcı argues, is structured through the logic and vocabulary of neoliberalism and perpetuates other forms of normativities and exclusions.[48] The urban trans activists display their political agency and oppositional consciousness through their critical conceptualization of Islam. Their critical language, regardless of whether they embrace Islam or not, confers on them an intelligible political positionality. In that sense, diversity, which has been rightly critiqued as a tool of neoliberalism for adopting a flattened version of difference and obscuring the structural workings of racism,[49] renders illegible the lived experiences of pious trans people whose ethical self-formations do not fit the parameters of secular agency and autonomy assumed to be cross-cultural and immanent to the trans subject. In other words, strategic diversity, to slightly misquote Gayatri Chakravorty Spivak, preserves the secular trans subject of the Global North or the secular Global North as subject by confirming, through a "diverse" and urban trans representation from Turkey, the universality of trans people's autonomy and sovereign agency.[50]

The responses in the video to the open-ended question "What is the role of religion and spirituality in your life?" indicate the multivalent ways in which the language and cultural capital of the secular Global North are translated into an Islamic national context by the urban trans activists. One of the interviewees, Destina, who identifies as a conservative Muslim, says: "I consider myself religious and conservative although I do not fulfill the religious duties perfectly. . . . Religion and spirituality play a major role in my life because I think that I have overcome many difficulties thanks to my faith."[51] Similarly to Destina, Selay also identifies as a believer in Islam. Moreover, she harshly condemns the brutalities and atrocities committed in its name: "I believe in Islam and Allah. I always pray to Allah. I believe in our prophet and other things too, but I do not believe in what they call Islam in 2011. If it is Islam, I am not a Muslim."[52] Selay's critique of how certain radical groups abuse Islam in the contemporary world is followed by her discussion of how "her" Islam is based on tolerance, compassion, altruism, and nonviolence. One can argue that Selay's and Destina's discourses about Islam can be read as manifestations of the minoritized subjects' attempts to disidentify with an orthodox and hegemonic religious tradition.[53] Their disidentificatory praxes can be compared to those of Muslim feminist writers who reclaim oral tradition to intervene in the supposedly closed debates in Islamic religious literature. Fatima Mernissi, for example, describes the Islam she inherited from her grandmother as "an occasion to journey to strange countries, to spread one's wings, and to discover love and enlightenment there."[54] Leila Ahmed also elaborates on the notion of Islam as an oral and aural heritage passed down from women to women through generations.[55] In the same vein as Muslim feminists who adhere to critical Islamic hermeneutics,[56] Selay and Destina understand Islam in a way that enables them to confront contemporary radical Muslims' amnesia and re-create a world in which they can spread their wings. Their self-reflexivity in relation to their critical embrace of Islam is informed by their activist language, cultural capital, urban location, and politics of resistance. Their pious acceptance of Islam does not disarticulate agency from autonomy or oppositional consciousness.

Selay's and Destina's feelings toward Islam and religion seem to be, on the surface, completely different from those of Esmeray, who says: "I do not think that any religion will make me happy. I feel like religion is the opium of the people." Having grown up in a Kurdish family in the city of Kars, a geography influenced, as she claims, by the political climate of the Soviet Union, Esmeray adopts an agnostic approach, claiming that we do not and cannot know whether Allah exists or not: "The only thing we know is that we want to be happy together in this world. That is what I believe in."[57] According to Esmeray, Islamic identity, in particular, and religious identity, in general, are not means through which her utopian and revolutionary vision can be realized. In her epistemic universe, religiosity emerges as a deterrent to the realization of that collectivist vision. In other words, for Esmeray, Islam turns out to be a category irreconcilable with her lived experience, activism, trans identity, and political objectives. Esmeray's irreligious positionality in the video complements the religiosity espoused by the other trans interviewees and thus serves to highlight Le Roux's commitment to strategic diversity. However, it is precisely this strategic diversity that erases the difference and re-centers the "same," that is, secular/liberal political agency. This erasure is enacted through a misreading of secular cultural capital as (ir)religious diversity, which, in turn, overdetermines the possibilities of inhabiting a religious trans positionality. Basing the strategic diversity on the conflation of the pious Muslim trans activists who adopt critical Islamic hermeneutics with so-called noncritical (and invisible on screen) pious trans people, Le Roux's activist project archives urban trans politics, activist language, and secular trans cultural capital at the expense of trans people whose ethical self-constitution and politics of piety dissociate agency from the language of resistance and subversion.

Le Roux's prioritization of urban trans activists in her collaborative project also raises issues as regards the divisions between the rural and the urban as well as the regional and the national. Çakırlar states that "rather than attempting to entirely contain the trans identity under the national referent of Turkey, [Le Roux's] project's core aim is to work with activists and address their struggle by creating a horizontal ethnographic setting."[58] I give credit to Le Roux for creating a horizontal ethnographic setting within which the trans activists are not used as tools to provide decontextualized and generalized information about what it means to be a trans person in Turkey. The setting enables the trans activists to share their wisdom and diverse forms of activist politics without appealing to the Global North's savior complex. However, the creation of this horizontal ethnographic space only becomes possible, I argue, through various forms of geopolitical and secular erasures, which challenges the argument that this multimedia project does not entirely contain the trans identity under the national referent of Turkey. First, Le Roux, by foregrounding the urban as the center of trans political life, conceptualizes the urban spaces in Turkey as the teleological and critical sites of modernity. The presence of a horizontal ethnographic setting conceals the role of the Eurocentric cultural capital and political language in engendering trans people's representation as critical national/transnational activists in urban spaces. Second, Le Roux's collaborative project couples oppositional political consciousness with urban geopolitics while privileging the critical trans public cultures of Turkey's global cities whose representational powers gain their currency through national and global referents. By reinforcing the link between urban critical political consciousness and national/transnational forms of activism, Le Roux's activist project leaves unquestioned how the absence of the nonmetropolitan and rural pious trans subject is central to the construction and global consumption of this horizontal ethnographic space.

In *Proudly Trans in Turkey*, the question of erasure is also obscured through the language of activist visibility, global human rights struggles, collaboration, and transnational solidarity. Berfu Şeker, in her interview with Le Roux on this multimedia project, defines Le Roux as a human rights activist whose work transcends boundaries.[59] In the interview, Şeker notes that Le Roux created and designed a similar project with African transgender activists in 2008, titled *Proudly African and Transgender*, and that while she was in Turkey in 2010 to attend an exhibition on this project, she got an invitation from transgender activists to create an analogous collaborative work.[60] To emphasize the collaborative and collective nature of her project, Le Roux stresses that Amnesty International Turkey and two Turkish trans organizations, Istanbul LGBTT and Pembe Hayat, will collectively own the copyrights to display the reproductions of the portraits of the trans activists in future exhibitions.[61] Le Roux's ethics of collaboration and collective work underscores her desire to avoid being seen as a white cisgender non-Turkish speaking outsider with a vested interest in looking in and extracting information from her subjects in the Global South.[62] Nonetheless, Le Roux's project's implication in the global neoliberal systems of LGBTQ funding and international human rights discourses as well as the transnational implications of her decontextualized and analogic activist praxes raise questions about the ethical foundations of her work and the excluded subjects of her "inclusive" secular politics.

Le Roux states that thanks to the contributions of Amnesty International Turkey, *Proudly Trans in Turkey* has more financial support than her previous project, *Proudly African and Transgender*.[63] This portrayal of Amnesty International Turkey as a benevolent and generous supporter of human rights activists, in general, and trans activists, in particular, sanitizes the operations of Amnesty International in the Global South as well as the political implications of this collaboration. Given that Amnesty International is an organization with a long history of biased reporting[64] in Muslim-majority countries and devastated war regions in the Global South as well as exploitative labor policies that have resulted in strikes in Turkey, one needs to interrogate at what cost, to whose benefit, to whose exclusion Amnesty International Turkey funds Le Roux's activist project and politics of visibility. What kind of cultural capital and political language are required to be visible as a trans activist in an Amnesty International–funded activist project? What political work does solidarity perform in this context? The invisibility of pious trans people who do not speak the critical language of global human rights constitutes the outer limits of Le Roux's activist archive. In this case, solidarity emerges as a diverse network consolidated through transnational neoliberal capital and predicated on the secular conceptions of autonomous agency and resistance. In other words, solidarity works as an alibi for the concurrent merging of neoliberal financial capital, liberal cosmopolitanism, and secular cultural capital.

Conclusion

At this point, a few clarifications are in order. First, a nonsecular transfeminist critique does not romanticize the peripheral and tangential relationship of the rural and the regional to the nation-state. As Gayatri Gopinath argues, the rural and the regional can be used to decenter and destabilize the dominant nationalist frameworks by "foregrounding 'other' narratives that tell an entirely different story of gender, sexuality, and nationalist subjectivity."[65] However, as Gopinath also reminds, their minoritized position vis-à-vis the nation-state does not mean that these spaces are "irreducibly particular [or] self-closed" but that "they are produced precisely by the collision of the local, the national, and the transnational."[66] In other words, pious trans people who do not occupy urban spaces or who have a tangential relationship with the ideological nation-state apparatuses cannot be understood as irreducibly particular or untouched by the global/transnational circulation of ideologies. In the same vein as urban trans political activists, rural pious trans people negotiate the local, the national, and the global processes in their ethical self-formation even though this negotiation does not necessarily follow the "political" constitution of agency-as-resistance. Secondly, a nonsecular transfeminist critique does not necessarily have an epistemic investment in "unearthing" alternative cartographies of trans or queer resistance to the national and global discursive traditions that the Western secular feminism considers nonliberal. Obviously, some pious trans people's discourses, acts, or embodied praxes might be "politically" intelligible to the extent that they fit the parameters of the trans activist language. However, it may well be that some of them embody and inhabit the politics in terms that are not easily translatable to the language of secular trans politics. Hence, I argue, the primary epistemic concern of a non-secular transfeminist critique is archival in that—rather than prioritizing how the "recovered" non-secular trans subject might offer us a new lens to understand trans religiosity and alternative forms of agency, which, as Rosalind C. Morris reminds us, would be tantamount to the replication of the masculine-imperialist ideology[67]—it interrogates what work the labels *activist*, *strategic*, and *political* perform in the vocabulary of secular trans politics as well as what kind of erasures/exclusions these labels authorize.

By focusing on the ways in which Eurocentric secular cultural capital is translated into an Islamic context to determine what counts as politically acceptable trans religious performance, a nonsecular transfeminist critique allows us to archive the transnational cartographies of secular erasure as well as the poly-vocality of trans (ir)religiosity. As I show in this article, trans people's narratives and performances reveal not only the irreducible heterogeneity of how they embody or refuse Islam but also the role of political/activist language in their embodied praxes. Analyzing their positions on the matter of religion outside of the secular prism of diagnostic reading opens up new and productive ways of thinking through this heterogeneity. The trans woman I saw in the nineties in a Mediterranean city of Anatolia or other trans people from the peripheries of the country who frequent mosques without necessarily frequenting legible activist and political spaces are reckoned with. Such a non-secular transfeminist analysis then ensures that the referential pious trans subject does not "disappear."

Şahin Açıkgöz is assistant professor of Islam, gender, and sexuality in the Department for the Study of Religion and a member of the executive committee of the Middle East and Islamic Studies Program at the University of California, Riverside.

Acknowledgments

I would like to express my immense gratitude to Melissa M. Wilcox, Joseph A. Marchal, and the anonymous reviewers for their comments, feedback, suggestions, and critical engagement with the early drafts of this article.

Notes

1. Throughout this article, I use terms such as *trans*, *transgender*, and *transsexual* frequently; however, this usage does not in any way suggest that all these terms are always interchangeable or that they have similar genealogies, connotations, significations, or political implications. Rather, it mostly reflects the choices made by the scholars/works analyzed in this article. Furthermore, my use of the expression "pious trans people" does not intend to homogenize or draw a singular portrayal of pious trans people given that piety, similarly to people who embrace it, embodies different affects in different geographies/histories. Piety can be personal or public, can have a geopolitically determined relationship with modernity, and can undoubtedly be shaped by, among other things, the dominant sects or madhhab in a specific context. For an insightful discussion on gender and piety in Shi'i Lebanon, see Deeb, *Enchanted Modern*.

2. I think of archives not merely as material repositories of texts, documents, audiovisual sources, etc., but also as incorporeal frameworks and discursive systems shaped by sociocultural capital and political economy, which render certain communities, subjects, figures, events, and objects (il)legible, (un)intelligible, and (in)visible in a given geographic space/historical period.

3. Altınay, "Reconstructing the Transgendered Self."

4. Wampler, "Trans-ing Religion."

5. Max Strassfeld and Robyn Henderson Espinoza build on the insights of Talal Asad and remind us that secularism is not secular and that it "functions as an unmarked (and thereby naturalized) form of white Protestantism disciplining (premodern, irrational, racialized) religion" ("Mapping Trans Studies in Religion," 285). That the secular cannot be understood independently of the religious is further discussed by Melissa E. Sanchez's insightful book *Queer Faith*, where she analyzes the theological roots of secular understandings of, among other things, sexuality and erotic accountability and demonstrates how "Christian theology has profoundly shaped Western secular descriptions of love and sexuality" (94).

6. Raymond, *Transsexual Empire*, 115.

7. Stone, "The *Empire* Strikes Back," 230.

8. Prosser, "Judith Butler," 259.

9. Butler, *Gender Trouble*.

10. Prosser, *Second Skins*; Namaste, *Invisible Lives*.

11. Prosser, "Judith Butler," 261.

12. Butler's more recent work, *Undoing Gender*, engages with the question of transness more comprehensively and addresses some of the concerns/critiques raised by trans scholars/activists against the prioritization of subversion and drag in their earlier work.

13. Prosser, *Second Skins*, 101.

14. Prosser, *Second Skins*, 101.

15. Prosser, *Second Skins*, 101.

16. C. Riley Snorton also critiques Prosser's prioritization of the bodily experience understood through a sexological prism at the expense of the psychic dimension. Highlighting the invisibility of the preoperative or nonoperative transsexual in Prosser's account, Snorton asks, "What happens when the story of the transsexual body does not evidence a clear break from a sexual ontological past?" ("'New Hope,'" 81).

17. Mahmood, *Politics of Piety*, 20–21.

18. Mahmood, *Politics of Piety*, 22.

19. Mahmood, *Politics of Piety*, 23.

20. Mahmood, *Politics of Piety*, 23.

21. Mahmood, *Politics of Piety*, 7.

22. Braidotti, "In Spite of the Times," 2.

23. Braidotti, "In Spite of the Times," 19.

24. Mahmood's non-secular conception of agency is more limited than Braidotti's theoretical framework given that the latter acknowledges posthumanism's relevance to the post-secular turn to reflect on the intersection between political subjectivity and biopolitical issues that are not usually categorized within the purview of the secular tradition in feminism. On the other hand, Braidotti's use of the term "postsecular" is problematic, at best, and an epistemic violence, at worst, given that the term not only naturalizes the Global North–centric temporal prism but also preserves the codification of the secular Global North as the subject looking in.

25. Vasilaki, "Politics of Postsecular Feminism," 106.

26. Vasilaki, "Politics of Postsecular Feminism," 115–116.

27. Vasilaki, "Politics of Postsecular Feminism," 110.

28. Vasilaki, "Politics of Postsecular Feminism," 118–19.

29. Vasilaki, "Politics of Postsecular Feminism," 110.

30. Bülent Ersoy has an extremely important place in the collective memory of the gender and sexual minorities from Turkey due to both her hypervisibility in Turkish visual/print media and her name's widespread association with anything that connotes gender and sexual nonconformity in the country. Like many queer- and trans-identified people growing up in Turkey, I used to get called "Bülent Ersoy" very frequently when I was bullied for my perceived femininity. Her name is used, in some cissexist and heterosexist circles of the society, as a form of insult similar to how *faggot* is used in English.

31. Altınay, "Reconstructing the Transgendered Self," 210–11.

32. My critique of Altınay's discussion of Ersoy's religious public persona as a strategic performance should not be taken to suggest that the purity of Ersoy's piety cannot be interrogated or that her decisions regarding public piety are never strategically influenced by local/national political forces. The fact that she has been a regular guest at the highly publicized iftar dinners organized by the AKP government and the Turkish president Recep Tayyip Erdoğan no doubt raises a lot of questions about her tenuous incorporation into neoliberal Islam in Turkey. For an insightful discussion on this, see Savcı, "Transing Religious Studies."

33. Julia Serano's book *Whipping Girl* elaborates on the trope of the deceptive transsexual in its critique of the dominant cultural and medical representations of trans women. In "Performing Translatinidad," Vek Lewis also examines how the trope of the deceptive transsexual operates in the dating reality show *There's Something about Miriam*.

34. Altınay, "Reconstructing the Transgendered Self," 214.

35. Altınay, "Reconstructing the Transgendered Self," 222.

36. Prosser, *Second Skins*.

37. Prosser, *Second Skins*, 14–15.

38. Altınay, "Reconstructing the Transgendered Self," 217.

39. Altınay, "Reconstructing the Transgendered Self," 217–18.

40. Altınay, "Reconstructing the Transgendered Self," 218.

41. Altınay, "Reconstructing the Transgendered Self," 220.

42. Prieur, *Mema's House*, 34, 140–41.

43. Lewis, "Sociological Work on Transgender in Latin America."

44. Çakırlar, "Transnational Pride."

45. Çakırlar, "Transnational Pride," 53.

46. Çakırlar, "Transnational Pride," 54.

47. Çakırlar is careful, though, to note that the presentation of the cultural alterity on screen in *Proudly Trans in Turkey* "still seems to prioritize a global/transnational gaze" and that the documentary "avoids a critical look at the inner tensions and conflicts of LGBTQ activism in Turkey" ("Transnational Pride," 54).

48. Savcı, "Who Speaks the Language of Queer Politics?," 373.

49. For more detailed discussion, see Mohanty, "Transnational Feminist Crossings"; and Ahmed, *On Being Included*.

50. Spivak, "Can the Subaltern Speak?," 22.

51. Le Roux, *Proudly Trans in Turkey*. All the translations in this article are mine unless stated otherwise.

52. Le Roux, *Proudly Trans in Turkey*.

53. José Esteban Muñoz discusses in detail the concept of disidentification by which he refers to the survival strategies that minoritized subjects practice in order to negotiate and navigate phobic/punitive majoritarian spheres (*Disidentifications*, 4).

54. Mernissi, *Veil and the Male Elite*, 63.

55. Ahmed, *Border Passage*, 125.

56. In terms of its translatability to secular political language, critical Islamic hermeneutics is similar to what Yolande Jansen describes as "Islamic secular hermeneutics" in her discussion on Saba Mahmood's critique of reformist approaches of Islam ("Postsecularism, Piety, and Fanaticism," 983). Jansen goes on to criticize Mahmood on the grounds that Mahmood replaces the secular-religious divide with a secularity-piety divide (977–98). I should note, however, that it is not my intention to replicate a pious-secular binary within the context of transness in this article. Rather, I am interested in interrogating what forms/kinds of pieties are translatable to, as well as legible in, the lexicon of secular trans politics. For a more detailed discussion on this topic, see Jansen, "Postsecularism, Piety, and Fanaticism"; and Mahmood, "Critiques of Secularism."

57. Le Roux, *Proudly Trans in Turkey*.

58. Çakırlar, "Transnational Pride," 51.

59. Şeker, *Başkaldıran Bedenler*, 252.

60. Şeker, *Başkaldıran Bedenler*, 251.

61. Şeker, *Başkaldıran Bedenler*, 266.

62. Şeker, *Başkaldıran Bedenler*, 258.

63. Şeker, *Başkaldıran Bedenler*, 266.

64. For instance, citing Elora Chowdhury, Lila Abu-Lughod reminds us of how the local campaigns, organizations, and efforts of dedicated Bangladeshi feminists to resolve the complex issue of acid violence were erased in the award given to the American documentary "Faces of Hope" by Amnesty International (*Do Muslim Women Need Saving?*, 14). Abu-Lughod's analysis also reveals the ways in which Amnesty International's fact sheet on honor crimes, titled "Culture of Discrimination," actively contributes to

the stigmatization of the Muslim-majority countries and trivialization of complex moral systems by characterizing the women living there as victims who have no moral agency (116).

65. Gopinath, "Queer Regions," 343.
66. Gopinath, "Queer Regions," 343.
67. Morris, introduction, 3.

References

Abu-Lughod, Lila. *Do Muslim Women Need Saving?* Cambridge, MA: Harvard University Press, 2013.

Ahmed, Leila. *A Border Passage: From Cairo to America—A Woman's Journey*. New York: Farrar, Straus and Giroux, 1999.

Ahmed, Sara. *On Being Included: Racism and Diversity in Institutional Life*. Durham, NC: Duke University Press, 2012.

Altınay, Rüstem Ertuğ. "Reconstructing the Transgendered Self as a Muslim, Nationalist, Upper-Class Woman: The Case of Bülent Ersoy." *WSQ*, no. 36 (2008): 210–29.

Braidotti, Rosi. "In Spite of the Times: The Postsecular Turn in Feminism." *Theory, Culture, and Society*, no. 26 (2008): 1–24.

Butler, Judith. *Gender Trouble: Feminism and the Subversion of Identity*. New York: Routledge, 1990.

Butler, Judith. *Undoing Gender*. New York: Routledge, 2004.

Çakırlar, Cüneyt. "Transnational Pride, Global Closets, and Regional Formations of Screen Activism: Documentary LGBTQ Narratives from Turkey." *South-North Cultural and Media Studies*, no. 31 (2017): 44–60.

Deeb, Lara. *An Enchanted Modern: Gender and Public Piety in Shi'i Lebanon*. Princeton, NJ: Princeton University Press, 2006.

Gopinath, Gayatri. "Queer Regions: Locating Lesbians in Sancharram." In *A Companion to Lesbian, Gay, Bisexual, Transgender, and Queer Studies*, edited by George Haggerty and Molly McGarry, 341–54. Chichester, UK: Wiley-Blackwell, 2008.

Jansen, Yolande. "Postsecularism, Piety, and Fanaticism: Reflections on Jürgen Habermas' and Saba Mahmood's Critiques of Secularism." *Philosophy and Social Criticism* 37 (2011): 977–98.

Le Roux, Gabrielle, dir. and artist. *Proudly Trans in Turkey: An Artistic Intervention for Social Justice*. Istanbul: Amnesty International Turkey, 2012.

Lewis, Vek. "Performing Translatinidad: Miriam the Mexican Transsexual Reality Show Star and the Tropicalization of Difference in Anglo-Australian Media." *Sexualities*, no. 12 (2009): 225–50.

Lewis, Vek. "Sociological Work on Transgender in Latin America: Some Considerations." *Journal of Iberian and Latin American Research*, no. 12 (2006): 77–89.

Mahmood, Saba. "Critiques of Secularism." *Philosophy and Social Criticism*, no. 37 (2011): 977–98.

Mahmood, Saba. *Politics of Piety: The Islamic Revival and the Feminist Subject*. Princeton, NJ: Princeton University Press, 2005.

Mernissi, Fatima. *The Veil and the Male Elite: A Feminist Interpretation of Women's Rights in Islam*. Reading, MA: Addison-Wesley, 1991.

Mohanty, Chandra. "Transnational Feminist Crossings: On Neoliberalism and Radical Critique." *Signs*, no. 38 (2013): 967–91.

Morris, Rosalind C. Introduction to *Can the Subaltern Speak? Reflections on the History of an Idea*, edited by Rosalind C. Morris, 1–18. New York: Columbia University Press, 2010.

Muñoz, José Esteban. *Disidentifications: Queers of Color and the Performance of Politics.* Minneapolis: University of Minnesota Press, 1999.

Namaste, Viviane. *Invisible Lives: The Erasure of Transsexual and Transgendered People.* Chicago: University of Chicago Press, 2000.

Prieur, Annick. *Mema's House, Mexico City: On Transvestites, Queens and Machos.* Chicago: University of Chicago Press, 1998.

Prosser, Jay. "Judith Butler: Queer Feminism, Transgender, and the Transsubstantiation of Sex." In *The Transgender Studies Reader*, edited by Susan Stryker and Stephen Whittle, 257–80. New York: Routledge, 2006.

Prosser, Jay. *Second Skins: The Body Narratives of Transsexuality.* New York: Columbia University Press, 1998.

Raymond, Janice G. *The Transsexual Empire: The Making of the She-Male.* Rev. ed. New York: Teachers College Press, 1994.

Sanchez, Melissa E. *Queer Faith: Reading Promiscuity and Race in the Secular Love Tradition.* New York: New York University Press, 2019.

Savcı, Evren. "Transing Religious Studies: Beyond the Secular/Religious Binary." *Journal of Feminist Studies in Religion*, no. 34 (2018): 63–68.

Savcı, Evren. "Who Speaks the Language of Queer Politics? Western Knowledge, Politico-Cultural Capital, and Belonging Among Urban Queers in Turkey." *Sexualities*, no. 19 (2016): 369–87.

Şeker, Berfu. *Başkaldıran Bedenler: Türkiye'de Transgender, Aktivizm ve Altkültürel Pratikler* (*Revolting Bodies: Transgender, Activism and Sub-cultural Practices in Turkey*). Istanbul: Metis Yayıncılık, 2013.

Serano, Julia. *Whipping Girl: A Transsexual Woman on Sexism and the Scapegoating of Femininity.* Emeryville, CA: Seal, 2007.

Snorton, C. Riley. "'A New Hope': The Psychic Life of Passing." *Hypatia*, no. 24 (2009): 77–92.

Spivak, Gayatri Chakravorty. "Can the Subaltern Speak?" In *Can the Subaltern Speak? Reflections on the History of an Idea*, edited by Rosalind C. Morris, 21–78. New York: Columbia University Press, 2010.

Stone, Sandy. "The *Empire* Strikes Back: A Posttranssexual Manifesto." In *The Transgender Studies Reader*, edited by Susan Stryker and Stephen Whittle, 221–35. New York: Routledge, 2006.

Strassfeld, Max, and Robyn Henderson Espinoza. "Mapping Trans Studies in Religion." *TSQ* 6, no. 3 (2019): 283–96.

Vasilaki, Rosa. "The Politics of Postsecular Feminism." *Theory, Culture, and Society*, no. 33 (2016): 103–23.

Wampler, Molly. "Trans-ing Religion: Is Religion Inclusive to the Transgender Community?" *Trail*, March 17, 2017. http://trail.pugetsound.edu/?p=13765.

Revisiting the Gay, Jewish Bicycle-Rider
John Boswell and the Uses of History

MAX STRASSFELD

ABSTRACT   This article examines the analogy between gays and Jews in John Boswell's scholarship in order to analyze the role of Jewishness in the construction of the field of history of
sexuality. Boswell argues that Jews and gays have a similar social status throughout history
until contemporary times, when gays continue to struggle while Jews have found a measure
of social acceptance. The difference between them, according to Boswell, is that Jews pass
down survival knowledge from within Jewish families, while gays are not generally born into
gay families. While critiquing the sexual, racialized, and gendered politics of Boswell's analogy,
this article will argue that the current antitrans political moment requires us to return to
the fundamental questions that Boswell poses about the relationship between history, the
historian, intergenerational knowledge transmission, and communal survival.

KEYWORDS   John Boswell, Jewish, trans, history

The work of John Boswell remains foundational in the study of religion and
sex. As Mark Jordan lays out in his foreword to the thirty-fifth anniversary
edition of *Christianity, Social Tolerance, and Homosexuality (CSTH)*, Boswell's
book was significant on several levels. Boswell composed a new grand narrative about the history of Christianity and sexuality, and his essential argument that the origins of homophobia in the West should not be simplistically
attributed to early Christianity was groundbreaking. In Boswell's analysis,
early Christianity emerges within the relatively permissive Greco-Roman
milieu, and only later (in the twelfth and thirteenth centuries) is there a historical shift toward intolerance of homosexuality. In other words, the idea that
the Christian Bible condemns homosexuality is a retroactive reading by later
Christians.[1]

   In arguing that the history of Christianity demonstrates varied attitudes
toward homosexuality, Boswell also undermined the assumption that gays
and religion are essentially in conflict.[2] To the extent that the field continues
to be compelled to make that fundamental point, Boswell's work remains
eerily relevant. As Joseph Marchal, one of the founding editors of this journal,
stated in an interview about *QTR*: "It's true that some have used religious

QTR • A Journal of Trans and Queer Studies in Religion • 1:1 • May 2024
DOI: 10.1215/29944724-11208938 © 2024 Max Strassfeld

argumentation to target queer and trans people, and that many are trauma-tized by religious narratives. . . . But it's equally true that many queer and trans people are religious and find community and affirmations in religions."[3] The fundamental notion that trans, queer, and religion are not inherently (essentially, eternally) opposed to one another still requires reiteration.

If Boswell's work is foundational in the formation of a field, it has also largely been discarded as a methodology for the study of the history of sexual-ity. Boswell has been criticized both for his treatment of gender, and for his insistence that "gay people" exist in history.[4] His approach sits uncomfortably alongside contemporary queer theory projects; his discussions of gay nor-malcy, for example, are at odds with strains of queer critique.[5] And yet Boswell's work is still compelling, as is his desire to provide gays with a past. His careful historical inquiry, coupled with his political commitments, has made Boswell's scholarship a model for later generations.[6] And the questions he raises, includ-ing fundamental questions about the utility of gay history, remain relevant today. In the current white supremacist and antitrans political environment, I share Boswell's questions about the purpose of (in my case Jewish/trans) his-tories and about the relationship between the historian, the political environ-ment, and the object of study.

For this inaugural issue of *QTR* it seemed fitting to revisit Boswell's schol-arship, and the figure of Jewishness, which has a central role in some of his argumentation. It would, of course, be fundamentally unfair to critique Boswell for lacking a contemporary trans Jewish studies ethos. But I am less interested in criticizing Boswell for eliding certain perspectives than I am in noting the ways these elisions shape his work. Because I seek to bring Boswell into new contexts, I also wish to consider both the potential benefits and pitfalls of that enterprise.

Building on the criticism of feminist scholars, I argue that Boswell's logics do not sufficiently consider race and processes of racialization, and that he does not grasp the import of his arguments in the context of contemporane-ous Jewish sexual politics. Having explored these elisions and the ways they constitute Jewishness in Boswell's work, I will, at the end of the essay, return to the fundamental questions that Boswell poses about the utility of gay his-tory from the perspective of the current political moment.

Judaism, Social Tolerance, and Homosexuality

While the broader political and activist implications of Boswell's work were largely directed toward a gay Christian audience, Boswell is also deeply inter-ested in European Jewish history.[7] A central moment in his introduction to *CSTH* is an extended analogy between gays and Jews. Boswell states:

> Most societies, for instance, which freely tolerate religious diversity also accept sexual variation, and the fate of Jews and gay people has been almost identical throughout European history, from early Christian hos-tility to extermination in concentration camps. The same laws which

oppressed Jews oppressed gay people; the same groups bent on eliminating Jews tried to wipe out homosexuality; the same periods of European history which could not make room for Jewish distinctiveness reacted violently against sexual nonconformity; the same countries which insisted on religious uniformity imposed majority standards of sexual conduct; and even the same methods of propaganda were used against Jews and gay people—picturing them as animals bent on the destruction of the children of the majority.[8]

In other words, sexual and religious diversity are often linked, which is an important insight all on its own. Moreover, the status of Jews and gays specifically fluctuates together throughout European history. Both groups are united by their shared experience of intolerance and regulation, to the extent that laws that address one group also tend to address the other. Finally, both Jews and gays are portrayed similarly at various points of history, often either as animals (or less than human) or as threats to minors.[9]

I want to notice two effects of this analogy between Jews and gay people. The first is that Boswell's interest in Judaism in this passage derives from parallels between Jewishness and gayness, rather than from Jewishness as a central object of study. I am not accusing Boswell of anti-Jewish sentiment. But his argumentation is, on occasion, clearly the product of a Christian perspective. Take, for example, Boswell's discussion of the verses in Leviticus that prohibit "lying with a man." His exegesis is generally nuanced, erudite, and presages some of the arguments biblical scholars will make about this verse.[10] His arguments end, however, with a demonstration of the way that Jewish law is largely rejected by early Christianity. In other words, Boswell's argument saves Christianity's status as non-homophobic by asserting that even if Leviticus is, in fact, prohibiting certain sex acts (if not homosexuality per se), it does not apply to Christians. This rescues Christianity, but at what cost?[11]

That Boswell focuses on Christianity is certainly fair—that is the topic of his book. But there is an unintended impact on the coherence of the gay Jew. It is not just that Boswell holds Jews and gays as distinct categories.[12] It is rather that a Jewish gayness ironically becomes less legible in this discussion of Leviticus. Jews become useful objects to think with.[13]

I want to draw our attention to a second important aspect of the analogy between gays and Jews, which is that the analogy eventually breaks down for Boswell. Boswell is interested in the question of how Jews have advanced their status in the contemporary US, while gays are still struggling to achieve the same advances. In later work, his interest in that question becomes more explicit:

This is why . . . Jews have generally been perceived as normal earlier than gay people in Western culture. It is not because Judaism is now better understood. . . . The reason that Jews achieve normal status before gay people is that religion is no longer part of the study of the normal. . . . The bodies that rule on normality are either uninterested in or afraid to take on religion.[14]

Boswell explains the advances Jews have made through secularization: the societal position of Jews advances in proportion to the marginalization of religion. While religion played an outsized role in defining normalcy in the past, the contemporary conflation of "normal" with "healthy" has, according to Boswell, shifted the power of the Church in this specific instance. Thus, the status of Jews has advanced and become decoupled from the social status of gays.[15]

Scholars of religion would now have much to say about the "secularization thesis" Boswell employs here.[16] But Boswell's implicit question is worth entertaining, whether or not his answer is entirely satisfying: Why has the status of the Jews progressed faster than the status of gays in the 1980s in the United States? For Boswell, this question is a historical one: What is it that decouples Jews from gays? But it is also implicitly the question of an activist—how do gays achieve the relative tolerance that Jews have? The problem with the question as framed, and its answer, is that both ignore the history of the whitening of certain groups of Jews within the US context. I will return to a discussion of race shortly as part of analyzing the unspoken substructure of Boswell's argumentation.

There is another obvious question that Boswell might have posed: Why is it that the statuses of Jews and gays are linked together historically? Subsequent work in the field addresses the relationship between queerness and Jewishness; the editors of *Queer Theory and the Jewish Question* describe their interest in exploring "the complex of social arrangements and processes through which modern Jewish and homosexual identities emerged as traces of each other."[17] In fact, this anthology was groundbreaking in part because it did not take the object of study ("queerness" or "Jewishness") for granted. In that same volume, Janet Jakobsen explores the analogy between Jews and gays in her brilliant essay entitled "Queers Are Like Jews, Aren't They?" In that essay, Jakobsen attends to the limitations of analogy as a form of political analysis and the dangers of analogizing between oppressions.[18] Many of the points Jakobsen makes about analogy speak directly to the challenges of the analogy between Jews and gays in Boswell's work.

If the analogy between Jews and gays seems to break down in the contemporary US context, Boswell also notes other ways in which Jews and gays do not function in parallel. According to Boswell, Jews are born into Jewish families that can pass down survival knowledge, unlike gays. Race (and processes of racialization) are at the heart of breaking the analogy between Jews and gays in both instances.

Race, Gender, Disability, and the "Chinese" Encyclopedia

Boswell's interest in the parallels between Jews and gays continued after *CSTH* was published. He delivered a lecture in 1986 at the University of Wisconsin-Madison titled "Jews, Gay People, and Bicycle Riders," which he edited into an essay that was published in 1989. In this talk (which was recorded for public television), Boswell asserts that the comparison between Jews and gays is not incidental to his project, but rather is a part of the intellectual intervention of his work.[19]

In "Jews, Gay People, and Bicycle Riders," Boswell offers a longue durée account of how taxonomies of normativity are organized in different eras. This is a related project to *CSTH*, but a shift from the initial frame of intolerance. He lays out different constructions of morality in the ancient (Greco-Roman) world, Catholic Europe, and the industrial West.

Boswell begins the talk by citing the example of a medieval Chinese encyclopedia. This encyclopedia stands in as a "foreign" taxonomical system:

> In its distant pages it is written that animals are divided into a) those that belong to the emperor; b) embalmed ones; c) those that are trained; d) suckling pigs; e) mermaids; f) fabulous ones; g) stray dogs; h) those that are included in this classification; i) those that tremble as if they were mad; j) innumerable ones; k) those drawn with a very fine camel's-hair brush; l) et cetera; m) those that have just broken the flower vase; n) those that in the distance resemble flies.[20]

The list is meant to be strange; it elicits laughter in the audience when Boswell quotes it in his talk. These categories of animals are different from any organizing system that his audience is supposed to be familiar with. For example, when the list mentions a category of animals owned by an emperor, it predicates its taxonomy on a particular political system.

Boswell borrows the description of the encyclopedia directly from Michel Foucault, who is himself quoting from the poet and essayist Jorge Luis Borges. In response to philosophical attempts to construct a universal order and taxonomy of the world, Borges cites a translation of a Chinese encyclopedia—the *Celestial Emporium of Benevolent Knowledge*.[21] He attributes the translation of that encyclopedia to Franz Kuhn, although that attribution (and the existence of the encyclopedia itself) have generally been called into question by scholars who believe that Borges fabricated the encyclopedia.[22] Borges presents us with a taxonomy of animals from the (historically, geographically) "distant" encyclopedia. This encyclopedia betrays an entirely different (and inscrutable) organizing principle. The category of "those [animals] that are included in this classification" intimates that there are animals that are not included in the encyclopedia's taxonomy, an allusion to the limits of the taxonomical enterprise itself.[23] Thus the Chinese encyclopedia, in Borges, functions as a critique of the project of universal taxonomy and points to some of the pitfalls of the taxonomical impulse.

Foucault chooses the example of the Chinese encyclopedia from Borges to begin his work *The Order of Things*. In Foucault's hands, the Chinese encyclopedia thematizes the ordering of knowledge and explores what is unthinkable or indecipherable within certain linguistic and epistemological frameworks. Foucault describes how the Chinese encyclopedia made him laugh, a laugh that disrupts the domestication of "wild" objects.[24] This use of "wild" functions as a kind of redoubling of the taxonomy of animality, and perhaps even plays with the way objects/animals enter into taxonomy in relation to their human usage; they are domesticated.

Foucault ties these reflections on the encyclopedia together with a consideration of the way the West imagines China as a culture that is "meticulous, the most rigidly ordered, the one most deaf to temporal events."[25] In other words, Foucault conveys a deliberate sense of an imagined China, inaccessible even from the Western perspective that imagined it, predicated on a series of metaphors (deafness, aphasia) that are used to describe this failure in perception. In Foucault, the language of the Chinese encyclopedia is racialized, orientalized, and enabled through metaphors of disability.[26]

It is from this convoluted genealogy that the encyclopedia makes its way to Boswell; Boswell cites directly from Michel Foucault's work.[27] When Boswell cites the encyclopedia, he also glosses its significance: "The fourteen animal categories . . . illustrate the caprices of taxonomy, and [Borges] deliberately attributed them to an ancient source to give them an air of authority."[28] According to Boswell, it is the ancientness of the encyclopedia that is important; historical distance is what demonstrates the contingency of taxonomy itself, and antiquity is given outsized weight.

For Boswell all taxonomies are contingent and potentially capricious, including both modern taxonomies and those from the past. This gloss of the encyclopedia supports his larger argument: he is concerned that a homophobic Christianity has been reified into a timeless moral stance. The Chinese encyclopedia is an example of the way taxonomies attempt to erase questions about their organization in an effort to naturalize their structures.

What Boswell's description ignores, however, is the orientalized production of "ancient" knowledge and the purported Chinese-ness of this fictional work. He leaves unexplained why the encyclopedia is Chinese; that is apparently self-evident. One could dismiss this citation of the encyclopedia as a simple framing device; Boswell opens with it and then largely ignores it until the end of his essay, where he spends less than a page exploring it. As a framing device, it works well to set up a conversation about the contingency of normativity. Still, his inattention to the invented Chinese-ness of the encyclopedia highlights Boswell's lack of engagement with race and racialization more generally.[29]

Even without a more robust analysis of race and religion, as the piece warrants, Jewishness itself and its complicated relationship to the category of race is its own form of unacknowledged presence. Processes of racialization help explain the divergence of the status of (white) Jews and gays that Boswell notices. In crafting the analogy between Jews and gays, Boswell effaces the complicated imbrications between his terms, and the way these categories emerge in relation to concepts of race and racialization.[30]

Reproducing Survival: The Gender and Racial Politics of the Analogy between Jews and Gays

Despite his analogy between Jews and gays, Boswell notes some important distinctions among the two groups. The first is the divergent status between the two in the modern era. I want to turn to the other main distinction he makes, namely that Jews are raised in Jewish families:

> Judaism . . . is consciously passed from parents to children, and it has been able to transmit, along with its ethical precepts, political wisdom gleaned from centuries of oppression and harassment: advice about how to placate, reason with, or avoid hostile majorities; how and when to maintain a low profile; when to make public gestures; how to conduct business with potential enemies. Moreover, it has been able to offer its adherents at least the solace of solidarity in the face of oppression.[31]

For Boswell, the importance of the fact that (some) Jews are raised in Jewish families is connected to the types of survival knowledge these families can transmit. The reproduction of Jewish knowledge is facilitated by these kinship networks, giving Jews both a sense of belonging and the skills to thrive in a hostile world. In Boswell's account, the reproduction of knowledge is part of the longevity of Jewishness.

By contrast, Boswell states, gay people generally do not have the benefit of being born into gay families. They are often isolated from friends and relatives because they are gay; rather than being a source of strength, kinship networks can be a source of pain. For Boswell, communities of gay people only tend to form within relatively tolerant times. In more difficult periods, gay people disappear into their private lives. So Boswell writes:

> When good times return, there is no mechanism to encourage steps to prevent a recurrence of oppression: no gay grandparents who remember the pogroms, no gay exile literature to remind the living of the fate of the dead, no liturgical commemorations of times of crisis and suffering. Relatively few gay people today are aware of the great variety of positions in which time has placed their kind.[32]

For Boswell, most gays lack an older generation to help them navigate the difficult times to come, or the historical memory to know how to organize to prevent those bad times from returning.[33] Boswell does not propose a progress narrative of history—instead he argues that in some ways, the status of gays has deteriorated. Still, it is worth noting that because Boswell understands the position of gays to be changeable, historical knowledge gains a particular significance.

This passage, published in 1980 on the precipice of what will become the "moral epidemic" over AIDS, is positively prescient.[34] But it is also an argument for the field of gay history. While Boswell never explicitly connects the dots for us in this introduction, I would argue that he understands gay historians as stepping into the void left by kinship networks; they function as the gay grandparents who "remember the pogroms." It is in this context, then, that we must read his insistence on a "gay" history; it is not just a "usable" past that he seeks to create, although he certainly does hope that his work will foment change in the Church. It is also that he understands history as a tool of contemporary survival.

Boswell's model of Jewishness is fraught even within its own time period. By tying cultural survival to Jewish families (and therefore Jewish reproduction), Boswell not only ignores the fact that not all Jews are born into Jewish families, but he also does not fully grasp the gendered and racialized dynamics of his discussion. In order to contextualize his argument about Jewish kinship, I want to survey some of the conflicts over Jewish reproduction that shape the time period in which Boswell wrote (and, in fact, continue to shape the politics of Jewish studies today).

The Jewish birth rate in the United States has attracted inordinate scholarly and popular interest. Jack Wertheimer is one of several scholars that has written prolifically on the subject in both academic and popular venues. Take, for example, his article in *Commentary* magazine from 2005. Wertheimer begins with an anecdote: "Not long ago, a Manhattan rabbi stunned his congregants by informing them that the future of the Jewish people would be secured not through trips to Israel, not through the battle against anti-Semitism, and not through the continued upward mobility of Jews, but in the bedroom."[35] Wertheimer, who agrees with this nameless Manhattan rabbi, is calling attention to a demographic "crisis" in Jews. Note the other aspects that are supposed to unite Jews and secure a Jewish future: Zionism, antisemitism, and continuing Jewish mobility. Zionism and antisemitism are sites of unacknowledged intra-communal tension in this passage. Even as Wertheimer rejects those bonds as the ones that will secure the future of Jews, presumably he includes the anecdote because each of the other features seemed more plausible to the congregants than the final one—reproduction.

Wertheimer argues that the Jewish future is imperiled because of a demographic problem linked to low birth rates. He cites data that suggests that Jewish women marry later. According to Wertheimer, this advanced maternal age leads to fewer children and smaller households, in numbers that do not match population replacement needs. He notes that the lower Jewish fertility rate is not new but rather began in the nineteenth century because of new economic opportunities, the accessibility of birth control, and higher educational attainment for women.[36] This creates, for Wertheimer, a demographic emergency and the need to advocate for "Jewish continuity."

Feminist scholarship has criticized the Jewish continuity movement, which has become a central term in Jewish communal life. In an article cowritten by Lila Corwin Berman, Kate Rosenblatt, and Ronit Stahl, the authors argue that not only has the narrative about Jewish "continuity" put pressure on (largely) women to reproduce in greater numbers, it has also created a culture of sexual harassment and assault in Jewish studies and Jewish communal institutions.[37] The authors trace the history of the rise of Jewish continuity discourse from the 1970s until the current day and describe the monumental edifice that has been built over the decades to monitor, survey, and support Jewish continuity, largely through the promotion of "family values" and the pressure to reproduce as an antidote to "assimilation." The result of these various efforts was to undermine women's sexual autonomy and authority, which created the institutional conditions in which sexual harassment flourished. The authors argue that continuity movements within Judaism supported a conservative gender and sexual politics.[38]

In a series of articles by Gilah Kletenik and Rafael Rachel Neis building on this feminist critique, the authors point to the neoliberal values that inhere in Jewish continuity discourse, including the way racism implicitly structures the regulation of the reproduction of Jewishness. Dynamics of race and class play out within the field itself, as white Jews have "more access, power, and authority to shape knowledge production."[39] The authors offer a profound critique of the ways that Jewish studies has become imbricated with the racialized cishet reproductive presumptions of continuity discourse.

It is in the context of this feminist, queer, and trans critique, then, that I want to briefly return to Wertheimer's arguments in a popular conservative Jewish magazine about Jewish continuity. In his call to support Jewish continuity by encouraging higher birth rates among Jewish women, Wertheimer consistently compares Jewish women to their "white, Gentile, counterparts."[40] The assumption that all Jewish women are white, on the one hand, and the unacknowledged racialized logic of a goal of white birth rates, on the other, actively positions whiteness as the measure for Jewish continuity. In other words, Wertheimer's arguments about continuity are not just gendered, focusing primarily on Jewish women. They are also racialized in structure, manifesting and preserving a (white) Jewish futurity. As Kletenik and Neis argue, continuity and reproduction not only represent a particular gendered and sexual politic, but a racialized one as well.[41]

In light of the gendered and racialized aspects of Jewish continuity, the reference to Jewish reproduction in Boswell's work touches on central tensions within both Jewish studies and Jewish communal contexts. Debates about Jewish continuity were already active in the time that Boswell would have been writing those passages. That Boswell did not always consider the gendered implications of his framing devices is a critique that has been levelled before, and Boswell himself was aware of this critique of his work.[42]

Bernadette Brooten has authored one of the most significant responses to Boswell on this front. While she lauds Boswell's contribution to the field, she argues that Boswell failed to take into account in his later work on same-sex unions the critique that he did not sufficiently address women in *CSTH*. She writes: "The entire thrust of Boswell's book is to lift up the astounding fact of official church recognition of same-sex unions. Why should the official recognition that forms the core of his book have been uninteresting to Christian women? And how did he ascertain that Christian women should have been content to forgo such recognition?"[43] When Boswell writes a book about same-sex unions but only describes unions between men, he is naturalizing and reiterating the exclusions directed at women. This is particularly frustrating for Brooten because Boswell cites evidence about women but fails to fully grapple with its significance.

In a brilliant reassessment of the field, Joseph Marchal places Brooten's work at the center of the history of sexuality.[44] Marchal is correcting for the way that scholarship about women (and the work of Brooten herself) has often been sidelined in narrating the development of the field. Marchal's correction, therefore, resituates the crucial importance of Brooten's approach. I am aware that in centering Boswell in this article, I am recapitulating the larger trend of sidelining scholarship by and about women. At the same time, Brooten's work specifically, and the feminist critiques of Boswell more generally, has inspired this reassessment of Boswell's work.

Boswell's analogy between Jews and gays looks quite different from a Jewish feminist analytic. Jews function to occlude a conversation about race and processes of racialization in Boswell's discussion. Jews stand in for (straight) reproduction and pass traditions down from within nuclear families. If the prospect of queer family and queer intergenerational learning is absent from Boswell's analogy, so too is a Jewishness that is not thoroughly domesticated.

Besides Brooten, historian Carolyn Dinshaw crafted one of the most significant receptions of Boswell's work.[45] In a talk originally presented in 1998 and later revised for her book *Getting Medieval*, Dinshaw formulates her theory of relationality with the past through an engagement with Boswell. In the talk version, Dinshaw also introduces a Jewish story about the reproduction of intergenerational knowledge.[46] She begins with a quotation from Marc Bloch, the French Jewish historian who was killed by the Nazis. The quote describes Bloch's young son asking his father, "What is the use of history?" Bloch's book, *The Historian's Craft*, was never finished because of the interruption of the war and Bloch's death.

This anecdote featuring a Jewish historian and the failure of history to reproduce implicitly comments on Boswell's links between Jews, history, and reproduction (although Dinshaw does not make that connection explicit herself.) Still, the story functions as a partial critique of Boswell's assumption that Jews can transmit history between generations. History is precarious in the face of violence; Marc Bloch's unfinished book haunts the text.

The violent interruption of Jewish historical reproduction frames the questions Dinshaw then asks: "But there are other kinds of affiliations, generations that are not traced via such traditional family relations. What is history for those of us whose lives are not oriented around generational reproduction of the traditional family, and what is the use of it? Whom can we ask? And who will ask *us*, in turn, to explain?"[47] Dinshaw, playing with Boswell's observation that gays do not necessarily reproduce gays, asks a question about the purpose of history within the bounds of queer kinship. She extends Boswell's yearning for intergenerational knowledge to build a different model of the production of history. In doing so, she leaves the equation between Jews and straight/traditional familial reproduction intact. But she pushes Boswell's question of the role of queer history in order to formulate her model of touching the past. In these various layers of Boswell's writing and reception, we can trace an unfurling imagined relationship between Jews, queers, and history.

In a seminal essay, Daniel Boyarin poses the question "are there any Jews in the history of sexuality?"[48] In the article, Boyarin explores biblical and rabbinic texts through the lens of Foucault's argument about the study of sexuality in the premodern period. Boyarin's question—are there any Jews in the history of sexuality—must be answered in the affirmative. Not just, as he argues, because of the way the biblical and rabbinic sources do not evince a category of sexuality but also because Jews have been at the center of the conceptualization of history in the field. There have always been Jews in the history of sexuality; Jews have been the backdrop to imagine a queerer past (and perhaps, future). Boswell seems nostalgic for aspects of "Jewish" knowledge transmission. This might, perhaps, also function as a nostalgia for a kind of imagined Jewish epistemology. The metaphor of the gay/Jewish grandmother who recollects the pogroms represents a communal memory used to guide Jewish resilience and resistance. History, in this formulation, becomes a kind of ancestral mode of knowing and perceiving the world. This mode of knowledge transmission is imbricated with conservative Jewish sexual and gendered politics in Boswell. But his questions still stand.

Coda: Groomers, Antitrans Politics, and the Uses of Histories

My goal in this essay was not to criticize Boswell per se. Rather, I have sought to revisit these debates within the history of sexuality to examine how Jewishness is used as a foil in the formulation of gay and then queer historical methodology and to play out the gendered and racialized implications of these arguments. In light of the current antitrans politics, which Jules Gill-Peterson has dubbed the creation of an "authoritarian cis state," these questions seem ever more relevant.[49] While Boswell's reliance on literal reproduction straightens Jewishness, the questions he raises about the utility of gay history and intergenerational knowledge continue to haunt me. I want to briefly take up these themes in relation to the targeting of trans youth, in order to leave us with a question about the use of trans Jewish histories within the context of contemporary attacks on intergenerational knowledge production and transmission.[50]

It needs to be acknowledged that there is no one narrative of Jewish or gay history nor even a single definition of the object of study. The "lachrymose" version of Jewish history, for example, in which Jewishness is constantly on the verge of disappearing, might be understood to fuel the Jewish continuity crisis. And as feminist scholars have demonstrated in their analysis of Jewish continuity movements, this way of telling the story has had violent impacts on Jewish women. Boswell is interested particularly in the history of European (Ashkenazi) Jewry, largely because this is his area of expertise; this is, however, a limited view of what constitutes "Jewish history."[51] It is crucial that we return to the role of history and our categories of study in this political moment, but I do not mean to suggest that there is a uniformity to "Jewish" or "trans" history nor that there is only one possible political use for history.

Recent legislative attacks on queer and trans rights have focused their efforts particularly on trans youth. Proposed bills restricting trans youth from participating in sports, and from accessing trans affirming medical care, have spread across the country. Often these bills are framed as protecting children. C. Heike Schotten has analyzed TERF political thought and named the confusion of the categories of oppressor and oppressed as a kind of extinction phobia.[52] It is within these logics that we regulate and police groups of (trans) children in order to protect (cis) children. Protecting children is a tacit way of advancing a "groomer" narrative.

While definitions of the term have varied, "groomers" usually refers to adults who "groom" children to be sexually assaulted and abused.[53] In a queer and trans context, the "groomer" accusation is also directly related to reproduction. As one tweet by the Christian nationalist handle AncestralVril put it: "Gen Z is overwhelmingly gay. Groomers can't reproduce so they recruit."[54] Thus "grooming" is an explanation meant to contextualize the perception that youth are coming out as trans and queer in greater numbers.[55] Queer and trans people must recruit the next generation, which is situated as a type of child abuse. In the broader political battles over education (such as the furor over the "don't say gay" bill), educating the next generation and intergenerational contact more broadly gets construed as a type of "grooming." It is here that Boswell's insistence on intergenerational knowledge transmission becomes so revealing; he links knowledge transmission with communal survival. The drive to suppress intergenerational trans and queer contact is a direct attack on queer and trans survival strategies.

Groomer content is often tacitly or expressly related to eugenic content. Other tweets from this user discuss an "international cabal of pedophiles," an accusation that is coded language to refer to Jews. In other words, trans people are pedophiles, and Jewish wealth and power is built on the traffic of children. The allegation that trans and queer people recruit vulnerable youth, therefore, is a racialized, gendered, sexual panic tied to antisemitism. It is a fear about the future of the United States, expressed as a fight for a white Christianity.[56]

Attacking trans youth while stigmatizing teaching about trans youth is nothing short of an all-out attack on a trans future. It is not an accident that these efforts are accompanied by a wholesale assault on the teaching of Black and Indigenous history; these are efforts bent on suppressing the passing down of skills meant to foster resilience and thriving in the next generations.

This functions as a broader politics of the eugenics of knowledge in the service of protecting (certain) children and securing a white Christian nationalist future.

I do not believe that I need the past to confirm my trans Jewish existence in the present. And I do not need the past to undermine the naturalization of the gender binary or of heterosexuality; I am convinced of the historical and cultural contingency of these terms already. I do not think historical work will sway bigots. If, according to Boswell, the passing down of knowledge is an important function of survival, then I wish to return us to the question, framed within our current punishing political environment:

What is the use of trans Jewish histories now?

Max Strassfeld is an associate professor of religious studies at the University of Arizona. They are the author of *Trans Talmud: Androgynes and Eunuchs in Rabbinic Literature* (2023).

Acknowledgments

I am grateful to have received a fellowship from the Hadassah-Brandeis Institute that supported the writing of this article, and I am also grateful for the intellectual engagement from the other HBI fellows. I wish to thank the anonymous reviewers, whose careful criticisms helped me to clarify and strengthen my argumentation. In addition to the reviewers, Cassandra Euphrat Weston and Ben Strassfeld provided crucial feedback that strengthened the argument and theoretical outlook—I am grateful to them both. Any errors, however, are mine.

Notes

1. Jordan, foreword.
2. Jordan, foreword.
3. Ober, "New Journal."
4. For an example of a critique of how Boswell addresses women, see Brooten, *Love Between Women*, 9–14. For a critique of Boswell's essentialism, see Halperin, *One Hundred Years of Homosexuality*, 41–54. Boswell has been pitted against Michel Foucault, and yet characterizations of a stark dichotomy between their approaches ignore the way that Boswell himself argues that certain social categories (like normativity) shift historically—in other words, that they are historically constructed.
5. See, for example, Boswell's remark: "In every way but one, most gay people are just like those around them" (*CSTH*, 16). Of course, Boswell is critiquing the contingency of "norms" even as he describes their regulatory force. But in doing so he also suggests gays are essentially "normal" except in one respect. For a classic critique of homonormativity, see Duggan, *Twilight of Equality?*, 43–67. From a trans studies perspective, see Stryker, "Transgender History."
6. Carolyn Dinshaw credits Boswell's work as the impetus for the foundational questions she raises in *Getting Medieval* (22–34).
7. For analyses of Boswell's reception in the gay community, see Schlager, "Reading *CSTH* as a Call to Action"; Jordan, "Both as a Christian and as a Historian."
8. Boswell, *CSTH*, 15–16.
9. Both queer theory and Jewish studies will take up the themes of animality and the harm posed to minors as central themes. On animality in queer and trans theory, see Chen, *Animacies*; Hayward and Weinstein, introduction. On animality in Jewish studies, see Cooper, "Writing Humanimals"; Lipton, *Dark Mirror*. On the queer and trans

potential to harm minors there is a seminal debate between José Esteban Muñoz and Lee Edelman. See Edelman, *No Future*; Muñoz, *Crusing Utopia*. In Jewish studies, see literature on the blood libel, such as Teter, *Blood Libel*.

10. In Boswell's analysis of Leviticus 18:22 and 20:13, he calls the book "the only place in the Old Testament where homosexual acts per se are mentioned" (*CSTH*, 100). Earlier in the chapter he also makes clear that the Bible does not contain an analogous term for "homosexual" in it, which is why he uses the phrase "homosexual acts" instead in the passage above (*CSTH*, 92). He suggests that the prohibition may have been intended mainly to separate Israelites from other peoples, based on his reading of the word *to'evah*, a term that has spawned much debate in biblical studies (*CSTH*, 100).

11. To his credit, Boswell does not blame Judaism for antihomosexual sentiment in the text (*CSTH*, 97). He also follows up the Jewish reception history of these verses, through their discussion in rabbinic literature and into medieval codes. This is quite different from Christian supercessionist arguments that tend to focus on the Hebrew Bible, and ignore any developments within Judaism that arise after the advent of Christianity. See Boswell, *CSTH*, 101n34. At the same time, Boswell seems to implicitly assume that Jews followed the law and were uniformly attached to it in this time period in his comparison with early Christians. This leaves Jewishness as largely univocal, a characterization that historians of the time period would reject.

12. In fact, Boswell explicitly notes that Jews can also be gay, although he makes a largely incoherent distinction between types of Jews: "Emphasizing the theological (as opposed to the ethnic) aspect of Judaism, and taking into account Judaism's own attitudes towards homosexuality, one might make the point that there are fewer Jewish (i.e., actively religious) gay people than there are gay Jews (persons of Jewish descent), although there are gay synagogues in the U.S. and many Reform synagogues welcome gay members" (Boswell, "Jews, Bicycle Riders, and Gay People," 206n4). This passage splits Judaism as a religion from Judaism as a (unified?) ethnicity. This ignores processes of racialization and the creation of a white Jewish ethnicity for some Jews. This assumption is not unique to Boswell. It is, however, indicative of a weakness of his argumentation, as I will discuss.

13. I am not accusing Boswell of antisemitism. His friend and colleague Ralph Hexter makes a point of Boswell's abhorrence of antisemitism in particular. See Hexter, "John Boswell's Gay Science."

14. Boswell, "Jews, Gay People, and Bicycle Riders," 1:07:01.

15. Boswell, "Jews, Gay People, and Bicycle Riders."

16. The literature on secularization is too vast to address here, but for a classic example, see Asad, *Formations of the Secular*. At the very least, Boswell's theory makes it difficult to explain social forces like Islamophobia.

17. Boyarin, Itzkovitz, and Pellegrini, *Queer Theory and the Jewish Question*, 1. Interestingly, Boswell's colleague Hexter, in defending Boswell from accusations of essentialism, cites the example of Jews: "While no one doubts that the history of the Jews has a coherence of a different sort from whatever problematic coherence a history of 'gay people' might have, for all sorts of reasons (temporal, geographical, definitional), it is worth pointing out that there is no little "construction" involved in the narration of the history of even so well- (and self-) identified a group" (Hexter, "John Boswell's Gay Science," 40). Boswell also agrees; he responds to his critics by noting the incoherency of many categories we use transhistorically, including "Jew." See "Jews, Bicycle Riders, and Gay People," 206n2. In this point I agree, although perhaps not in the ways he intends; "Jews" is as equally incoherent a historical category as "gays" is.

18. Jakobsen, "Queers Are Like Jews, Aren't They?," esp. 65--72.

19. For example, he tells the audience that the original plan for *CSTH* was an extended analysis of the parallels between Jews and gays ("Jews, Gay People, and Bicycle Riders"). Boswell's analogy between Jews and gays inspired other writers; Gore Vidal wrote an essay that was both critical of Boswell's use of the term "gay" and inspired by the analogy. See Vidal, "Pink Triangle and Yellow Star." Hexter cites this essay in "John Boswell's Gay Science," 37, 51–52.

20. Borges, "John Wilkins' Analytical Language," 103.

21. The "Chinese" encyclopedia first appears in Borges's essay "John Wilkins' Analytical Language," which explores the work of the seventeenth-century philosopher. Wilkins attempted to create a universal language and imagines a taxonomy whereby he divides the universe into forty classes of objects. Borges describes how every class of objects had a prefix associated with it, made up of a consonant and a vowel. So linguistic meaning is supposed to be tied directly to the syllables of the word itself; the word is no longer an abstract sign but contains its own taxonomy of meaning. For a close reading of Borges's essay, see Duszat, "Foucault's Laughter."

22. Franz Kuhn was a translator of Chinese philosophical works into German (and was later targeted by the Nazis). Borges was aware of Kuhn's work; he reviewed some of Kuhn's translations. See Hubert, "Sinology on the Edge." For a reading of the Chinese encyclopedia that argues it was only partially fictional, see Youxiang, "Explicating the Classification."

23. Borges raises larger theoretical questions about the nature of taxonomy. He reflects at the end of the essay: "Obviously there is no classification of the universe that is not arbitrary and conjectural. The reason is very simple: we do not know what the universe is" ("John Wilkins' Analytical Language," 231). It is worth noting briefly some of the limitations of Borges's critique. He begins by complaining how "we have all suffered those unappealable debates in which a lady . . . swears that the word *luna* is more (or less) expressive than the word *moon*" (229). In other words, women stand in for the illogic of the relationship between signifier and signified.

24. Foucault, *Order of Things*, xv–xxiv. There is too much literature on the interpretation of the Chinese encyclopedia in Foucault's thought to list exhaustively here. For a piece that summarizes the two main branches of interpretation, see Wicks, "Literary Truth." Foucault's reference to being "accustomed to tame the wild profusion of existing things" may be deliberately using language of domestication to describe this taxonomy of animals, which does have a category of "tame" animals (*Order of Things*, xv). On Foucault, animality, and the Chinese encyclopedia, see Huot, "Chinese Dogs and French Scapegoats." It also may not be an accident that Foucault uses the example of aphasics in this section of the text; although much scholarship on animality disputes this claim, language is often used as the defining distinction between humans and animals. An aphasic human disrupts those divides.

25. Foucault, *Order of Things*, xx.

26. The relationship between D/deaf community and disability is contested ground. On this question, see Davis, *Enforcing Normalcy*; Burch and Kafer, *Deaf and Disability Studies*. On the influence of Foucault's work on Said and the connection to orientalism, see Bhatnagar, "Uses and Limits of Foucault."

27. Boswell's footnote suggests that he did not consult Borges directly but rather translated the passage from Foucault's French (Boswell, "Jews, Bicycle Riders, and Gay People," 226n35). This citation from Foucault is yet another example that undermines the misconception that Boswell and Foucault were diametrically opposed to one another, which has to do with the reception history of each scholar and the furor that arises over the essentialist/social constructionist debate. In an interview after the publication of Boswell's book, Foucault himself describes how Boswell's work influenced his thinking.

See O'Higgins, "Sexual Choice, Sexual Act." For an overview of that debate and Boswell's place in it, see Kuefler, *Boswell Thesis*, 1–34.

28. Boswell, "Jews, Bicycle Riders, and Gay People," 226. This quotation is from the published version of the essay, rather than the earlier talk. He does make changes between the recorded talk and the essay version, but the Chinese encyclopedia appears in both.

29. There are ways that racialization does appear in Boswell's essay. In the talk, Boswell makes a distinction between those subsets of the population that are deemed "different but equal" and those that are "inferior insiders" and uses the caste system as an example. The final published version of the essay changes the language of "different but equal" to "distinguishable insider." Presumably, Boswell recognized the way "different but equal" is freighted language in a US context, where "separate but equal" is a hallmark phrase from the 1896 Supreme Court decision that upheld segregation. Boswell seems remarkably sanguine about the possibility of "different but equal" leading to true equality, in the way that certain kinds of distinguishing characteristics (such as left-handedness) have become morally neutral. Moreover, using caste as the example displaces problems of hierarchy and racialization elsewhere. The relationship of the caste system to race is a source of ongoing scholarly and popular debate. See, e.g., the controversy that surrounded Isabel Wilkerson's book, *Caste*.

Boswell also retells a joke that appears in the Katherine Anne Porter novel *Ship of Fools*. The joke features a conversation between two passengers aboard a ship, one of whom is antisemitic. His (unsympathetic) listener finally interjects, "You're right. It's all their fault. It's the Jews and the bicycle riders." Confused, the Nazi sympathizer asks why the bicycle riders are responsible for society's ills. His interlocuter replies: "Why the Jews?" (Boswell, "Jews, Bicycle Riders, and Gay People," 227). In Boswell's hands this is a joke about the irrationality of intolerance, but it is also an oblique reference to the racialization of Jewishness under Nazi ideology.

30. The literature on the topic of Jews and racialization is too vast to summarize here. For a recent analysis of the culpability of Jews in the incarceration of Japanese Americans during World War II, which contains a survey of the literature, see Eisenberg, "State of the Field." On the question of studying Jews of color and the occlusion of the topic within Jewish studies, see Gordon, "Rarely Kosher."

31. Boswell, *CSTH*, 16.

32. Boswell, *CSTH*, 16–17.

33. Familial knowledge transmission is, of course, a fairly narrow concept of how survival skills are passed down in any community, including gay communities. See, as one small example, the pamphlet produced by the New York chapter of the Mattachine Society on what to do if you are arrested ("If You Are Arrested . . ."). For a classic description of the lesbian bar scene as a center of lesbian knowledge transmission, see Kennedy and Davis, *Boots of Leather, Slippers of Gold*. At the same time, any discussion of intergenerational knowledge transmission in queer communities inevitably gets tied to controversies over intergenerational sex and the accusation that queer and trans people are predators. I will discuss contemporary "grooming" accusations.

34. On the term "moral epidemic" and the response to HIV, see Petro, *After the Wrath of God*, 1–17.

35. Wertheimer, "Jews and the Jewish Birthrate," 39.

36. Wertheimer, "Jews and the Jewish Birthrate," 40. Wertheimer implicitly defends this line of argumentation by asserting that modern Orthodox women do not lag behind their counterparts in educational attainment and yet manage higher fertility rates. This is a tacit defense against accusations of sexism.

37. Berman, Rosenblatt, and Stahl, "Continuity Crisis." Keren McGinity, the author of several central texts on Jews and intermarriage, wrote a response to the piece, asking

the authors to consider the role of the "continuity crisis" in cementing traditional masculine roles; see McGinity, "Unfinished Business." This builds on her research found in her monograph; see McGinity, *Marrying Out.*

38. Berman, Rosenblatt, and Stahl, "Continuity Crisis," 186. The authors also describe how the rise of the study of Jewish demographics happened at the same time as white Jews in the United States were experiencing a status shift in the post-WWII era. Rising levels of acceptance of Jews were tied to rising Jewish fears of assimilation.

39. Kletenik and Neis, "What's the Matter with Jewish Studies?"; see also Kletenik and Neis, "Decolonizing Jewish Studies Part II."

40. Wertheimer, "Jews and the Jewish Birthrate," 40.

41. Kletenik and Neis, "What's the Matter with Jewish Studies?" The racialization of Jewish continuity politics could be contextualized within a broader panic about a "white future" in US politics. Three years after the National Jewish Population Survey that accelerated the panic about Jewish survival, Charles Murray wrote an editorial in the *Wall Street Journal* called "The Coming White Underclass," in which he argued that out-of-wedlock birth rates are the reason why Black people underperform economically when compared to their white counterparts. Noting the rise of "illegitimate" births among whites, Murray calls for the institution of "family values" in order to save the white character of the United States. Thus Jewish efforts at controlling reproduction might be better understood both as part of the process of racializing Jewishness and as participating in a broader white eugenic US discourse. See Murray, "Coming White Underclass." For a critique of Murray's work see Fields and Fields, *Racecraft,* 12–15. For an analysis of the way Murray was taken up in US sexual politics, see Moslener, *Virgin Nation,* 109–30.

42. The preface to *CSTH* contains a paragraph explaining why the book does not focus on women; he laments the way that the sources were primarily written by men and about men (xvii). In the question-and-answer section of his lecture on Jews and gays, one of the first questions is about the status of women. Boswell, while apologetic, refers to the limitations of the sources again, and the need for more research in the future ("Jews, Gay People, and Bicycle Riders").

43. Brooten, *Love between Women,* 12.

44. Marchal, *Appalling Bodies,* 16–21.

45. Dinshaw, "Touching on the Past"; Dinshaw, *Getting Medieval,* 22–34.

46. Dinshaw, "Touching on the Past." In *Getting Medieval,* she includes the Marc Bloch quote as an epigraph at the beginning of her introduction (1), but does not include the anecdote itself within her section on Boswell.

47. Dinshaw, "Touching on the Past," 57.

48. Boyarin, "Are There Any Jews?" He is citing Foucault, *History of Sexuality.*

49. Gill-Peterson, "Cis State."

50. There is a thriving field of trans historians addressing the question of the use of history in the current political moment. Both C. Riley Snorton and Gill-Peterson, for example, have brilliantly considered the implications of their historical analysis for contemporary political struggle. See Snorton, *Black on Both Sides,* vii–xiv; Gill-Peterson, *Histories of the Transgender Child,* 195–209. There is also a burgeoning subfield of trans history more generally. See, for example, the special issue of *TSQ* on trans history, DeVun and Tortorici, "Trans*historicities." Emily Skidmore has an excellent genealogy of the development of the field, with explanations of the importance of the work of Susan Stryker, Joanne Meyerowitz, and Clare Sears; see Stryker, *Transgender History*; Meyerowitz, *How Sex Changed*; Skidmore, "Recovering a Gender-Transgressive Past"; Sears, *Arresting Dress.* This is not a comprehensive list; the roundtable discussion in the special issue of *TSQ* helps to outline major directions in the field; see Bychowski, "'Trans*historicities': A Roundtable Discussion."

51. It is not an accident that both Boswell and Dinshaw refer to the Holocaust—Boswell in his citation of the joke about bicycle riders and Jews and Dinshaw in her citation of Marc Bloch's work. Using the Holocaust as a stand-in for Jewish history tends to reiterate an Ashkenazi focus, whether or not the Holocaust was actually only a European phenomenon. For one analysis of the broader impact of the Holocaust, see Boum and Stein, *The Holocaust and North Africa*. For an engagement with US history that is not Ashkenazi-focused, see Soomekh, *Sephardi and Mizrahi Jews in America*. For a collection of primary sources of Jews in the Americas (that emphasizes sources from Latin America and the Caribbean in addition to the United States and Canada), see Brodsky and Liebman, *Jews across the Americas*. This is far from a comprehensive list of challenges to Ashkenazi/white/European focused versions of Jewish history, but it is meant to suggest some recent directions of research.

52. Schotten, "TERFism, Zionism, and Right-Wing Annihilationism." In this article, Schotten traces TERF theology to Jewish Zionist lesbian separatist thought, as opposed to the traditional narratives that tend to locate TERF theology as originating out of Catholicism, with the work of Mary Daly and Janice Raymond.

53. For a discussion of the definition of grooming, see Craven, Brown, and Gilchrist, "Sexual Grooming of Children."

54. AncestralVril, "Gen Z." This tweet was cited in the study on "groomers," "Digital Hate." Another recent tweet from this user bemoans the Weimar Republic and celebrates its end; the account is openly antisemitic.

55. Gill-Peterson contests the perception that trans youth are a "new" problem. See Gill-Peterson, *Histories of the Transgender Child*.

56. Lore/tta LeMaster writes about the way "groomer" rhetoric projects apocalypticism onto trans bodies. See LeMaster, "Interrogating 'the End.'"

References

@AncestralVril. "Gen Z." Twitter, June 1, 2022, 10:15 a.m. https://twitter.com/AncestralVril/status/1532003025304297472.

Asad, Talal. *Formations of the Secular: Christianity, Islam, Modernity*. Stanford, CA: Stanford University Press, 2003.

Berman, Lila Corwin, Kate Rosenblatt, and Ronit Y. Stahl. "Continuity Crisis: The History and Sexual Politics of an American Jewish Communal Project." *American Jewish History* 104, nos. 2–3 (2020): 167–95.

Bhatnagar, Rashmi. "Uses and Limits of Foucault: A Study of the Theme of Origins in Edward Said's 'Orientalism.'" *Social Scientist* 14, no. 7 (1986): 3–22. https://doi.org/10.2307/3517247.

Borges, Jorge Luis. "John Wilkins' Analytical Language." In *Selected Non-Fictions*, edited by Eliot Weinberger, translated by Esther Allen, Suzanne Jill Levine, and Eliot Weinberger, 229–33. New York: Penguin, 1999.

Boswell, John. *Christianity, Social Tolerance, and Homosexuality: Gay People in Western Europe from the Beginning of the Christian Era to the Fourteenth Century*. Chicago: University of Chicago Press, 1980.

Boswell, John. "Jews, Bicycle Riders, and Gay People: The Determination of Social Consensus and Its Impact on Minorities." *Yale Journal of Law and Humanities* 1, no. 2 (1989): 205–28.

Boswell, John. "Jews, Gay People, and Bicycle Riders." *Nothing to Hide*. Lecture on public access WYOU Community Television, Madison, WI, April 25, 1986. https://www.youtube.com/watch?v=DwEAZNdJ-J4.

Boum, Aomar, and Sarah Abrevaya Stein, eds. *The Holocaust and North Africa*. Stanford, CA: Stanford University Press, 2019.

Boyarin, Daniel. "Are There Any Jews in 'The History of Sexuality'?" *Journal of the History of Sexuality* 5, no. 3 (1995): 333–55.

Boyarin, Daniel, Daniel Itzkovitz, and Ann Pellegrini, eds. *Queer Theory and the Jewish Question*. New York: Columbia University Press, 2003.

Brodsky, Adriana M., and Laura Arnold Liebman, eds. *Jews across the Americas: A Sourcebook. 1492–Present*. New York: New York University Press, 2023.

Brooten, Bernadette. *Love between Women: Early Christian Responses to Female Homoeroticism*. Chicago: University of Chicago Press, 1996.

Burch, Susan, and Alison Kafer, eds. *Deaf and Disability Studies: Interdisciplinary Perspectives*. Washington, DC: Gallaudet University Press, 2010.

Bychowski, M. W., Howard Chiang, Jack Halberstam, Jacob Lau, Kathleen P. Long, Marcia Ochoa, C. Riley Snorton, Leah DeVun, and Zeb Tortorici. "'Trans*historicities': A Roundtable Discussion." In DeVun and Tortorici, "Trans*historicities."

Chen, Mel. *Animacies: Biopolitics, Racial Mattering, and Queer Affect*. Durham, NC: Duke University Press, 2012.

Cooper, Andrea Dara. "Writing Humanimals: Critical Animal Studies and Jewish Studies." *Religion Compass* 13, no. 12 (2019): e12341. https://doi.org/10.1111/rec3.12341.

Craven, Samantha, Sarah Brown, and Elizabeth Gilchrist. "Sexual Grooming of Children: Review of Literature and Theoretical Considerations." *Journal of Sexual Aggression* 12, no. 3 (2006): 287–99. https://doi.org/10.1080/13552600601069414.

Davis, Lennard. *Enforcing Normalcy: Disability, Deafness, and the Body*. London: Verso Books, 1995.

DeVun, Leah, and Zeb Tortorici, eds. "Trans*historicities." *TSQ* 5, no. 4 (2018): 515–719.

"Digital Hate: Social Media's Role in Amplifying Dangerous Lies about LGBTQ+ People." Center for Countering Digital Hate and the Human Rights Campaign, August 10, 2022. https://hrc-prod-requests.s3-us-west-2.amazonaws.com/CCDH-HRC-Digital -Hate-Report-2022-single-pages.pdf.

Dinshaw, Carolyn. *Getting Medieval: Sexualities and Communities, Pre- and Postmodern*. Durham, NC: Duke University Press, 1999.

Dinshaw, Carolyn. "Touching on the Past." In *The Boswell Thesis*, edited by Matthew Kuefler, 57–73. Chicago: University of Chicago Press, 2005.

Duggan, Lisa. *The Twilight of Equality? Neoliberalism, Cultural Politics, and the Attack on Democracy*. Boston: Beacon, 2003. http://archive.org/details/twilightofequalioolisa.

Duszat, Michael. "Foucault's Laughter: Enumeration, Rewriting, and the Construction of the Essayist in Borges's 'The Analytical Language of John Wilkins.'" *Orbis Litterarum* 67, no. 3 (2012): 193–218.

Edelman, Lee. *No Future: Queer Theory and the Death Drive*. Durham, NC: Duke University Press, 2004. https://www.dukeupress.edu/no-future.

Eisenberg, Ellen. "State of the Field: Jews and Others." *American Jewish History* 102, no. 2 (2018): 283–301. https://doi.org/10.1353/ajh.2018.0022.

Fields, Barbara J., and Karen E. Fields. *Racecraft: The Soul of Inequality in American Life*. Brooklyn: Verso Books, 2022.

Foucault, Michel. *The History of Sexuality, Volume 1: An Introduction*. Translated by Robert Hurley. New York: Vantage Books, 1990.

Foucault, Michel. *The Order of Things: An Archaeology of the Human Sciences*. Translated by Alan Sheridan. London: Routledge, 2002.

Gill-Peterson, Jules. *Histories of the Transgender Child*. Minneapolis: University of Minnesota Press, 2018.

Gill-Peterson, Jules. "The Cis State." *Sad Brown Girl* (blog), April 14, 2021. https:// sadbrowngirl.substack.com/p/the-cis-state.

Gordon, Lewis R. "Rarely Kosher: Studying Jews of Color in North America." *American Jewish History* 100, no. 1 (2016): 105–16. https://doi.org/10.1353/ajh.2016.0006.

Halperin, David M. *How to Do the History of Homosexuality*. Chicago: University of Chicago Press, 2002.

Halperin, David M. *One Hundred Years of Homosexuality : And Other Essays on Greek Love*. New York: Routledge, 1990.

Hayward, Eva, and Jami Weinstein. "Introduction: Tranimalities in the Age of Trans* Life." *TSQ* 2, no. 2 (2015): 195–208. https://doi.org/10.1215/23289252-2867446.

Hexter, Ralph. "John Boswell's Gay Science: Prolegomenon to a Re-reading." In *The Boswell Thesis*, edited by Matthew Kuefler, 35–57. Chicago: University of Chicago Press, 2006.

Hubert, Rosario. "Sinology on the Edge: Borges's Reviews of Chinese Literature (1937–1942)." *Variaciones Borges*, no. 39 (2015): 81–101.

Huot, Claire. "Chinese Dogs and French Scapegoats: An Essay in Zoonomastics." In *Foucault and Animals*, edited by Matthew Chrulew and Dinesh Joseph Wadiwel, 37–59. Leiden, Netherlands: Brill, 2016.

Jakobsen, Janet. "Queers Are Like Jews, Aren't They? Analogy and Alliance Politics." In *Queer Theory and the Jewish Question*, edited by Daniel Boyarin, Daniel Itzkovitz, and Ann Pellegrini, 64–89. New York: Columbia University Press, 2003.

Jordan, Mark. "'Both as a Christian and as a Historian': On Boswell's Ministry." In *The Boswell Thesis*, edited by Matthew Kuefler, 88–110. Chicago: University of Chicago Press, 2006.

Jordan, Mark. Foreword to *Christianity, Social Tolerance, and Homosexuality*, 35th anniv. ed., by John Boswell, xv–xxi. Chicago: University of Chicago Press, 2015.

Kennedy, Elizabeth Lapovsky, and Madeline D. Davis. *Boots of Leather, Slippers of Gold: The History of a Lesbian Community*, New York: Routledge, 1993.

Kletenik, Gilah, and Rafael Rachel Neis. "Decolonizing Jewish Studies Part II: A Response to the Backlash." *Religion Dispatches*, May 5, 2021. https://religiondispatches.org/decolonizing-jewish-studies-part-ii-a-response-to-the-backlash/.

Kletenik, Gilah, and Rafael Rachel Neis. "What's the Matter with Jewish Studies? Sexism, Harassment, and Neoliberalism for Starters." *Religion Dispatches*, April 19, 2021. https://religiondispatches.org/whats-the-matter-with-jewish-studies-sexism-harassment-and-neoliberalism-for-starters/.

Kuefler, Mathew, ed. *The Boswell Thesis: Essays on Christianity, Social Tolerance, and Homosexuality*. Chicago: University of Chicago Press, 2006.

LeMaster, Lore/tta. "Interrogating 'the End,' Becoming 'the End.'" *Review of Communication* 22, no. 2 (2022): 153–56. https://doi.org/10.1080/15358593.2022.2074800.

Lipton, Sara. *Dark Mirror: The Medieval Origins of Anti-Jewish Iconography*. New York: Henry Holt, 2014.

Marchal, Joseph. *Appalling Bodies: Queer Figures before and after Paul's Letters*. Oxford: Oxford University Press, 2019.

Mattachine Society of N.Y. "If You Are Arrested . . . : The Pocket Lawyer." https://www.nypl.org/events/tours/audio-guides/treasures-audio-guide-verbal-descriptions/item/5524.

McGinity, Keren R. "American Jewry's #MeToo Problem: A First-Person Encounter." *Jewish Telegraphic Agency* (blog), June 21, 2018. https://www.jta.org/2018/06/21/ny/american-jewrys-metoo-problem-a-first-person-encounter.

McGinity, Keren R. *Marrying Out: Jewish Men, Intermarriage, and Fatherhood*. Bloomington: Indiana University Press, 2014.

McGinity, Keren R. "The Unfinished Business of the Sexual Revolution." *American Jewish History* 104, no. 2 (2020): 207–13.

Meyerowitz, Joanne. *How Sex Changed: A History of Transsexuality in the United States.* Cambridge, MA: Harvard University Press, 2002.

Moslener, Sara. *Virgin Nation: Sexual Purity and American Adolescence.* Oxford: Oxford University Press, 2015.

Muñoz, José Esteban. *Cruising Utopia: The Then and There of Queer Futurity.* New York: New York University Press, 2009.

Murray, Charles. "The Coming White Underclass." *Wall Street Journal*, October 29, 1993.

Ober, Holly. "New Journal Will Spotlight Queer and Trans Religious Studies Scholarship." *UC Riverside News*, February 2, 2022. https://news.ucr.edu/articles/2022/02/02/new-journal-will-spotlight-queer-and-trans-religious-studies-scholarship.

O'Higgins, James. "Sexual Choice, Sexual Act: An Interview with Michel Foucault." *Salmagundi*, nos. 58–59 (1982–83): 10–23.

Petro, Anthony M. *After the Wrath of God: AIDS, Sexuality, and American Religion.* Oxford: Oxford University Press, 2015.

Porter, Katherine Anne. *Ship of Fools.* Boston: Little, Brown, 1962.

Pushaw, Christina. "Anti-Grooming Bill." Twitter, March 4, 2022, 6:33 p.m. https://twitter.com/christinapushaw/status/1499890719691051008.

Schlager, Bernard. "Reading *CSTH* as a Call to Action: Boswell and Gay-Affirming Movements in American Christianity." In *The Boswell Thesis*, edited by Mathew Kuefler, 74–88. Chicago: University of Chicago Press, 2006.

Schotten, C. Heike. "TERFism, Zionism, and Right-Wing Annihilationism: Toward an Internationalist Genealogy of Extinction Phobia." *TSQ* 9, no. 3 (2022): 334–64. https://doi.org/10.1215/23289252-9836022.

Sears, Clare. *Arresting Dress: Cross-Dressing, Law, and Fascination in Nineteenth-Century San Francisco.* Perverse Modernities. Durham, NC: Duke University Press, 2014.

Skidmore, Emily. "Recovering a Gender-Transgressive Past." In *A Companion to American Women's History*, 2nd ed., edited by Nancy A. Hewitt and Anne M. Valk, 209–22. Hoboken, NJ: John Wiley and Sons, 2020.

Snorton, C. Riley. *Black on Both Sides: A Racial History of Trans Identity.* Minneapolis: University of Minnesota Press, 2017.

Soomekh, Saba, ed. *Sephardi and Mizrahi Jews in America: The Jewish Role in American Life.* West Lafayette, IN: Purdue University Press, 2015.

Stryker, Susan. *Transgender History: The Roots of Today's Revolution.* 2nd ed. New York: Seal, 2017.

Stryker, Susan. "Transgender History, Homonormativity, and Disciplinarity." *Radical History Review* 2008, no. 100 (2008): 145–57. https://doi.org/10.1215/01636545-2007-026.

Teter, Magda. *Blood Libel: On the Trail of an Anti-Semitic Myth.* Cambridge, MA: Harvard University Press, 2020.

Vidal, Gore. "Pink Triangle and Yellow Star." In *Pink Triangle and Yellow Star and Other Essays (1976–1982)*, 167–84. New York: HarperCollins, 1983.

Wertheimer, Jack. "Jews and the Jewish Birthrate." *Commentary* 120, no. 3 (2005): 39–44.

Wicks, Robert. "Literary Truth as Dreamlike Expression in Foucault's and Borges's 'Chinese Encyclopedia.'" *Philosophy and Literature* 27, no. 1 (2003): 80–97. https://doi.org/10.1353/phl.2003.0032.

Wilkerson, Isabel. *Caste: The Origins of Our Discontents.* New York: Random House, 2020.

Youxiang, Tu. "Explicating the Classification of the Chinese Encyclopedia Enumerated by Borges." *Theory, Culture, and Society* 24, nos. 7–8 (2007): 310–11.

Shame

JOY LADIN

Woe to the one who says to a father,
"What have you begotten?"
or to a mother,
"What have you brought to birth?"
—Isaiah 45:10

"I Was Shamed By My Whole Town for Getting an Abortion"
—https://www.cosmopolitan.com/politics/a27572832/i-had
-abortion-in-alabama/

Ashamed of what you are and aren't,
you struggle to stay connected,
part of the family, part of the culture
that sometimes makes you feel like a monster,
telling yourself
you're the opposite of brave,
that whatever you are is the opposite
of what I meant to make.
How dare you question
what I create?
Your shame and your panic,
your sex and your rage,
where you're broken
and where you break—
I bore them, I bear them, I open the gates
of privilege and stigma
so even you can see
the image—my image—
in which you are created.
You can hide from everyone, child,
but you can't hide from me.

QTR • A Journal of Trans and Queer Studies in Religion • 1:1 • May 2024
DOI: 10.1215/29944724-11208947 © 2024 Joy Ladin

I'm your calamity and your queen,
the truth from which there's no protection,
the heaven that stretches equally
over victory and shame.
I foretold you long ago. Declared
to the ends of the earth
I would be your potter
and you would be my clay.
A storehouse I'd fill with treasure.
A habitation for my name.
Matter fashioned into revelation.
A cloud
from which I rain.

Joy Ladin has published ten books of poetry, including National Jewish Book Award winner *The Book of Anna* (2007), Lambda Literary Award finalists *Transmigration* (2009) and *Impersonation* (2015), and her most recent work, *Shekhinah Speaks* (2022). She has also published a memoir, *Through the Door of Life: A Jewish Journey between Genders* (2013), and a book of trans theology, *The Soul of a Stranger: Reading God and the Torah from a Transgender Perspective* (2018). Her writing is available at https://joyladin.wordpress.com.

Acknowledgments
This poem previously appeared in *Shekhinah Speaks* (Chicago: selva oscura, 2022) and has been reprinted with permission.

CREATIVE CONTRIBUTION

Resounding Shadows
A Visual Journey through
{spirit   forged}

SA SMYTHE

ABSTRACT This creative-critical essay is a refracted meditation on the spirit of sound and shadow-work through SA Smythe's original sound composition and performance activation *{spirit   forged}* (2023), with accompanying visual documentation. The work was in part a response to Amartey Golding's Spring 2023 installation, *In the comfort of embers*, commissioned by the Power Plant Contemporary Art Gallery in Tkaronto. Smythe reflects on the ecology of thought that laid the foundation for their own transmedia theories and practices, including moments of ancestral whispers, the interplay of light and darkness, sonic alchemy, and abiding reverence for the problematic of Black belonging. Delving into sound and its intimate vessels in a meditation on cultural memory, "Resounding Shadows" revels in liminal fusion of form, inviting the reader to join the traversal of spirit work where personal and collective journeys intertwine.

KEYWORDS spirit, resonance, shadow, Caribbean, performance, belonging

> *resound* (v): to produce or become filled with sound;
> to become renowned

> Let our rejoicing rise
> high as the list'ning skies
> let it resound loud as the rolling sea
> —James Weldon Johnson, "Lift Ev'ry Voice and Sing"

Across the yawn of ancestry and violence, the long shadows of grief and transformation engendered by the weathers that weather us well beyond our corporeal shells, how do we resound ourselves and Self? Whither the capacity to shore up enough shelter along the seas of our collective spirit when the container of our fleshly form remains insufficient?

The seeds of those questions have gnawed at me, taking root across the network of my life's work. These seeds got another field in which to flourish when I was invited to produce *{spirit   forged}*, a soundscape composition and live performance activation for Amartey Golding's installation, *In*

QTR • A Journal of Trans and Queer Studies in Religion • 1:1 • May 2024
DOI: 10.1215/29944724-11208956 © 2024 SA Smythe
119

Figure 1. Gathering behind the shadows. Amartey Golding's The Being and SA Smythe, *{spirit   forged}* (2023). Photograph by Hyerim Han. Courtesy of The Power Plant Contemporary Art Gallery.

the comfort of embers. Both installation and performance were curated and programmed by Joséphine Denis, then assistant curator for special projects at the Power Plant Contemporary Art Gallery in Tkaronto, Canada. What follows is a journey aided by the visual documentation of that work, interwoven with meditations of the memories, elements, and kin that engendered it.

In one beginning, I hear an echo of this memory. There's me, age seven or eight, craning my neck toward my great uncle's old Victrola-styled phonograph. A multitoned cabinet of rich, worn wood around my height hulked in the corner of my family's parlor, filling the room with sounds ranging from dub to rocksteady to calypso to gospel soul, especially on Saturday afternoons. *One step . . . beyond!* cried Prince Buster on the eponymous B-Side to his 1964 record, *Al Capone*. It was a sort of proto-ska and sound system number replete with unrestrained horns on the largely instrumental track aside from the reverbed herald of the title shouted over intervals. I can hear the iconic *chug-a-*

chck, chug-a-chck, chug-a-chck that Buster popularized along with other jaunty toasting—a Jamaican iteration of rap, scat, and beatboxing—ring out, a little tinny from the record spinning atop the cabinet. I would always stand near it, hovering on the periphery of the buzzing social life and adult conversation that the space harbored. I'd inch toward the dampening doors until I caught the eye of some auntie or other and was inevitably shooed away, lest I break or spill something. Sometimes I'd go unnoticed enough to peer into the horn, close enough to let my breath fall flatly down into the imperceptible dark of the grill, studying the contraption, curious about what made it churn on its own like that, a small eternity after one of my relatives, usually a man of my grandfather's generation, stopped winding the arm that usually stood at haughty attention on one side.

One step beyond . . . Soon enough, we'd hear it: the sound of the stylus hitting the run-out area, that space on a vinyl record between the end of the music and the center label. It sounded like wood chips quietly popping in a dancing fire. I called it "dread wax" then, after mishearing "dead wax," the colloquial description of that strip of material. It evoked for me the gurgling sounds I'd hear from the grill outside, hood propped up against the limestone and elevated on top of cement blocks, scenes of cracked pimiento seeds and other seasons splayed out atop a fresh piece of fish—always under twelve inches long, per tradition—as my Rasta uncle, my mother's older brother, patiently attended the helm. It seemed magical to me, an arcane and Babylon thing, the way the vinyl would spin and its handle would move independently. *How does it do that?* I'd wonder, sometimes aloud. *Ah jus suh it go*, they'd say, a wearisome refrain and an eternally unsatisfying response commonly doled out to we children. Once, I asked an older cousin who was visiting us up in the bush, in a litany of my infamous *whys*. *Muss ah di duppy dem*, he enthused, wide-eyed and vexatious. I'd mostly learned not to believe him by then, but still. Duppies?! One never knew what could be haunting a place like this, this town in Cockpit Country, where our first maroons fled into a hard-fought freedom, whose name we yet struggle to pronounce. For a while after that, whenever someone opened the cabinet to turn a record over, I would hold vigil, *just in case*, until someone came along to lift the needle and return the spirits into their dark silence. I kept a few of my treasures underneath for a time, some shells from the river, fool's gold, a marble, a palm frond carefully folded into a cross. My first altar, a conspiracy colluding underneath sound with literal ghosts in the machine making mischief and memory. Felled by murder or disease, distanced by the theft of time and the collective sensorium's divorcement by modernity, there's no one with whom I might replay the shared memories to see if I got it right. But that's not the question worth inhabiting. *One step beyond!* Decades later for the performance of *{spirit   forged}*, I remain gripped by the echo, seduced by the abeyance of precision.

I posed the question, "How might we resound with deep intention?," ever obsessed with the questions surrounding who, how, and where *we* be. To whom we belong and what stories undergird the stakes of those attachments. The

Figure 2. Seated at the sound altar. SA Smythe, *{spirit   forged}* (2023). Photograph by Hyerim Han. Courtesy of The Power Plant Contemporary Art Gallery.

verb *resound* denotes "to sound again" or "to sing the praises of." Its adjective, *resounding*, adds dynamic depth, invoking sonic emphasis to convey something unmistakable, indelible, something superlative or otherwise significant. The prefix *re-* signals a return to some originary place, as well as an undoing or evolution from those once-familiar grounds. The production of *{spirit   forged}* was thus a resounding experiment, a memory-bound and spirit-forward study in sounding, again and otherwise. The soundscape for the live performance composed a multichannel sound field that I dubbed the "Hearkener's Nexus." It utilized the [proclivity] machine that I previously codesigned with Tina Tallon, a creative technologist and sound artist with whom I was able to collaborate and learn from during our year in Italy as individual recipients of the 2021–22 Rome Prize (in Musical Composition and Modern Italian Studies) awarded by the American Academy in Rome. The [proclivity] machine was developed for the world premiere of */proclivity/*, a performance commissioned by Black Italian curator and artistic director Johanne Affricot. It was presented in the historic all-Black artist exhibition *Sediments: After Memory* (2022) for her Black-led curatorial team at Spazio Griot's first-of-its-kind takeover of the Mattatoio Museum in Rome. Tallon and I used the open-source environment and visual programming language Pure Data, which I have since supplemented with Ableton and Audacity for subsequent digital productions. The physical aspect of the Hearkener's Nexus included a sound field's asymmetrical speaker placement throughout the installation, mostly tucked into various corners on the floor and in the shadowy edges toward the ceiling. I further arranged the soundscape and performance space with live instruments (a violin, a theremin, percussive finger bells, syncopated voice and breath work, and ocarinas from my father's hometown of Puerto Limón).

The base notes of the soundscape were layered from field recordings of found objects and substances, reverberating across the audio channels as though responding to one another's calls. For the antiphonal rejoinder, I mixed prearranged instrumentation that swelled into improvised interludes. I took turns with the live instruments and a loop pedal that allowed freedom to improvise the order and return of certain sounds and distortions. There was also the fleeting top note of the audience's intermittent percussion (a clap, a shake of the bell, a throat clearing), enduring witness as we journeyed through the gallery. I solicited impromptu storytelling besides my own; as my echoey prerecorded voice implored, *Tell me a story*, or asked, *Who is your story?*, I spent a few moments waiting with an outstretched microphone and a patient gaze. I quickly spliced some of that as the composition's outro, saving it all for later iterations of the Hearkener's Nexus, the field of which (spatial, sonic, and otherwise) gets more intricate and entangled with every performance—like interdependent life does the more it is lived.

The ninety-minute score integrated sampled recitations of more stories, arranged into a type of recitative (a *récitatif*, between song and speech) to my choreographed gestures of sound and shadow-work. The resulting atmosphere felt both overflowing and sparse, responsive and fractal. We bore witness, committed to the possibility of kin beyond ken and in pursuit of the body as a divining rod. It was a joy, a balm to allow ritual and re-memory to serve as collaborative guides through Golding's transatlantic and transcultural offering, which guided and transformed me in return such that suddenly, *we*.[1] We be the ghosts. We resound the machine.

....

Ancestrally kinetic, historic, and rooted—which is to say, embodied by the seeded grace of sacred African and Afro-diasporic reworlding practices—this piece sought spirit as the catalyst that has wrought (forged) elemental convergences that have ushered us, a *we*, forth. Fundamentally, it was a challenge to

Figure 3. An offering of protection from four continents. SA Smythe, *{spirit forged}* (2023). Photograph by Hyerim Han. Courtesy of The Power Plant Contemporary Art Gallery.

relinquish any aloof or distanced awareness of public from the Self. To allow myself the healing space of discomposure. I had to work my way through the shadow of the vestibular, as in Hortense Spillers in "Mama's Baby, Papa's Maybe." Through the "light beyond metaphor" in Derek Walcott's "The Sea Is History." In the marrow of a Black trans nonbinary body nominally mine, I am intimately familiar with the vestibule. Parts of me remain coercively interstitialized as and against the gender line, Black on all sides, beached and shoaled and thus attuned to similarly vast and indeterminate things. In the mediated confluence of performance, I succumbed deeper into the space of the emblematic interstitial: the antechamber to the door of no return, the passage, the score, the Self. Elements and noumena coursing through the space between us required an urgent adjustment, a disorientation imagining that no such space exists. In the spirit of Black traditions like call and response, this performance activation was an opportunity to sound (out) and feel through a presentation of physical and ephemeral Black and trans diasporic memory work and other methods into a conversation (a dwelling, an assembly), into an installation saturated with reflections about history, violence, materiality, the body, masculinity, and domination. Loving possibility and healing emerge in careful relation, adorning our bodies as capacious and atomic instruments. Sounding again to a syncopated grief and history's ruptured beat, we began counting out a measure of what Ashon Crawley has also hailed as otherwise possibility.[2] The apparent chasm between the curlicue brackets of {spirit   forged} is an invitation. A place held. An affirmation that possibility matters, one step beyond. The stories of "our" "own" particles friction "there," take up room "then." Of all the forms and versions (selves, mediums, genres, borders) I've worked in relation to, sound art–performance has offered the most concentrated tinctures of the possible.

In one beginning, the elements. As his title gestures, the element of fire is a leitmotif throughout Golding's installation of video, photography, narrative, and conditionally wearable garments. One, *Chainmail 3 (Puffer Jacket)*, is a 166-kilogram structure that the audience can touch and wear; the other is a handcrafted garment held in humanoid shape by a mannequin and featuring hundreds of thousands of strands of human hair designed and maintained in various protective styles. Specifically, Golding hails the embers, those small and usually waning portions of a fire that lingers on. The possible seed for another roaring blaze, always a nod on the verge of creation and destruction.[3] In response, I turn to the spirit of water, which holds a similarly infinite dyad. It is an element that heals, purifies, destroys, overwhelms. Fire is in part a thermal and radiant source of energy, producing heat and light. Water also conveys kinetic energy. As the lands across our planet continue to freeze and overheat in extremis, as volcanoes erupt, wildfires and storms rage and seas boil, as the physical uninhabitability spreads toward the ontological one on this earth, as flora and fauna rebel, refuse, and herald the ongoing catastrophe, it is clear we are in medias res to multiple elemental reckonings. They are in turns incalculable, imminent, necessary, and utterly devastating. The majority of us do not need these reminders that we have been asymmetrically bestowed, but we must bear witness nevertheless.

The ecology of the soundscape and activation considers harboring memory the way that water does, considers the fires this time and the next. Waterways abound into every horizon. "The sea is history," averred Caribbean poet and playwright Derek Walcott in his eponymous poem. "All beginning in water, all ending in water," muses Dionne Brand in *A Map to the Door of No Return*.[4] Behold these resounding elements, these energetic fountains. Witness with Lucille Clifton's observation in "the mississippi river runs into the gulf" that "every water is the same water coming round." There is something seductive in the wry litany, the gentle admonishment in antagonism of Time's feckless hold as "everyday someone is standing on the edge / of this river, staring into time, / whispering mistakenly: / only here. only now."[5] To have a knowledge about the futility of the experience of finite physical life in tandem with the compulsion to repeat it anyway: written confluently—that is, flowing along the same rivers of realization, or concurrently oriented toward shared ecological and genealogical sense, Alexis Pauline Gumbs urges us in *Undrowned: Black Feminist Lessons from Marine Mammals* to "trust that all water touches all water everywhere."[6] Healing is as inevitable as the tide, in Golding's self-descriptions of his work. Stuck on by what C. Riley Snorton marks in "The Gospel of Thon" (alternately known as "Nonbinary Archives and the Grammar of Experience") as the *when* of nonbinary experience, I aspire to breathe life into that inevitability: who needs *when*, when we know *that*?

In one beginning, always the breath. So be it. Let the expansion and deflation of lungs resound, loud as the rolling sea. After all, we yearn for a respite that is already ours, for freedom by every name, a clearing place to escape the constant nonconsensual noise of organized abandonment, the cacophony of catastrophe. To *we*. The concept of it in some nondual spiritual traditions is always that the Self, which we imagine as bound/binding in familiar syntax, is always already unfettered. There in the breath, underneath the soft hum of eyelids closed in the comfort of a single ember as the whole flame, a solitary wave as a whole sea. Realize, then, that the ecology of we and the individuated contours of our emotions-thoughts-energies, our sense-selves can readily attune to the heartbeat of this world; moreover, they are a crucial piece of the un-cartographic orientation to the next. You are a part of this cycle, this we in process. We might follow Romain Rolland and acknowledge this assemblage as oceanic feeling.[7] Whoever you are now is in deep relation with the eternity of what has always been there. Do you wish someone (past, present, or future) was with you? Take one step beyond. Who says they aren't?

After a journey through the expanse of the otherwise brightly lit gallery, it begins again. A murmur. A dim corridor. A thick darkness creeps up the installation's deep, crimson walls such that you feel the need to squint to see the ceiling or into the distance as your eyes search for any small, tangible thing

Figure 4. A chiaroscuro into the vestibular. SA Smythe, *{spirit forged}* (2023). Photograph by Hyerim Han. Courtesy of The Power Plant Contemporary Art Gallery.

in the void. The darkness is thicker than what your eyes allow. There is something beyond it, you're sure, as sounds creep around the corner. Crackling, humming, mechanically deepened voices blend their lowest pitches with the pitch of the dark, setting the tone and symbolizing the liminal threshold between the known and the unknown just below the surface of visual perception. In this space of ritual, the audience members instinctively sidle up together and eventually come shoulder to shoulder, looking side to side for where to stand. Soft murmurs continue.

The you in the neophyte we is slowly getting immersed in a rapture of collective making, where boundaries blur and energies converge. Barefoot in a zaffer-colored floor-length hooded robe of crushed velvet, whose hem trails an ocean behind me, I take up a five-count measure and emerge from a gallery vestibule, marking time and people with subtle steps and gestures from my hands wrapped in laced gloves. With the flick of a wrist, the curled stroke of an index finger begins brushing against the air, the wall space in between people, beckoning to cast their gazes deeper into the dark. From beneath the folds of soft fabric come the bronze and gold and silver finger bells. I shake them to the measure I made, and place a few into the hands of those with the most unwavering eye contact, those whose shadow-kissed faces seem like kindred in possibility, for the time being. Some of us will come to lay them at the feet of the Hair Garment, some of us take them home. Drawing back the hood from my head reveals a chain-mail headpiece, links matching the Puffer Jacket suspended in the air within. I gather some of the fabric of my rope and regard the stories of multiple presences sewn into the hem. No one follows. I turn back and hold the same calculating index finger to my lips, the other index finger toward the dark. Susurrations eke out and crescendo from the soundscape echoing into the corridor from the indecipherable fog. Crunching leaves, crackling kindling, urgent talking, and deep-pitched humming that seems to interrupt itself. A shriek of laughter. All gather toward a harmonious chorus. This is the first wave of intermittent repetitive gestures choreographed to mirror and/or precede the the Hearkener's Nexus, disrupting the temporal order of the traditional call and response. Sometimes the response augurs the call.

We round the corner toward the embers of light that flicker forth from a large installation screen featuring Golding's three short films. Sonically dowsing the moody flames visualized on screen and mimicked in the soundscape (shaking wax paper like a rug, sprinkling fistfuls of rice grains onto a sheet of aluminum), a rush of ocean water flows on its own cue, frolicking into an irreverent wind, simmering into silence as my uncle's digitally distorted drawl rises into focus, stretched and slowed right after beginning to share a story, a series of moments in a prerecorded conversation during his childhood in Lowe River and Spanish Town: *Suh mi just wan fi seh sum'n bout growing up in Jamaica . . .* The story continues, audibly though indiscernibly, as you realize that ears strain to hear the message.

How to resound a sustaining story, relishing the stakes of our magnitude and bond? We have many recipes for the Blackhood, this we of us. The animating force of Gwendolyn Brooks and her South Side, Derek Walcott's Saint Lucia, my father's Costa Rica, Glissant's Caribbean, Golding's Scotland, my Wales. His Ghana, our Jamaica. Our Xaymaca. The "there" from whence Mahmoud Darwish comes.[8] A mango tree tended by mother's father's mother, one they say came true and grew as tall as it was because after some relative tossed the pit into the ground, she claimed responsibility to and for it, nurturing it into sweetness until it blessed my generation. Across the ongoing antagonisms of this world as the sociogenic principles bleed (us) into ontogenetic ones, there lies a shadow realm of spirit and its demands. It grabs the edges of our stories with its carnivalesque teeth. We see the shadows. We (think) we are working to access them. We are, as ever, wrought—and distraught—in return.

Figure 5. Communing with The Being. SA Smythe, *{spirit   forged}* (2023). Photograph by Hyerim Han. Courtesy of The Power Plant Contemporary Art Gallery.

The freedom in performance includes bringing in collaborators from every realm, especially gestural, spiritual, sonic, and in this instance with the audience members previously hailed to match the frequencies of certain sounds, atmospheric storytelling featuring the clear upturned vocals of dear friend Nalo Hopkinson reading an excerpt of a poem from her father, Slade Hopkinson, "The Madwoman of Papine: Two Cartoons with Captions" conversing through the narrative epigraph of her short story, "A Habit of Waste":[9]

> These are the latitudes of the ex-colonised,
> of degradation still unmollified,
> imported managers, styles in art,
> second-hand subsistence of the spirit,
> the habit of waste,
> mayhem committed on the personality,
> and everywhere the wrecked or scuttled mind.
> Scholars, more brilliant than I could hope to be,
> advised that if I valued poetry,
> I should eschew all sociology.[10]

In the beginning, beyond a threshold, circling the duality of light and darkness meets me as I delve deeper into my vestibular role. I enter the space on the other side of the looping video installation—one side awash in dim and shifting concentrations of light as the other is pitched with textured shadows in the dark. Deeper still into shadows at work. Shedding the robe with slow, elongated shrugs to reveal a reflective bronzed body suit, my searching and deliberate movements cast intricate shadows into that space, meeting and merging with other shadows, making more shadows that occasion us to linger over hidden and plural aspects of Self, the transformative power of embracing the shadows within. The veil has been lowered. The chainmail headdress I wore in the corridor was to be relinquished to a waiting busk, clear and glowing perpendicular to the layout. The boundaries between performer and viewer continue to waiver as we witness the hair sculpture together, witness each other witnessing it while my fingers play an invisible piano in the air and I lift my head. The resonance of the experience lingers in the shared space, then (and now, and here). Verbal quietude as a distilled flapping of wings and the crinkling of dried palm leaves soar across one audio channel. Somewhere, in the darkest corner, marimbas and other percussive gourds mirror heartbeats, pulse against one another. A deep, foundational bass vibrates against the walls; your own heartbeat cannot help but match it. These sounds remain for the rest of the performance, and long after, even when other sounds and rhythms ebb and flow. They invite us to witness *with* and *as* in the space of invocation of the depths of an inner darkness, where healing and growth intertwine.

All the while, Golding's three videos continue to play on, with "Bring Me to Heal 1," featuring a parable that he penned about the Running Horse and the Goose, interspliced with dreamlike scenes of The Being (interpreted by

Figure 6. Shedding the Self in search of spirit. SA Smythe, *{spirit   forged}* (2023). Photograph by Hyerim Han. Courtesy of The Power Plant Contemporary Art Gallery.

Amartey's brother and professional ballet dancer, Solomon Golding) wearing the hair garment as flesh and appendages. Nalo Hopkinson's processed voice returns, processed vocals are doubled up, converted to a deeper pitch, and delayed, reproducing in themselves in resounding chorus. My collaborators included my Caribbean kin (Nalo, Uncle Errol, Amartey, and other *Idren*), with the ancestral spirits working through and around us in this collaborative atelier of becoming through performance.

    {spirit   forged} was as much a collaboration as an accountable sonic relationship to the community of the Self. After all, "I" is as much of a fantastic

spiritual fiction as "solo" ever was. Perhaps it is rather one of our most sacred collaborations, obscured by the dispossessive grammars that we have inherited. Those of us enmeshed in the radical density of Black life know this fiction well. Sylvia Wynter tells us that stories are as much a part of what makes us who, what, and when we are. "Human beings are magical," she says in an essay on the Caribbean rethinking of modernity writ large.[11] "Bios and Logos. Words made flesh, muscle and bone animated by hope and desire, belief materialized in deeds, deeds which crystallize our actualities." Across space-time, Ben Okri agrees, identifying stories as "infinite seeds that we have brought with us through the millennia of walking the dust of the earth."[12]

Dreadspeak (also known as Iyraric, a creolized blend of "standard" patois/ Jamaican Creole, Amharic, and other liturgical phrases and elements borrowed from English and Ge'ez) refers to "I and I" with a measured reflection of spiritual oneness, a trinity portending spirit and/as/with Self. A soul-level harmony of noumenal and phenomenal possibility—a spiritual collaboration. It makes sense to refuse an over-deterministic attachment to refuse pronouns, belaboring them as particularly relevant, as their import has been outsized and sharpened into weapons in a culture war in defense of something that language could never possess. I (and I) still feel this collaborative weight in the singular *they*, the pronoun that increasingly drums anti-Black trans antagonists into a frenzy. They diminish *we*, willing us into oblivion with accusations of ungrammatical being—too right, but for the wrong reasons. They are defenders of the desires to the disimaginative coloniality, which is both unimaginative and disincentivizes imagination. The unmitigated rupture of this proscriptive hegemonic and fearful reality is part of the collaborative referent, that *we* that keeps ringing out.

I collaborate with Caribbean men telling the parable to one another around a campfire. With The Being who walked in the garment we see, traipsing urgently through London's Victoria and Albert Museum, at times luxuriating at the threshold of history with the cudgel of their Black androgyny. Their body cast in protective hairstyle communicates the need for protection. We share that need, and we share that shadow, with me approximating touch in different directions, adding texture to the tendrils of hair silhouetted on the haloed spot lit on crimson wall. The lowered pitch of Nalo's sweet voice reading a condescending character, winds itself around the snippets of my uncle's mischievous storytelling. Through my arrangement, another narrative emerges, one of gender expanse and aporia.

> She was wearing the body I used to have . . .
> . . . boyish beauty . . .
> So den . . . den yuh no wah him tell mi seh? . . .

The immersive sound channels shift and pace quickens as I traipse from the dark into the brighter space, the audience following closely behind, uncertain that they should. Do we always follow where the spirit leads?

Figure 7. A vestibular defiance. SA Smythe, *{spirit   forged}* (2023). Photograph by Hyerim Han. Courtesy of The Power Plant Contemporary Art Gallery.

Figure 8. A desperate attunement. SA Smythe, *{spirit   forged}* (2023). Photograph by Hyerim Han. Courtesy of The Power Plant Contemporary Art Gallery.

It has been said that I crave certain kinds of structure, with a compunction toward a deluded safety in ordering a disordered world. Yet endings are what I continue to resist, circling them in infinitely smaller orbit. Even now, I linger in the space of that exhibition, the space of every soundscape, performance, classroom, marathon phone call with a confidante across continents, childhood race up a coconut tree. Both Vladmir and Estragon, I struggle to sustain the willful and errant choice to continue, even as the struggle appears increasingly absurd. The melody picks up from the looped violin I laid down earlier

Figure 9. The message received. SA Smythe, *{spirit forged}* (2023). Photograph by Hyerim Han. Courtesy of The Power Plant Contemporary Art Gallery.

throughout the gallery. I reach toward The Being's garment once more, feet fixed in the Puffer Jacket's shadow. I still cannot reach it. My wrist goes limp near the floor, hovering above where the shadow of the two garments almost meet. The rest of me crumbles in futility, taking me to an exasperated place that echoes Dionne Brand's narrator in *Land to Light On*, who announces "I don't want no fucking country." Her litany being the inability to perfect "my own shadow, my violent sorrow, my / individual wrists."[13]

Overcome with emotion and memories of alienation and all kinds of quiet despair, I break down under the sweat and the lights, gritting my teeth and collapsing under Golding's Puffer Jacket (Chainmail 3). As I'm unexpectedly wracked with sobs, the soundscape decomposes with me, frenetic, splitting and achingly soft. Nalo's voice interrupts in her character's partial accusation: *When it was my body* . . . as I sit within the three-shadow nexus of the chainmail; arched back, look upward and to the left (where The Being's garment is held on a pedestal). *{spirit forged}* was not merely a performance but an immersive journey through the tapestry of my own Black trans spirituality, memories, ancestry, and the ethereal and material transformations conjured through imaginative Black and/as trans collaboration. Golding's *In the comfort of embers* offered a vessel to a vessel, an experience that transcended the physical and allowed me to excise what lingers in the shadows above and underneath, where shadows danced, identities intertwined, and spirits resounded, and a "we" of witness was transitionally born(e). The spirit we forge in the midst of Black gathering, in commitment to Black testimony, and toward a sustainable horizon of Black belonging, is a spirit that lingers. To speak of Self now, is to speak of the infinite story held on the verge of every future echo that stares back, expectantly, patiently just the same.

Mekatelyu sum'n else . . .

Figure 10. The Self was always the spirit. SA Smythe, *{spirit forged}* (2023). Photograph by Hyerim Han. Courtesy of The Power Plant Contemporary Art Gallery.

Well then, tell me something, then. Next to a hearth of our own making. We will weave another Hearkener's Nexus, a field of attunement. I hear in you the echo of a future memory. A story begins again, different this time. Right before you return to yourself, the surrounding sound one last refrain, my uncle's deep island drawl folds an offering into itself above the higher-pitched gusts of my measured breaths, one step beyond:

Hear mi nuh?

SA Smythe is a transmedia storyteller, multi-instrumentalist, critical theorist, and educator. They are based in Tkaronto, where they work as assistant professor of Black studies and the archive and as founding director of the Collaboratory for Black Poiēsis at the University of Toronto.

Acknowledgments

I continue to be grateful for the opportunity to witness and respond to the *In the comfort of embers* installation featuring video, sculpture, photography works by Amartey Golding, curated by Joséphine Denis for the Spring 2023 exhibition at The Power Plant Contemporary Art Gallery in Tkaronto. Thank you to Nalo Hopkinson and Uncle Errol for harmonizing their stories with mine and for resounding home. Thank you to Courtney Desiree Morris and Autumn Knight for their respective kindred and witness as I conceived the performance, sound composition, and choreography for {spirit   forged}. Deep gratitude to the editors of *QTR* for their patience as I struggled to return to this meditation on spirit and collaboration while reeling from a fresh wave of genocide and other modes of dispossession and to Ashon Crawley for the invitation and years of collaboration into a joyous patchwork of friendship, a delectable we, a blueprint for otherwise possibility.

Notes

1. See Shockley, *suddenly we.*
2. Crawley, *Blackpentecostal Breath.*
3. Golding, *In the comfort of embers.*
4. Brand, *Map to the Door of No Return*, 6.
5. Clifton, "mississippi river runs into the gulf."
6. Gumbs, *Undrowned*, 32.
7. Freud, *Civilization and Its Discontents*, 8.
8. Darwish, "I Come from There."
9. Hopkinson, *Skin*, 183–202.
10. Hopkinson, *Skin*, 183.
11. Wynter, "The Pope Must Have Been Drunk, the King of Castile a Madman," 35.
12. Okri, "Under the Sun."
13. Brand, *Land to Light On*, 48.

References

Brand, Dionne. *Land to Light On*. Toronto: McClelland and Stewart, 1997.

Brand, Dionne. *A Map to the Door of No Return: Notes to Belonging*. Toronto: Vintage Canada, 2002.

Brooks, Gwendolyn. "Paul Robeson." In *The Essential Gwendolyn Brooks*, edited by Elizabeth Alexander. New York: Library of America, 2005.

Clifton, Lucille. "the mississippi river empties into the gulf." In *How to Carry Water: Selected Poems of Lucille Clifton*, 176. Rochester, NY: BOA Editions, 2020.

Crawley, Ashon T. *Blackpentecostal Breath: The Aesthetics of Possibility*. New York: Fordham University Press, 2016.

Darwish, Mahmoud. "I Come from There." In *The Bed of the Stranger*. Translated by Anton Shammas. Beirut: Riad El-Rayyes Books, 1999.

Freud, Sigmund. *Civilization and Its Discontents*. New York: W. W. Norton, 1962.

Glissant, Édouard. *Poetics of Relation*. Ann Arbor: University of Michigan Press, 1997.

Golding, Amartey. *In the comfort of embers*. Installation, Power Plant Contemporary Art Gallery, Toronto, Spring 2023.

Gumbs, Alexis Pauline. *Undrowned: Black Feminist Lessons from Marine Mammals*. Chico, CA: AK, 2020.

Hopkinson, Nalo. "A Habit of Waste." In *Skin Folk*, 183–202. New York: Warner Aspect, 2001.

Hopkinson, Slade. "The Madwoman of Papine: Two Cartoons with Captions." In *Skin Folk*. New York: Warner Aspect, 2001.

Okri, Ben. "Under the Sun: A Meditation by Ben Okri on Stories." *Irish Times*, November 4, 2015. https://irishtimes.com/culture/books/under-the-sun-a-meditation-by-ben-okri-on-stories-1.2416769.

Shockley, Evie. *suddenly we*. Middletown, CT: Wesleyan University Press, 2023.

Snorton, C. Riley. "Nonbinary Archives and the Grammar of Experience." Unpublished manuscript, 2021.

Spillers, Hortense J. "Mama's Baby, Papa's Maybe: An American Grammar Book." *Diacritics* 17, no. 2 (1987): 64–81. https://doi.org/10.2307/464747.

Walcott, Derek. *The Poetry of Derek Walcott, 1948–2013*. London: Faber and Faber, 2019.

Wynter, Sylvia. "The Pope Must Have Been Drunk, the King of Castile a Madman: Culture as Actuality and the Caribbean Rethinking of Modernity." In *Reordering of Culture: Latin America, the Caribbean and Canada in the 'Hood*, edited by A. Ruprecht and C. Taiana, 17–41. Ottawa: Carleton University Press, 1995.

"I Am at Peace with Being a Hole"
The Raptures and Ruptures of Queer Diasporic Life

ISAIAH FROST RIVERA

Circuits of the Sacred: A Faggotology in the Black Latinx Caribbean
Carlos Ulises Decena
Durham, NC: Duke University Press, 2023. 208 pp.

In his multisensory affirmation of Black queer cosmologies, Carlos Ulises Decena mobilizes his personal journey as a working-class queer immigrant scholar to illustrate the transmogrification of Blackness in Afrodiasporic spiritual cultures and sensorial conceptions of the self. Defining "faggotology," or "pensar maricón," as a "mystical bottoming" (11) that embraces the liberatory wisdom of hemispheric spiritual knowledge, Decena engages intuitive sites of queer Afro-Caribbean divinity that disavow academic transparency and respectability. Here, he conceives of Blackness as "in transit," using circuits to observe how Blackness is refracted through "contradictory grids of intelligibility" (6) across physical differences, cultural contexts, and sociopolitical histories. By animating disparate epistemologies, structures of feeling, and tensions that flow between internal and external connection networks, Blackness as a circuit seeks a more nuanced approach to transnational discourses in which "Black" may in fact be a flattening or distorting identity category rather than an opening for subjective, even salacious, permutations. Thus, by cataloging his own fragmented path toward a fuller understanding of his Black queer subjectivity, Decena produces an intergenerational, genre-blurring text that praises the inherent sacredness of daily diasporic life, encouraging readers to name "our lusty, funky, and stank quests to freak through our bodies" (9) and cherish the cosmological revelations that ensue.

Circuits of the Sacred is divided into four parts: its chapters, or "narrative nodes" (7), are spread out nonsequentially in order to activate "conocimiento," a form of "inarticulable ancestral wisdom" (163n53) that "turn[s] intellectual labor into a mystical quest" (11). In "Part 0: Orígenes (Origins)," Decena lays out

QTR · A Journal of Trans and Queer Studies in Religion · 1:1 · May 2024
DOI: 10.1215/29944724-11208965 © 2024 Isaiah Frost Rivera

the fundamental shape of the text, followed by a narrative homage to his ancestral genealogy via his upbringing in Santo Domingo. "Part I: Caminos" shifts to Decena's experiences within academic spaces. Chapter 2, "Bridge Crónica: A Triptych, with Elegguá," performs a ritual tribute to the deity of roads and paths, charting Decena's own distorted self-actualization as a working-class Afro-Caribbean scholar divorced from his cultural lineage, underscoring the contradictory imbrication of Blackness and faggotology. Chapter 3, "Experiencing the Evidence," teases out intuition and embodied knowledge through Decena's titular inversion of historical positivism, establishing faggotology as "an otherwise morphology for being and knowing the divine" (57) that prioritizes the body's capacity to retain and rupture histories of everyday life.

"Part II: Dos Puentes, Tránsitos" continues to tease out the ineffable, diffractive qualities of faggotology. Chapter 4, "Loving Stones: A Transnational Pataki," deploys travel narratives to explore transnational forms of Santería through a Marxist analysis of otases, or ritual stones, and their messy relationship with commodity fetishism. Chapter 5, "¡Santo! Repurposed Flesh and the Suspension of the Mirror in Santería Initiation," features a side-by-side personal narrative structure that juxtaposes a fictionalized account of Decena's formative years with evocations of his initiation as a Santería priest, further linking the body's intuitive apprehension of dislocated histories with modes of mystical knowledge.

Finally, "Part III: Traces" puts faggotology into practice, which is where Decena's methodology most impresses. Chapter 6, "Indecent Conocimientos: A Suite Rasanblaj in Funny Keys," features several narrative passages embodying an *"erotics of intimacy"* which "conceives of unexpected sites of pleasure in the body" (127). Here, Decena fully leans into the antirespectability of faggotology, positioning illuminating contemplations of trance possession alongside breathtakingly detailed accounts of sexual encounters with strangers to highlight how intimacies between precarious bodies constitute a critical, and political, form of worship. In "Epístola al Futuro/An Epistle to the Future," Decena closes with a heartfelt address to his own children that functions "as gospel for the black queer children of the future" (157), recombining ancestral wisdom with the cosmological inheritance of future generations.

Decena's work will undoubtedly find favor among diasporic scholars of sexuality, religion, and spirituality, though it remains to be seen how Blackness as a circuit will contribute to emerging debates about the implicit anti-Blackness of "Brownness" as an essentialized racial category among Caribbean Latinx groups. *Circuits* shies away from a deeper analysis of such slippages in Latin American/Dominican national identity; however, Decena's theorization lends itself to a deconstruction of this obfuscating trend endemic in Latinx studies, more directly critiqued by scholars such as Christopher L. Busey, Carolyn Silva, Laura Grappo, and Ren Ellis Neyra. Describing Blackness "as the cut, wound, and raja with specific historical and geopolitical coordinates on the island of my biological birth" (9), Decena's text will also appeal to Black and Afro-Latinx studies scholars interested in what Lorgia García Peña terms "the vaivenes [comings and goings] of Black Latinidad in the twenty-first century."[1] Queer studies scholars will similarly appreciate faggotology as an oppositional, if utopic, approach to collective queer self-conception that dwells in performative excess and waste, somewhat akin to what Bobby Benedicto terms "queer of color negativity," through which one renegotiates "the burden of repairing the very world that demands [their] annihilation."[2]

Disability studies scholars will likely be drawn to Decena's deconstruction of wholeness as an "*enclosure*" that reduces the body to "an instrument of contact with sentience" (4). Rather than being "en paz conmigo mismo (at peace with myself)" (4), Decena asserts: "I am at peace with being a hole. A black (w)hole" (5), riffing off Evelynn Hammonds's foundational essay on the absent presence of Black women's sexuality, though curiously omitting Jennifer C. Nash's arguably more germane "Black anality" expansion, which centers the anus as "a space of play, pleasure, desire, and delight for black subjects."[3] Considering (anal)ogies abound in *Circuits*, including Decena's description of rimming as "the touch of the divine in the gutter—a flower mapped on the asshole one licks" (154), I couldn't help but wonder what faggotology might have gained from the cosmological valences of a distinctly *Black queer* anality. Nonetheless, Decena's strategic methodological openings, as it were, exude a rapturous, sacred vulnerability that effectively undergirds his ritual subversion of heteronormative hegemony.

I have no doubt more bountiful points of departure will emerge among future readers, who will certainly be as provoked and challenged as I was by Decena's ambitious, at times unwieldy, but largely successful scholarly reckoning with liberatory queer Afro-Latinx and Caribbean futures.

Isaiah Frost Rivera (he/they), born and raised in Staten Island, is a scholar, maker, and Black digital speculator pursuing his PhD in the African and African Diaspora Studies program at the University of Texas at Austin. They hold a BA from CUNY Brooklyn College in English with a double minor in LGBTQ studies and Puerto Rican and Latino studies, an MA in Latin American and Caribbean regional studies from Columbia University, and an MA in English from Lehigh University. His research interests include queer and trans Afrodiasporic expressive cultures, archival ethics, and the intersections between metamodern horror and retributive justice.

Notes

1. Peña, Translating Blackness, 22.
2. Benedicto, "Agents and Objects of Death," 278.
3. Hammonds, "Black (W)holes and the Geometry of Black Female Sexuality"; Nash, "Black Anality," 456.

References

Benedicto, Bobby. "Agents and Objects of Death: Gay Murder, Boyfriend Twinning, and Queer of Color Negativity." *GLQ* 25, no. 2 (2019): 273–96.

Hammonds, Evelynn. "Black (W)holes and the Geometry of Black Female Sexuality." *differences* 6, nos. 2–3 (1994): 126–45.

Nash, Jennifer C. "Black Anality." *GLQ* 20, no. 4 (2014): 439–60.

Peña, Lorgia García. *Translating Blackness: Latinx Colonialities in Global Perspective.* Durham, NC: Duke University Press, 2022.

BOOK REVIEW

A Proximate Language, Approximate Language

BESHOUY BOTROS

Queer Companions: Religion, Public Intimacy, and Saintly Affects in Pakistan
Omar Kasmani
Durham, NC: Duke University Press, 2022, xvi + 208 pp.

In Arabic, "reading" comes close to "close"; the words are almost adjacent in any competent dictionary. The imperative forms of the verbs "to read" (*iqra'* اِقْرأ) and "to come close" (*iqrab* اِقرب) are proximate, not because they are etymologically related, but simply because they share their first three letters. Both imperatives start with alif ا, continue with qaf ق and reh ر, and then the word forks; if it ends with the first letter of the alphabet, alif, it forms اِقرأ, "read," the injunction at the beginning of the Quran, قرآن. If it ends with the second, beh, it becomes اِقرب, "to come close"; one diacritic shift makes the adjective "closer" (*aqrab* آقرب). These words introduce a hermeneutics of close reading in Arabic, making legible the charge of Omar Kasmani's *Queer Companions: Religion, Public Intimacy, and Saintly Affects in Pakistan*.

    Queer Companions opens with قُرب, the Urdu word from Arabic meaning "intimacy, closeness, affective nearness, trust" (1), to meditate on the relationships the book analyzes: those between Kasmani and the fakirs, his ascetic interlocutors in Sehwan; between these actors and the saint La'l Shahbaz Qalandar, the polymorphous subject of Sufi, Shia, and Shivaite devotion; and between the fields of queer and religious studies. Kasmani takes up "the epistemological work of regathering intimacy in ways that do not squarely home in its Euro-American genealogies and secular orientations" (2). "An intersex child who abandons home, an unchaperoned mother of eight, an ascetic who gives up celibacy for a girl he loves" (26), and others are the book's protagonists, and Kasmani narrates their relations to Lal and to sites across the town's pilgrimage route. In so doing, Kasmani is decidedly not "queering" the figure of the fakir, but instead theorizing queer relationality and un-straight affordances as they emerge in his engagement with his interlocutors and in their

QTR • A Journal of Trans and Queer Studies in Religion • 1:1 • May 2024
DOI: 10.1215/29944724-11208974 © 2024 Beshouy Botros
This is an open access article distributed under the terms of a Creative Commons license (CC BY-NC-ND 4.0).

encounters with Lal, their broader devotional communities, and the Pakistani state, whose presence is increasingly felt in the shrine's administration. Drawing on fifteen months of fieldwork spanning 2009–2018, Kasmani provides generous and generative chronicles of politics and piety in Sehwan.

The first chapter follows Baba-Akram, or Baba, across dreamscapes and landscapes. Baba was a fifty-year-old intersex, *khwaja-sara* fakir whose dreams led them to Lal. Kasmani's attention to these visions, "infrastructures of the imaginal," builds on work by scholars of Islam such as Amira Mittermaier who have illustrated that the imaginal is not unreal, but rather "a distinct and betwixt realm of perception" that "correlates forms of seeing and varieties of perception across wakefulness and dreaming." (37). This approach marks a reformulation of the fundamental tool of ethnography, observation, which is recast in Sufi terms to account for the comingling between dreamlands and the physical realm. Recognizing that fakirs can be treated as quintessential objects of anthropological inquiry, Kasmani strives to produce a Sufist ethnography, not an ethnography of Sufism. He is careful to avoid "queer-jacketing" Baba, who might be subject to an identitarian reading fixated on their gender expression. Kasmani notes certain sartorial details and how Baba interchangeably uses masculine and feminine registers when speaking, but it is not the fact of their gender expression that informs a queer reading. Rather it is Baba's trajectory, which spans the beginning of the Pakistani state's administration of shrines in 1960; their being led to Lal through visions and songs; and their moves away from their biological family and a socially prescribed future as *khwaja-sara* that evince unstraight affordances.

The next two chapters follow two mothers, Amma and Zaheda, in the durbar and courtyard of the shrine, which had metal detectors installed after a 2017 suicide bombing. Kasmani furthers his analysis of the proximity between saintly and state institutions by attending to these women's corporeal and affective lives. He narrates Amma's communion with Lal via a male cohabiting spirit and how she earns a living within an ecology of local spiritual guides and healers, one that persists alongside state-managed donation sites. Through Zaheda, Kasmani introduces the term *bhes*, meaning both "guises" and "disguises." Fakirs assume a habitus that makes palpable their ascetic devotion through citations of other fakirs and saintly tropes. Kasmani recounts instances in which Zaheda was not recognized as a fakir, including one in which they were together and a shrine visitor mistook him for the spiritual guide. Thinking through her practice of endurance, Kasmani extends and challenges Saba Mahmood's pathfinding *The Politics of Piety* through his critical attention to the state's attempts to govern religiosity and delineation of how nonnormative Islamic devotional practices fit within the matrix of gendered embodiment and subject formation. By analyzing the Pakistani state's attempts to shape the affective landscape of religiosity, Kasmani also provides apertures to consider the state's management of sexuality beyond biopolitical frames, which tend to assume secularity.

The final two ethnographic chapters take us to a *kafi*, or fraternal fakir lodge, where Murad's renouncing of celibacy and marriage to a girl half his age sparked intrigue, and to a graveyard where the fakirs Jamal and Bibi interface with fairies in a hetero-temporal worlding with saints. Narrating Murad's scandal and its impacts on the lodge, Kasmani illustrates how "ideas around sexual intimacy inflect fakir narratives on intimacy with saints" and furthers two key insights: that saintly intimacy is at odds with the economies of the heterosexual family and that unstraight affordances "not only support otherwise ways of being in the world, but can also work against intimacy" (109). Kasmani thus traces the contours of saintly affects and contributes to a critical return to intimacy as an object of inquiry across Black and queer studies.

Kasmani concludes *Queer Companions* with a theoretical coda and the word *suhbet* صحبت, Urdu from Arabic meaning "companionship," "conversation," "cohabitation," "spiritual meeting," "sex." Kasmani articulates companionship as an ethic of study that prioritizes the intereptetive cross-pollination of *queer* and *religion*, as opposed to an "Islamicizing of queer" (153, 157). He also joins scholars working to unyoke queer hermeneutics from their Euro-American settings. Scholars working in area studies have experience accompanying one another across seemingly disparate geographies. One can look to historians of Iran at home in Burma or China, anthropologists of West Africa deeply read in South Asian historiography, or Caribbeanists following currents in Indian Ocean studies. Practices such as these, of being mutually informed and in intentional relation, undergird *Queer Companions*' methodological challenges and theoretical promises. If queer truly travels as a hermeneutic, it ought to inspire invocations of *qurb* and other vernacular terms to inform readings of the poetics of relation in seemingly disparate contexts. As an epistemic project, "queer companionship" is multilingual and at least biliterate. So go on, reader: *lánzate*, lance yourself; *iqrab*, come close; *iqra'*.

Beshouy Botros is a PhD student working across the History and Women's, Gender, and Sexuality Studies Departments at Yale University. Botros is researching sexuality, race, and trans* medicine in Northern Africa, is more broadly interested in cultural and intellectual history, and can be reached at beshouy.botros@yale.edu.

2 04